Accounting Workbook
FOR DUMMIES®

by John A. Tracy, CPA

WILEY

Wiley Publishing, Inc.

Accounting Workbook For Dummies®

Published by
Wiley Publishing, Inc.
111 River St.
Hoboken, NJ 07030-5774
www.wiley.com

Copyright © 2006 by Wiley Publishing, Inc., Indianapolis, Indiana

Published by Wiley Publishing, Inc., Indianapolis, Indiana

Published simultaneously in Canada

For general information on our other products and services, please contact our Customer Care Department within the U.S. at 877-762-2974, outside the U.S. at 317-572-3993, or fax 317-572-4002.

For technical support, please visit www.wiley.com/techsupport.

Wiley also publishes its books in a variety of electronic formats. Some content that appears in print may not be available in electronic books.

Library of Congress Control Number is available from the publisher.

ISBN-13: 978-0-471-79145-4

ISBN-10: 0-471-79145-8

Manufactured in the United States of America

10 9 8 7 6 5 4

1B/TR/QR/QY/IN

WILEY

About the Author

John A. Tracy (Boulder, Colorado) is Professor of Accounting, Emeritus, at the University of Colorado in Boulder. Before his 35-year tenure at Boulder, he was on the business faculty for 4 years at the University of California in Berkeley. He has served as staff accountant at Ernst & Young and is the author of several books on accounting and finance, including *Accounting For Dummies, The Fast Forward MBA in Finance, How To Read a Financial Report,* and *How to Manage Profit and Cash Flow* with his son Tage Tracy. Dr. Tracy received his BSC degree from Creighton University 50 years ago this year, and earned his MBA and PhD degrees from the University of Wisconsin. He is a CPA (inactive) in Colorado.

Dedication

In memory of Gordon B. Laing, the original editor of my *How to Read a Financial Report* — a gentleman and editor of the first rank.

Author's Acknowledgments

I'm deeply grateful to everyone at Wiley Publishing, Inc. who helped produce this book. Their professionalism, courtesy, and good humor were much appreciated. My editors, Tim Gallan and Elizabeth Rea, were exceptional. It was a pleasure working with them. I owe them a debt I cannot repay. So a simple but heartfelt "thank you" will have to do.

This book would not have been possible but for the success of my *Accounting For Dummies* (Wiley, 3rd Edition, 2005). I owe Wiley Publishing, Inc. and the several editors on the three editions of the book an enormous debt of gratitude, which I am most willing to acknowledge. Thanks to all of you! I hope I have done you proud with *Accounting Workbook For Dummies*.

Publisher's Acknowledgments

We're proud of this book; please send us your comments through our Dummies online registration form located at www.dummies.com/register/.

Some of the people who helped bring this book to market include the following:

Acquisitions, Editorial, and Media Development

Senior Project Editor: Tim Gallan

Acquisitions Editor: Stacy Kennedy

Senior Copy Editor: Elizabeth Rea

Editorial Program Coordinator: Hanna K. Scott

Technical Editor: Jill Gilbert Welytok

Editorial Manager: Christine Meloy Beck

Editorial Assistants: David Lutton, Nadine Bell, Erin Calligan

Cartoons: Rich Tennant (www.the5thwave.com)

Composition Services

Project Coordinator: Michael Kruzil

Layout and Graphics: Lauren Goddard, Denny Hager, Stephanie D. Jumper, Barry Offringa, Lynsey Osborn, Heather Ryan

Proofreaders: Jessica Kramer

Indexer: Estalita Slivoskey

Publishing and Editorial for Consumer Dummies

Diane Graves Steele, Vice President and Publisher, Consumer Dummies

Joyce Pepple, Acquisitions Director, Consumer Dummies

Kristin A. Cocks, Product Development Director, Consumer Dummies

Michael Spring, Vice President and Publisher, Travel

Kelly Regan, Editorial Director, Travel

Publishing for Technology Dummies

Andy Cummings, Vice President and Publisher, Dummies Technology/General User

Composition Services

Gerry Fahey, Vice President of Production Services

Debbie Stailey, Director of Composition Services

Contents at a Glance

Table of Contents

Introduction

....

First of all, I have to admit that accounting has an image problem. Be honest: What's the first thing that pops into your mind when you see the word "accountant"? You probably think of a nerd wearing a green eyeshade who has the personality of an undertaker (no offense meant to undertakers, of course). Well, I've never worn a green eyeshade in my life, and I can assure you that I'm not a nerd. I own an iPod, I have a good sense of humor, and in addition to being an accounting professor for more than 40 years, I've also held several administrative positions. But to be honest, I was somewhat of a nerd when I decided to go into accounting. (I have pictures to prove it.)

I was a freshman at Iowa State University studying engineering but not liking it too well. On a whim, I dropped into the student counseling office and took some tests. The result was that they told me that I was a reasonably well-adjusted 18-year-old (little did they know), I had an IQ sufficient for what they were about to recommend (but they never told me my IQ), and I should switch to accounting. I was floored. Accounting? Well, I took the counselors' advice and changed my major to accounting, and I've never regretted it.

Explaining accounting for nonaccountants is one of my passions in life, and I've written several books on the topic. About a decade ago, I had the opportunity to write *Accounting For Dummies* (Wiley), which is now in its third edition. One of my other books is *How To Read A Financial Report* (Wiley), which has been in print more than 25 years. This book, *Accounting Workbook For Dummies,* fills a gap in my other books: They don't have questions and exercises. This book offers plenty of questions to test and improve your understanding of accounting.

This book offers a different take on accounting — one that offers new insights and perspectives. Having taught accounting for over 40 years, I have a pretty good idea of how the subject is taught. I don't go out of my way to be contrary or confrontational, but accounting isn't an exact science. Accounting is full of controversy and differences of opinion. In this book, I state my opinions forcefully and (I hope) clearly.

The spirit of this book is illustrated in two stories. One concerns the young and eager musician on her first trip to New York City, who gets off the train at Grand Central Terminal and asks the first person she meets on the street: "How do you get to Carnegie Hall?" The answer is: "Practice, practice, practice!" The second story concerns the legendary UCLA basketball coach John Wooden. At the first practice of each year, he taught the players how to tie their shoes so that they wouldn't come loose during a game.

About This Book

Whether it's a small mom and pop business or the gargantuan General Electric, every business keeps track of its financial activities and its financial condition. You can't run a business without an accounting system that tells you whether you're making a profit or suffering a loss, whether you have enough cash to continue or your checking account balance is approaching zero, and whether you're in good financial shape or are on the edge of bankruptcy.

Accounting Workbook For Dummies is largely about *business accounting*. It explains how business transactions are recorded in the accounts of a business and the financial statements that are prepared for a business to report its profit and loss, financial condition, and cash flows. It also explains how business managers use accounting information for decision making. (The book doesn't delve into business income taxation, which is the province of professional accountants.)

Most business managers have limited accounting backgrounds, and most have their enthusiasm for learning more about accounting well under control. But, down deep, they're likely to think that they should know more about accounting. Business managers should find this book quite helpful even if they just dip their toes in.

If you're a business bookkeeper or accountant, you can use this book to review the topics you need to know well. It can help you upgrade your accounting skills and savvy and lay the foundation for further advancement. One great thing about *Accounting Workbook For Dummies* is that it offers alternative explanations of accounting topics that are different from the explanations in standard accounting textbooks. The many questions and problems (with clearly explained answers) offer an excellent way to test your knowledge, and nobody knows your exam scores but you.

If you're a student presently enrolled in a beginning accounting course, you can use this book as a supplementary study guide to your textbook, one that offers many supplementary questions and exercises. Perhaps you took an accounting course a few years ago and need to brush up on the subject. This book can help you refresh your understanding of accounting and help you recall things forgotten.

Foolish Assumptions

Mastering accounting is like mastering many subjects: First, you must understand the lingo and the fundamentals. In accounting, you have to work problems to really get a grasp of the topic and technique. Passive reading just isn't enough. In writing this book, I assumed that you aren't a complete accounting neophyte. I designed the book as a second step that builds on your basic accounting knowledge and experience. If you have no previous exposure to accounting, you may want to consider first reading *Accounting For Dummies* (Wiley).

You don't have to be a math wizard to understanding accounting; basic high school algebra is more than enough. However, you do have to pay attention to details, just as you have to pay close attention to the words when you study Shakespeare. Accounting involves calculations, and using a business/financial calculator is very helpful. In my experience, many people don't take the time to learn how to use their calculators. But that's time well spent. In many of the questions and problems posed throughout the book, I explain how to use a business calculator for the solution.

How This Book Is Organized

Accounting Workbook For Dummies consists of four parts that cover topics including recordkeeping basics, financial statements, accounting for business managers, and investment accounting. I wrap it all up with some advice about financial statements and tips for management accounting.

Part 1: Business Accounting Basics

The general theme of the chapters in this part is how an accountant records the transactions of a business (its financial activities) in an accrual-basis accounting system and how the effects of transactions are reported in the three primary financial statements of a business — the income statement, the balance sheet, and the statement of cash flows. This part also includes a review of the bookkeeping cycle, from recording original entries through the adjusting and closing entries at year-end.

Part 11: Preparing Financial Statements

This part examines the accounting issues and procedures involved in preparing the three primary financial statements of a business. Compared with the standard textbook approach to these topics, I put much more emphasis on the interconnections between the three financial statements. The statements fit together like a tongue-and-groove joint, and the chapters focus on these connections. This part closes with the decisions every business must make in choosing which accounting methods to use for recording profit.

Part 111: Managerial, Manufacturing, and Capital Accounting

This part of the book examines how managers use accounting information when making business decisions. In addition to financial statements, managers need profit models for their decision-making analysis, and accountants should take the lead in designing useful profit models for managers. This part also explains how the product cost of manufactures is determined and the difficult accounting issues involved in measuring product cost. The last chapter of this part discusses the accounting measurement of interest and return on investment. Most people have a basic understanding of interest and return on investment, but when it gets right down to a specific situation, they're fuzzy on the details.

Part 1V: The Part of Tens

Like all *For Dummies* books, *Accounting Workbook For Dummies* ends with a couple chapters that provide tips to help you recall and apply important points sprinkled throughout the book. The editors have decreed that there shall be ten of these tips in each chapter. I provide two such chapters in this book — one being ten things you should know about business financial statements, and one being a ten-point checklist for management accountants.

Icons Used In This Book

Throughout this book, you can find useful "pointers" that save you the trouble of buying a yellow highlighter pen and using sticky notes. These icons draw your attention to certain parts of the text. Think of them as road signs on your journey through accounting.

This icon marks the spot of an example question that explains and illustrates an important point. The answer follows the question. It's a good idea to make sure that you understand the answer before attempting the additional questions on the topic. To get the most out of the example questions, don't read the answer right away. First, try to answer the question, and then compare my answer with yours and how you got it.

This icon points out information that you probably would have underlined or highlighted while reading. These points are worth remembering. When reviewing each chapter, read everything with this icon attached in order to get the essentials.

I use this icon to indicate that I'm building on your background in accounting. Instead of starting at ground zero, I assume that you already know basic points about the topic. If this book were an elevator, this marker would mean that you're ascending from the first floor to the second floor.

Simply put, this icon is a red flag that means "Watch out." This warning sign means that the topic being explained is a serious and troublesome issue in accounting, so you should pay close attention and handle it with care.

Where to Go from Here

Accounting Workbook For Dummies is designed to maximize modularity. Each chapter stands on its own feet to the fullest extent possible. Of course, it makes sense to read the chapters in order, but you can jump around as the spirit moves you.

You may be a business investor who's interested in interpreting return on investment (ROI) (Chapter 12), or you may want to review manufacturing cost accounting (Chapter 11). You may be a business manager who needs to know about analyzing profit behavior (Chapter 10), or you may be confused about cash flow (Chapters 7 and 8). If you're a student studying for your first accounting exam, I suggest that you start with Part I and read the chapters in order.

In my view, a business/financial calculator has become as essential as a TV remote control, and I highly recommend that you invest in one (a business/financial calculator, that is, not a remote control). Hewlett-Packard (HP) and Texas Instruments (TI) make very good ones. If you can avoid it, don't buy the cheapest model; the next one up usually has better financial functions and a good display. At the time of writing this chapter, my favorite two calculators are the HP 17B and the TI BA II.

Part I
Business Accounting Basics

The 5th Wave   By Rich Tennant

"Lucky for us—our Net Income column ended directly over a 'Triple Word Score' square."

In this part . . .

Accountants are the scorekeepers of business. Without accounting, a business couldn't function; it wouldn't know whether it's making a profit; and it wouldn't know its financial condition. Bookkeeping — the recording-keeping part of accounting — must be done well to make sure that all the financial information needed to run the business is complete, accurate, and reliable. This part of the book walks you through the basic bookkeeping cycle — from making original entries through adjusting entries, to financial statements. Before jumping into the mechanics of bookkeeping, however, I explain the financial effects and the manifold effects of sales and expenses on assets and liabilities.

Chapter 1

Elements of Business Accounting

In This Chapter

▶ Working with the accounting equation

▶ Understanding the differences between cash- and accrual-basis accounting

▶ Examining the three primary business financial statements

▶ Seeing the effects of crooked accounting on financial statements

The starting point in accounting is identifying the *entity* being accounted for. A business entity can be legally organized as a *partnership, corporation, limited liability company*, or other structures permitted by law. Alternatively, a business entity simply may consist of the business activities of an individual, in which case it's called a *sole proprietorship*. Regardless of how the business entity is legally established, it's treated as a separate entity or distinct person for accounting purposes.

Keeping the Accounting Equation in Balance

If you've ever studied accounting, you probably recall the *accounting equation:*

Assets = Liabilities + Owners' equity

The accounting equation says a lot in very few words. It's like the visible part of an iceberg — a lot of important points are hidden under the water. Notice the two sides to the equation: assets on one side and the *claims* against the assets on the other side. These claims arise from credit extended to the business (liabilities) and capital invested by owners in the business (owners' equity). (The claims of liabilities are significantly different than the claims of owners; liabilities have seniority and priority for payment over the claims of owners.)

Suppose a business has $10 million total assets. These assets didn't fall down like manna from heaven (as my old accounting professor was fond of saying). The money for the assets came from somewhere. The business's creditors (to whom it owes its liabilities) may have supplied, say, $4 million of its total assets. Therefore, the owners' equity sources provided the other $6 million.

Business accounting is based on the two-sided nature of the accounting equation. Both assets *and* sources of assets are accounted for, which leads, quite naturally, to *double entry accounting*. Double entry, in essence, means two-sided. It's based on the general economic exchange model. In economic transactions, something is given and something is received in exchange. For example, I recently bought an iPod from Apple Computer. Apple gave me the iPod and received my money. Another example involves a business that borrows money from its bank. The business gives the bank a legal instrument called a *note* promising to return the money at a future date and to pay interest over the time the money is borrowed. In exchange for the note, the business receives the money. (Chapter 3 explains how to implement double entry accounting.)

EXAMPLE

Q. Is each of the following equations correct? What key point does each equation raise?

a. $250,000 Assets = $100,000 Liabilities + $100,000 Owners' equity

b. $2,345,000 Assets = $46,900 Liabilities + $2,298,100 Owners' equity

c. $26,450 Assets = $675,000 Liabilities – $648,550 Owners' equity

d. $4,650,000 Assets = $4,250,000 Liabilities + $400,000 Owners' equity

A. Each accounting equation offers an important lesson.

a. Whoops! This accounting equation doesn't balance, so clearly something's wrong. Either liabilities, owner's equity, or some combination of both is $50,000 too low, or the two items on the right-hand side could be correct, in which case total assets are overstated $50,000. With an unbalanced equation such as this, the accountant definitely should find the error or errors and make appropriate correcting entries.

b. This accounting equation balances, but, wow! Look at the very small size of liabilities relative to assets. This kind of contrast isn't typical. The liabilities of a typical business usually account for a much larger percentage of its total assets.

c. This accounting equation balances, but the business has a large negative owners' equity. Such a large negative amount of owners' equity means the business has suffered major losses that have wiped out almost all its assets. You wouldn't want to be one of this business's creditors (or one of its owners either).

d. This accounting equation balances and is correct, but you should notice that the business is *highly leveraged,* which means the *ratio of debt to equity* (liabilities divided by owners' equity) is very high, more than 10 to 1. This ratio is quite unusual.

1. Which of the following is the normal way to present the accounting equation?

   a. Liabilities = Assets – Owners' equity

   b. Assets – Liabilities = Owners' equity

   c. Assets = Liabilities + Owners' equity

   d. Assets – Liabilities – Owners' equity = 0

Solve It

2. A business has $485,000 total liabilities and $1,200,000 total owners' equity. What is the amount of its total assets?

Solve It

3. A business has $250,000 total liabilities. At start-up, the owners invested $500,000 in the business. Unfortunately, the business has suffered a cumulative loss of $200,000 up to the present time. What is the amount of its total assets at the present time?

Solve It

4. A business has $175,000 total liabilities. At start-up, the owners invested $250,000 capital. The business has earned $190,000 cumulative profit since its creation, all of which has been retained in the business. What is the total amount of its assets?

Solve It

Distinguishing Between Cash- and Accrual-Basis Accounting

Cash-basis accounting refers to keeping a record of cash inflows and cash outflows. An individual uses cash-basis accounting in keeping his checkbook because he needs to know his day-to-day cash balance and he needs a journal of his cash receipts and cash expenditures during the year for filing his annual income tax return. Individuals have assets other than cash (such as cars, computers, and homes), and they have liabilities (such as credit card balances and home mortgages). Hardly anyone I know keeps accounting records of their noncash assets and their liabilities (aside from putting bills to pay and receipts for major purchases in folders). Most people keep a checkbook, and that's about it when it comes to their personal accounting.

Although it's perfect for individuals, cash-basis accounting just doesn't cut it for the large majority of businesses. Cash-basis accounting doesn't provide the information that managers need to run a business or the information needed to prepare company tax returns and financial reports. Some small personal service businesses (such as barber shops, lawyers, and real estate brokers) can get by using cash-basis accounting because they have virtually no assets other than cash and they pay their bills right away.

The large majority of businesses use *accrual-basis accounting*. They keep track of their cash inflows and outflows, of course, but accrual-basis accounting allows them to record all the assets and liabilities of the business. Also, accrual-basis accounting keeps track of the money invested in the business by its owners and the accumulated profit retained in the business. In short, accrual-basis accounting has a much broader scope than cash-basis accounting.

A big difference between cash- and accrual-basis accounting concerns how they measure annual *profit* of a business. With cash-basis accounting, profit simply equals the total of cash inflows from sales minus the total of cash outflows for expenses of making sales and running the business, or, in other words, the net increase in cash from sales and expenses. With the accrual-basis accounting method, profit is measured differently because the two components of profit — sales revenue and expenses — are recorded differently.

When using accrual-basis accounting, a business records sales revenue when a sale is made and the products and/or services are delivered to the customer, whether the customer pays cash on the spot or receives credit and doesn't pay the business until sometime later. Sales revenue is recorded before cash is actually received. The business doesn't record the cost of the products sold as an expense until sales revenue is recorded, even though the business paid out cash for the products weeks or months earlier. Furthermore, with accrual-basis accounting, a business records operating expenses as soon as they're incurred (as soon as the business has a liability for the expense), even though the expenses aren't paid until sometime later.

Cash-basis accounting doesn't reflect economic reality for businesses that sell and buy on credit, carry inventories of products for sale, invest in long-lived operating assets, and make long-term commitments for such things as employee pensions and retirement benefits. When you look beyond small cash-based business, you quickly realize that businesses need the comprehensive recordkeeping system called accrual-basis accounting. I like to call it "economic reality accounting."

The following example question focuses on certain fundamental differences between cash-basis and accrual-basis accounting regarding the recording of sales revenue and expenses for the purpose of measuring profit.

Q. You started a new business one year ago. You've been very busy dealing with so many problems that you haven't had time to sit down and look at whether you made a profit or not. You haven't run out of cash (which for a start-up venture is quite an accomplishment), but you understand that the sustainability of the business depends on making a profit. The following two summaries present cash flow information for the year and information about two assets and a liability at year-end:

Revenue and Expense Cash Flows For First Year

$558,000 cash receipts from sales

$375,000 cash payments for purchases of products

$340,000 cash payments for other expenses

Two Assets and a Liability at Year-End

$52,000 receivables from customers for sales made to them during the year

$85,000 cost of products in ending inventory that haven't yet been sold

$25,000 liability for unpaid expenses

Compare the profit or loss of your business for its first year according to the cash- and accrual-basis accounting methods.

A. Profit according to cash-basis accounting equals the cash inflow from sales minus the total of cash outflows for expenses (and the total of cash outflows for expenses equals the purchases of products plus other expenses). Thus, under cash-basis accounting, your business has a $157,000 loss for the year ($558,000 sales revenue – $715,000 expenses = $157,000 loss).

Under accrual-basis accounting, you record different amounts for sales revenue and the two expenses, which are calculated as follows:

$558,000 cash receipts from sales + $52,000 year-end receivables from customers = $610,000 sales revenue

$375,000 cash payments for purchases of products – $85,000 year-end inventory of unsold products = $290,000 cost of products sold expense

$340,000 cash payments for other expenses + $25,000 year-end liability for unpaid expenses = $365,000 other expenses

Deducting cost of products sold and other expenses from sales revenue gives a net loss of $45,000 ($610,000 sales revenue – $290,000 cost of products sold – $365,000 other expenses = $45,000 net loss for year).

To answer Questions 5 through 8, please refer to the summary of revenue and expense cash flows and the summary of two assets and a liability at year-end presented in the preceding example question.

5. What would be the amount of accrual-basis sales revenue for the year if the business's year-end receivables had been $92,000?

6. What would be the amount of accrual-basis cost of products sold expense for the year if the business's cost of products held in inventory at year-end had been $95,000?

7. What would be the amount of accrual-basis other expenses for the year if the business's liability for unpaid expenses at year-end had been $30,000?

Solve It

8. Based on the changes for the example given in Questions 5, 6, and 7, determine the profit or loss of the business for its first year.

Solve It

Summarizing Profit Activities in the Income (Profit & Loss) Statement

As crass as it sounds, business managers get paid to make profit happen. Management literature usually stresses the visionary, leadership, and innovative characteristics of business managers, but these traits aren't worth much if the business suffers losses year after year or fails to establish sustainable profit performance. After all, businesses are profit-motivated, aren't they?

It's not surprising that the *income statement* takes center stage in business financial reports. The income statement summarizes a company's revenue and other income, expenses, losses, and bottom-line profit or loss for a period. The income statement gets top billing over the other two primary financial statements (the balance sheet and the statement of cash flows), which I discuss later in this chapter. The income statement is referred to informally as the *Profit & Loss* or *P&L statement,* although these titles are seldom used in external financial reports. (Alternatively, it may be titled *Earnings Statement* or *Statement of Operations.*)

Financial reporting standards demand that an income statement be presented in quarterly and annual financial reports to owners. But financial reporting rules are fairly permissive regarding exactly what information should be reported and how it's presented (see Chapter 5 for the full scoop on income statement disclosure).

Q. Take a look at this extremely abbreviated and condensed income statement for a business's most recent year. (***Note:*** A formal income statement in a financial report must disclose more information than this.)

Income Statement for Year

Sales revenue	$26,000,000
Expenses	24,310,000
Net income	$1,690,000

This business sells products, which are also called *goods* or *merchandise*. The cost of products sold to customers during the year was $14,300,000. Expand the condensed income statement to reflect this additional information.

A. Income statement reporting requires a company to show the cost of goods (products) sold as a separate expense and deduct it immediately below sales revenue. The difference must be reported as *gross margin* (or *gross profit*). Therefore, the condensed income statement should be expanded as follows:

Income Statement for Year

Sales revenue	$26,000,000
Cost of goods sold	14,300,000
Gross margin	$11,700,000
Other expenses	10,010,000
Net income	$1,690,000

9. One rule of income statement reporting is that interest expense and income tax expense be reported separately. The $10,010,000 "Other expenses" in the income statement for the answer to the example question includes $350,000 interest expense and $910,000 income tax. Rebuild the income statement given the information for these additional two expenses. *Hint:* Profit before interest expense is usually labeled "operating earnings," and profit after interest and before income tax expense is usually labeled "earnings before income tax."

Solve It

10. No specific rule governs income statement disclosure of advertising expense. Suppose the $10,010,000 "Other expenses" in the income statement for the answer to the example question includes $5,000,000 of advertising expense. Would you favor reporting this as a separate expense in the income statement? *Hint:* This question calls for your opinion only.

Solve It

11. No specific rule governs income statement disclosure of executive-level compensation. Suppose the $10,010,000 "Other expenses" in the income statement for the answer to the example question includes $3,000,000 of executive-level compensation that includes both base salaries and generous bonuses. Would you favor reporting this as a separate expense in the income statement? *Hint:* This question calls for your opinion only.

Solve It

12. Please refer to the income statement for the answer to the example question. Suppose the business distributed $650,000 cash to its shareowners from its profit (net income) for the year. Is this cash disbursement treated as an expense?

Solve It

Assembling a Balance Sheet

The *balance sheet* is one of the three primary financial statements that businesses report (the other two being the income statement and the statement of cash flows). It's also called the *financial condition statement* or *statement of financial position*. The balance sheet summarizes the assets, liabilities, and owners' equity accounts of a business at an instant in time. Prepared at the close of business on the last day of the profit period, the balance sheet presents a "freeze frame" look at the business's financial condition.

Preparing and reporting a balance sheet takes time, so by the time you read a balance sheet, it's already somewhat out-of-date. The business's stream of activities and operations doesn't stop, which means that from the date at which the balance sheet was prepared to when you read it, the business will have engaged in many transactions. These subsequent transactions may have significantly changed its financial condition. For more on the balance sheet, turn to Chapter 6.

In accounting, the term *balance* refers to the dollar amount of an account, after recording all increases and decreases in the account caused by business activities. The balance sheet reports the balances of asset, liability, and owners' equity accounts, but it also refers to the equality, or balance, of the accounting equation (see the section "Keeping the Accounting Equation in Balance" earlier in this chapter).

Q. The following list summarizes the assets and liabilities of a business at the close of business on the last day of its most recent profit period:

Amounts owed by customers to the business: $485,000

Cost of unsold products (that will be sold next period): $678,000

Cash balance on deposit in checking account with bank: $396,000

Amounts owed by business for unpaid purchases and expenses: $438,000

Notes payable to bank (on which interest is paid): $500,000

Original cost of long-term operating assets that are being depreciated over their useful lives to the business: $950,000

Accumulated depreciation of long-term operating assets: $305,000

Using this information, prepare the business's balance sheet.

A.

Cash	$396,000	Accounts Payable	$438,000
Accounts Receivable	$485,000	Notes Payable	$500,000
Inventory	$678,000	Owners' Equity*	$1,266,000
Fixed Assets (Net of Accumulated Depreciation)	$645,000		
Total Assets	$2,204,000	Total Liabilities and Owners' Equity	$2,204,000

*Owners' equity is determined by deducting the sum of liabilities from total assets.

Note: This balance sheet isn't classified into current assets and current liabilities. Also, owners' equity isn't classified. (Chapter 6 explains the balance sheet in greater detail.)

Use the balance sheet shown in the preceding example to answer Questions 13 through 16.

13. Suppose $950,000 of owners' equity consists of profit earned and not distributed by the business. What is this amount usually called in the balance sheet? And, what is the other amount of owners' equity called in the balance sheet?

14. It appears that the business can't pay its liabilities. The two liabilities total $938,000, but the business has a cash balance of only $396,000. Do you agree?

15. Can you tell the amount of profit the business earned in the period just ended?

16. In a balance sheet, assets usually are listed in the order of their "nearness" to cash. Cash is listed first, followed by the asset closest to being converted into cash, and so on. Is the sequence of assets according to normal rules for presenting assets in balance sheets?

Solve It

Partitioning the Statement of Cash Flows

You could argue that the statement of cash flows is the most important of the three primary financial statements. Why? Because in the long run everything comes down to cash flows. Profit recorded on the accrual basis of accounting has to be turned into cash — and the sooner the better. Otherwise, profit doesn't provide money for growing the business and paying distributions to owners.

By themselves, the income statement and balance sheet don't provide information about the cash flow generated by the business's profit-making, or *operating,* activities. But people who use financial reports (business managers, lenders, and investors) want to see cash flow information. In short, financial reporting standards require a statement of cash flows. The statement begins with reporting the cash flow from operating activities and also reports the other sources and uses of cash during the period, which are divided into the following:

- ✔ **Investing activities:** Include the purchase and construction of long-term operating assets such as land, buildings, equipment, machinery, vehicles, and tools. If a business realizes cash from the disposal of such assets, the proceeds are included in this category of cash flows.

- ✔ **Financing activities:** Include borrowing money from debt sources and paying loans at maturity as well as raising capital from shareowners and returning capital to them. Cash distributions from profit are included in this category of cash flows.

Q. The statement of cash flows for a business's most recent year is presented as follows. Based on the information provided, is it possible to determine the amount of cash flow from operating activities?

Cash flow from operating activities:		?????
Cash flow from investing activities:		
Capital expenditures	($2,345,000)	
Proceeds from disposal of real estate	$225,000	($2,120,000)
Cash flow from financing activities:		
Increase in debt	$1,625,000	
Issue of capital stock shares	$550,000	
Cash dividends to shareholders	($400,000)	$1,775,000
Net cash increase during year		$355,000

A. You can determine the amount of cash flow from operating activities by the following calculations:

$2,120,000 net cash needed for capital expenditures + $355,000 cash balance increase = $2,475,000 total cash needed

$2,475,000 total cash needed – $1,775,000 net cash provided from financing activities = $700,000 cash flow from operating activities

Cash flow from operating activities is explained in more detail in Chapter 8.

You can condense a statement of cash flows, such as the one for the example, into its four basic components as follows (negative numbers appear in parentheses):

Cash flow from operating activities	$700,000
Cash flow from investing activities	($2,120,000)
Cash flow from financing activities	$1,775,000
Net increase in cash during the year	$355,000

If you know three of the four components in a condensed statement of cash flows, you can determine the fourth factor. Suppose you know the increase or decrease in cash during the year (which is easy enough to determine by comparing the ending cash balance with the beginning cash balance). And suppose you can quickly determine the cash flow from investing activities and the cash flow from financing activities (because there aren't many transactions of these two types during the year). Knowing these three factors, you can quickly determine the cash flow from operating activities. The remainder of the increase or decrease in cash during the year is attributable to operating activities.

Questions 17 through 20 give you three of the four components in a condensed statement of cash flows and ask you to solve for the unknown factor.

17. Three of the four components of cash flow for the year of a business are as follows:

Cash flow from operating activities	$450,000
Cash flow from investing activities	($725,000)
Cash flow from financing activities	$50,000
Net increase (decrease) in cash during the year	????

Determine the increase or decrease in cash during the year.

18. Three of the four components of cash flow for the year of a business are as follows:

Cash flow from operating activities	$2,680,000
Cash flow from investing activities	????
Cash flow from financing activities	$1,250,000
Net increase (decrease) in cash during the year	$400,000

Determine cash flow from investing activities for the year.

19. Three of the four components of cash flow for the year of a business are as follows:

Cash flow from operating activities	$650,000
Cash flow from investing activities	($925,000)
Cash flow from financing activities	????
Net increase (decrease) in cash during the year	($65,000)

Determine cash flow from financing activities for the year.

Solve It

20. Three of the four components of cash flow for the year of a business are as follows:

Cash flow from operating activities	????
Cash flow from investing activities	($480,000)
Cash flow from financing activities	($150,000)
Net increase (decrease) in cash during the year	$150,000

Determine cash flow from operating activities for the year.

Solve It

Tracing How Dishonest Accounting Distorts Financial Statements

It goes without saying that a business should keep its accounting system as honest as the day is long. In preparing its financial statements, a business should be forthright and not misleading. As the late sportscaster Howard Cosell would say, "Tell it like it is." I regret to tell you that some businesses cheat in their accounting and financial reporting. Now, there's cheating and then there's *real* cheating. So what's the difference?

Many businesses perform cosmetic surgery on their accounts, touching up their financial condition and profit performance. This practice is popularly called *massaging the numbers*. Professional investors (as in mutual fund managers) and lenders (as in banks) know that a certain amount of accounting manipulation goes on by many businesses, and as a practical matter not much can be done about it.

On another level, some businesses resort to *accounting fraud* to put a better sheen on profit performance and conceal financial problems. Accounting fraud is popularly called *cooking the books*. Think of massaging the numbers as fibbing or putting a spin on the truth and accounting fraud as out-and-out lying with the intent to deceive and mislead. In recent years the incidence of accounting fraud has risen alarmingly. (Do Enron, WorldCom, and Waste Management ring any bells?) Accounting fraud is illegal and perpetrators are subject to prosecution under criminal law. Plus, victims can sue the persons responsible for the fraud.

Q. Suppose a business has engaged in some accounting fraud to boost its profit for the year just ended. Assume that the business didn't commit any accounting fraud before this year (which may not be true, of course). As the result of fraudulent entries in its accounts, the $2,340,000 bottom-line profit reported in its income statement was overstated $385,000. How does this dishonest accounting distort the business's balance sheet?

A. Owners' equity is overstated $385,000 because profit increases owners' equity. And the overstatement of profit may have involved the overstatement of assets, the understatement of liabilities, or a combination of both. To correct this error, owners' equity should be decreased $385,000. As well, assets should be decreased $385,000, or liabilities should be increased $385,000 (or some combination of both).

---

21. Suppose a business commits accounting fraud by deliberately not writing down its inventory of $268,000, which is the cost of certain products that it can no longer sell and will be thrown in the junk heap. How should its balance sheet be adjusted to correct for this accounting fraud, ignoring income tax effects? (Use the answer template provided.)

Solve It

Cash	Accounts Payable
Accounts Receivable	Notes Payable
Inventory	Owners' Equity
Fixed Assets (Net of Accumulated Depreciation) ____	
Total Assets	Total Liabilities and Owners' Equity

22. Suppose a business commits accounting fraud by deliberately not recording $465,000 liabilities for unpaid expenses at the end of the year. How should its balance sheet be adjusted to correct for this accounting fraud, ignoring income tax effects? (Use the answer template provided.)

Solve It

Cash	Accounts Payable
Accounts Receivable	Notes Payable
Inventory	Owners' Equity
Fixed Assets (Net of Accumulated Depreciation) ____	
Total Assets	Total Liabilities and Owners' Equity

Answers to Problems on Elements of Business Accounting

The following are the answers to the practice questions presented earlier in this chapter.

1 Which of the following is the normal way to present the accounting equation?

    c. Assets = Liabilities + Owners' equity

The other three accounting equations are correct from the algebraic equation point of view. However, the accounting equation is usually shown with assets on one side and the two broad classes of claims against the assets on the other side. *Note:* You see answer (b) (Assets – Liabilities = Owners' equity) when the purpose is to emphasize the *net worth* of a business, or its assets less its liabilities.

2 A business has $485,000 total liabilities and $1,200,000 total owners' equity. What is the amount of its total assets?

Total assets = $1,685,000, which is the total of $485,000 liabilities plus $1,200,000 owners' equity.

3 A business has $250,000 total liabilities. When it was started the owners invested $500,000 in the business. Unfortunately, the business has suffered a cumulative loss of $200,000 up to the present time. What is the amount of its total assets at the present time?

Total assets = $550,000, which is the total of $250,000 liabilities plus $300,000 owners' equity.

Notice that the original $500,000 that the owners invested in the business is reduced by the $200,000 cumulative loss of the business, and owners' equity is now only $300,000.

4 A business has $175,000 total liabilities. Originally, at the time of starting the business, the owners invested $250,000 capital. The business has earned $190,000 cumulative profit since it started (all of which has been retained in the business). What is the total amount of its assets?

Total assets = $615,000, which is the total of $175,000 liabilities and $440,000 owners' equity.

Notice that in addition to the original $250,000 capital invested by owners, the business has earned $190,000 profit, so its total owners' equity is $440,000.

5 What would be the amount of accrual-basis sales revenue for the year if the business's year-end receivables had been $92,000? (For the original numbers, see the section "Distinguishing Between Cash- and Accrual-Basis Accounting.")

Sales revenue ($558,000 cash receipts + $92,000 year-end receivables) = $650,000

6 What would be the amount of accrual-basis cost of products sold expense for the year if the business's cost of products held in inventory at year-end had been $95,000? (For the original numbers, see the section "Distinguishing Between Cash- and Accrual-Basis Accounting.")

Cost of products sold ($375,000 cash payments – $95,000 year-end inventory) = $280,000

7 What would be the amount of accrual-basis other expenses for the year if the business's liability for unpaid expenses at year-end had been $30,000? (For the original numbers, see the section "Distinguishing Between Cash- and Accrual-Basis Accounting.")

Other expenses ($340,000 cash payments + $30,000 year-end liability) = $370,000

8   Based on the changes to the example given in Questions 5, 6, and 7, determine the profit or loss of the business for its first year.

In this case, the total of the two expenses (cost of products sold and other expenses) happens to be $650,000, which is exactly equal to sales revenue. So the business *breaks even* for the year. This outcome is unusual, of course; the total of expenses for the year is almost always different than total sales revenue for the year.

9   One rule of income statement reporting is that interest expense and income tax expense be reported separately. The $10,010,000 "Other expenses" in the income statement for the answer to the example question includes $350,000 interest expense and $910,000 income tax. Rebuild the income statement given the information for these additional two expenses. *Hint:* Profit before interest expense is usually labeled "operating earnings," and profit after interest and before income tax expense is usually labeled "earnings before income tax."

Income Statement for Year

Sales revenue	$26,000,000
Cost of goods sold	14,300,000
Gross margin	$11,700,000
Other expenses	8,750,000
Operating earnings	$2,950,000
Interest expense	350,000
Earnings before income tax	$2,600,000
Income tax expense	910,000
Net income	$1,690,000

Burying interest expense or income tax expense in a broader expense category such as "other expenses" or "general expenses" is unacceptable. Interest and income tax expenses are reported toward the bottom of the income statement. They're viewed as *nonoperating expenses,* which means that they depend on how the business is financed and its income tax situation.

10   No specific rule governs income statement disclosure of advertising expense. Suppose the $10,010,000 "Other expenses" in the income statement for the answer to the example question includes $5,000,000 of advertising expense. Would you favor reporting this as a separate expense in the income statement? *Hint:* This question calls for your opinion only.

Well, there's no rule against disclosure of advertising expense — that's for sure. Because it's such a large expense, I favor disclosing it in the income statement. But most businesses are very sensitive about disclosing their advertising expense and, in fact, don't disclose this expense in their income statements.

11   No specific rule governs income statement disclosure of executive-level compensation. Suppose the $10,010,000 "Other expenses" in the income statement for the answer to the example question includes $3,000,000 of executive-level compensation that includes both base salaries and generous bonuses. Would you favor reporting this as a separate expense in the income statement? *Hint:* This question calls for your opinion only.

Oh boy! This is a hot potato question. I'm all for open, frank, and transparent disclosure in financial reports, but this is like believing in Santa Claus. Most businesses are very reluctant to disclose executive-level compensation in their income statements or elsewhere in their financial reports. With no rule forcing such disclosure in their income statements, most businesses don't reveal this piece of information. You can ask for executive-level compensation information if you're on the board of directors of the business, but as an outside shareowner, don't expect to get this information.

12 Please refer to the income statement for the answer to the example question. Suppose the business distributed $650,000 cash to its shareowners from its profit (net income) for the year. Is this cash disbursement treated as an expense?

No, cash distributions from profit to the shareowners of a business aren't an expense. In other words, net income is before any distributions to shareowners.

Income statements generally don't disclose information regarding distributions from profit (net income) during the year. To be more accurate, I should say that an income statement doesn't *have to* disclose this information. However, some businesses don't end their income statements at bottom-line net income: They add net income to the retained earnings balance at the start of the year and deduct distributions from net income during the year to arrive at the year-end balance of retained earnings. But such disclosure isn't common practice. Distributions from net income usually are reported in a separate financial statement called the Statement of Changes in Owners' Equity, which I discuss in Chapter 8.

13 Suppose $950,000 of owners' equity consists of profit earned and not distributed by the business. What is this amount usually called in the balance sheet? And, what is the other amount of owners' equity called in the balance sheet?

The $950,000 of owners' equity over and above the amount of capital invested by the owners typically is called *retained earnings*. To be more precise, business corporations and limited liability companies use this term. (If a business is organized legally as a partnership, it follows different practices for reporting the partners' equity.)

14 It appears that the business can't pay its liabilities. The two liabilities total $938,000, but the business has a cash balance of only $396,000. Do you agree?

A business isn't expected to hold cash equal to the total of its liabilities. In my opinion, this business wouldn't be judged insolvent, although this judgment depends on how conservative or strict you are in evaluating solvency. The business's cash flow prospects are the key factor. The accounts receivable will be collected in the short-run, and this incoming cash will be available for paying the business's liabilities. Also, the inventory held by the business will be sold during the short-run and will generate cash flow.

15 Can you tell the amount of profit the business earned in the period just ended?

No, a balance sheet doesn't report profit (net income) for the most recent period. You look to its income statement for this key figure.

16 In a balance sheet, assets usually are listed in the order of their "nearness" to cash. Cash is listed first, followed by the asset closest to being converted into cash, and so on. Is the sequence of assets according to normal rules for presenting assets in balance sheets?

Yes, the sequence is correct according to conventional rules for reporting assets in a balance sheet. Cash is listed first, followed by assets according to their "nearness" to cash. In the example, the business doesn't have short-term investments in marketable securities. So, its accounts receivable asset is listed second, after cash, because these receivables will be collected in the short-term. Inventory is listed after accounts receivable because this asset consists of products that have to be sold before they can be converted into cash.

17 Based on the three of four components of cash flow for the year of a business that follow, determine the increase or decrease in cash during the year.

Cash flow from operating activities	$450,000
Cash flow from investing activities	($725,000)
Cash flow from financing activities	$50,000
Net increase (decrease) in cash during the year	????

Cash decreased $225,000 during the year.

18 Based on the three of four components of cash flow for the year of a business that follow, determine cash flow from investing activities for the year.

Cash flow from operating activities	$2,680,000
Cash flow from investing activities	????
Cash flow from financing activities	$1,250,000
Net increase (decrease) in cash during the year	$400,000

Cash flow from investing activities for the year is a *negative* $3,530,000. In other words, the net cash *decrease* from investing activities was $3,530,000 during the year.

19 Based on the three of four components of cash flow for the year of a business that follow, determine cash flow from financing activities for the year.

Cash flow from operating activities	$650,000
Cash flow from investing activities	($925,000)
Cash flow from financing activities	????
Net increase (decrease) in cash during the year	($65,000)

Cash flow from financing activities for the year is $210,000. In other words, the net cash increase from financing activities was $210,000 during the year.

20 Based on the three of four components of cash flow for the year of a business that follow, determine cash flow from operating activities for the year.

Cash flow from operating activities	????
Cash flow from investing activities	($480,000)
Cash flow from financing activities	($150,000)
Net increase (decrease) in cash during the year	$150,000

Cash flow from operating activities for the year is $780,000. In other words, the net cash increase from sales and expense (operating) activities was $780,000 during the year.

21 Suppose a business commits accounting fraud by deliberately not writing down its inventory of $268,000, which is the cost of certain products that it can no longer sell and will be thrown in the junk heap. How should its balance sheet be adjusted to correct for this accounting fraud, ignoring income tax effects?

The changes in the balance sheet to correct the fraudulent error are:

Cash		Accounts Payable	
Accounts Receivable		Notes Payable	
Inventory	($268,000)	Owners' Equity	($268,000)
Fixed Assets (Net of Accumulated Depreciation)	_____		_____
Total Assets	($268,000)	Total Liabilities and Owners' Equity	($268,000)

22 Suppose a business commits accounting fraud by deliberately not recording $465,000 liabilities for unpaid expenses at the end of the year. How should its balance sheet be adjusted to correct for this accounting fraud, ignoring income tax effects?

The changes in the balance sheet to correct the fraudulent error are:

Cash		Accounts Payable	$465,000
Accounts Receivable		Notes Payable	
Inventory		Owners' Equity	($465,000)
Fixed Assets (Net of Accumulated Depreciation)	_____		_____
Total Assets		Total Liabilities and Owners' Equity	

Chapter 2

Financial Effects of Transactions

• •

In This Chapter
▶ Identifying business transactions
▶ Examining the financial effects of revenue and expenses
▶ Getting a handle on the composite effect of profit and loss

• •

*T*he following three financial statements are the financial anchors and reference points of every business:

 ✔ **Balance sheet:** Summarizes the business's assets, liabilities, and owners' equity at the end of a period

 ✔ **Income statement:** Summarizes the profit-making transactions of the business for a period of time; also known as the profit and loss (P&L) statement

 ✔ **Statement of cash flows:** Summarizes the business's cash transactions for the same period of time

The first job of accounting is to faithfully record all the transactions of the business so that you then can prepare the financial statements listed above from the transaction records. If you're more the visual type, try this on for size:

Transactions → Accounting process → Financial statements

Transactions are the heartbeat of every business, which is why accountants, above all else, must know how to record them. This chapter separates business transactions into their main types and pays particular attention to how profit-making transactions — specifically, sales and expenses — impact the financial condition of a business.

Note: I do *not* use debits and credits (see Chapter 3) in this chapter. Instead, this chapter keeps the focus on the balance sheet, which is the summary of the financial condition of a business.

Classifying Business Transactions

Businesses are profit-motivated, so one basic type of transactions is obvious: *profit-making transactions.* In a nutshell, profit-making transactions consist of making sales and incurring expenses. Well, if you want to be picky, a business may have other income in addition to sales revenue, and it may record losses in addition to expenses. But the bread and butter profit-making activities of a business are making sales and keeping expenses under control. The profit-making transactions of a business over a period of time are reported in its *income statement* (which I cover in more detail in Chapter 1).

A business's other transactions fall into three basic categories:

✔ **Set-up and follow-up transactions for sales and expenses:** Includes collecting cash from customers after sales made on credit are recorded; the purchase of products (goods) that are held for some time before being sold, at which time the expense is recorded; and making cash payments for expenses some time after the expenses are recorded

✔ **Investing activities (transactions):** Includes the purchase, construction, and disposals of long-term operating assets such as buildings, machinery, equipment, and tools

✔ **Financing activities (transactions):** Includes borrowing money and repaying amounts borrowed; owners investing capital in the business and the business returning capital to them; and making cash distributions to owners based on the profit earned by the business

Investing and financing activities of a particular period are reported in that period's *statement of cash flows* (see Chapter 1). In contrast, set-up and follow-up transactions for sales and expenses stay in the background, meaning that they are *not* reported in a financial statement. Nevertheless, these transactions are essential to the profit-making process.

Consider, for instance, the purchase of products for inventory. As far as profit is concerned, nothing happens until the business makes a sale of that inventory and records the cost of goods sold expense against the revenue from the sale. Because the business needs to have the products available for sale, the purchase of inventory is the important first step, or set-up transaction.

In understanding accounting, you first need to be very clear about which type of transaction you're looking at.

Q. During the year, a business engaged in the following transactions:

a. Borrowed money from a lender (for example, a bank)

b. Purchased products that it put in inventory to be sold to customers at a later date

c. Bought new delivery trucks that will be used for several years

d. Sold to customers products that had been held in inventory

For each transaction, identify which type of transaction it is according to the four basic types:

• Profit-making activities (sales and expenses)

• Set-up and follow-up transactions for sales and expenses

• Investing activities

• Financing activities

A. The transactions and types match up as follows:

a. Financing activities

b. Set-up and follow-up transactions for sales and expenses

c. Investing activities

d. Profit-making activities

Purchasing and constructing assets that have multi-year lives are long-term investments, which are classified as investing activities.

1. A business's shareowners invest additional capital in the business. Which type of transaction is this?

Solve It

2. A business records employees' wages and salaries for the period. Which type of transaction is this?

Solve It

3. A business records the cost of electricity and gas used during the period. Which type of transaction is this?

Solve It

4. A business pays a vendor for a previous purchase of products bought on credit. Which type of transaction is this?

Solve It

Seeing Both Sides of Business Transactions

The accountant's job is to capture all the transactions of the business, determine the financial effects of every transaction, record every transaction in the business's accounts, and from the accounts prepare the financial statements.

To carry out their mission, accountants must understand how transactions (and certain other events) affect the financial condition of the business. To illustrate the impact of transactions, consider the case of a business that has been in operation for many years. Its condensed balance sheet at the start of the year appears in Figure 2-1.

Condensed Balance Sheet

Figure 2-1: Condensed balance sheet of a business.

Cash	$250,000	Operating liabilities		$350,000
Receivables	$300,000	Interest-bearing liabilities		$500,000
Inventory	$400,000	Owner's invested capital		$250,000
PP&E, net	$550,000	Owner's retained earnings		$400,000
Assets	$1,500,000	= Liabilities and Owner's Equity		$1,500,000

Most businesses report more than just the four kinds of assets shown in Figure 2-1, but these four are the hard-core assets of a business that sells products. ("PP&E" stands for *property, plant, and equipment,* which is the generic name for the long-term operating assets of a business. The term "net" means that the amount of accumulated depreciation that has been recorded up to this time is deducted from the cost of the assets.)

Liabilities are divided into two types based on their sources:

✔ Those that arise out of operating activities

✔ Those that result from borrowing money on interest-bearing debt

Operating liabilities are short-term and do not bear interest. Owners' equity is shown in two different accounts in Figure 2-1. The first is for capital invested in the business by its owners. This source of owners' equity is segregated from the other owners' account, which expresses profit that has been earned and retained by the business.

In Figure 2-1, you can see that the total assets and the total liabilities plus owners' equity appear below the line. This information is the accounting equation of the business. The accounting equation is in balance, as it should be, of course.

Q. Refer to the eight basic accounts presented in the condensed balance sheet shown in Figure 2-1 — the four assets, the two liabilities, and the two owners' equities. How does each of the following transactions change the company's financial condition?

a. The business borrows $500,000 and signs a legal instrument called a *note payable* to the lender, promising to pay interest over the life of the loan and to return $500,000 at a future date.

b. The business invests $250,000 in a new machine that it will use for several years and pays for the purchase with a check.

c. The business owners invest an additional $750,000 in the business to aid in its growth and expansion.

d. The business distributes $100,000 of the profit it earned during the year to its shareowners.

A. **a.** *Condensed Balance Sheet*

Cash	+$500,000	Operating liabilities	
Receivables		Interest-bearing liabilities	+$500,000
Inventory		Owners' invested capital	
PP&E, net		Owners' retained earnings	
Assets	+$500,000 =	Liabilities and Owners' Equity	+$500,000

No interest expense is recorded when the money is borrowed because interest is a time charge for using borrowed money. Interest expenses will be recorded in each future period the money is borrowed, starting at the time the money is borrowed.

b. *Condensed Balance Sheet*

Cash	–$250,000	Operating liabilities	
Receivables		Interest-bearing liabilities	
Inventory		Owners' invested capital	
PP&E, net	+$250,000	Owners' retained earnings	
Assets	=	Liabilities and Owners' Equity	

There is no change in total assets but rather an exchange among assets: Cash decreases $250,000 with the cost of the new machine. Keep in mind that the cost of the machine will be charged as a depreciation expense over future periods in which the machine is used.

c. *Condensed Balance Sheet*

Cash	+$750,000	Operating liabilities	
Receivables		Interest-bearing liabilities	
Inventory		Owners' invested capital	+$750,000
PP&E, net		Owners' retained earnings	
Assets	+$750,000 =	Liabilities and Owners' Equity	+$750,000

d. *Condensed Balance Sheet*

Cash	–$100,000	Operating liabilities	
Receivables		Interest-bearing liabilities	
Inventory		Owners' invested capital	
PP&E, net		Owners' retained earnings	–$100,000
Assets	–$100,000 =	Liabilities and Owners' Equity	–$100,000

Profit is recorded in owners' retained earnings. Profit increases this account, and distributions from profit decrease the account.

5. Suppose that all revenue transactions during the year increase cash and that all expense transactions during the year decrease cash. In other words, suppose no other assets and no operating liabilities are affected by the profit-making activities of the business during the year (this scenario isn't realistic and is assumed only for this problem). The net income (bottom-line profit) of this atypical business for the year is $950,000. How does profit change its financial condition?

Solve It

Condensed Balance Sheet

Cash	Operating liabilities
Receivables	Interest-bearing liabilities
Inventory	Owners' invested capital
PP&E, net	Owners' retained earnings
Assets =	Liabilities and Owners' Equity

6. During the year, a business borrowed $850,000 and used $750,000 of those funds to invest in new long-term operating assets. How do these actions change its financial condition?

Solve It

Condensed Balance Sheet

Cash	Operating liabilities
Receivables	Interest-bearing liabilities
Inventory	Owners' invested capital
PP&E, net	Owners' retained earnings
Assets =	Liabilities and Owners' Equity

7. A freak flood caused extensive damage to inventory. Unfortunately these losses weren't insured, and the business had to write off $175,000 of its inventory. Ignoring the income tax effects of this write-off, how does this event change the business's financial condition?

Solve It

Condensed Balance Sheet

Cash	Operating liabilities
Receivables	Interest-bearing liabilities
Inventory	Owners' invested capital
PP&E, net	Owners' retained earnings
Assets =	Liabilities and Owners' Equity

8. A note payable liability came due (meaning it reached its maturity date) during the year, and the business decided not to renew (or *rollover*) this loan. Accordingly, the business paid $500,000 to the lender, and the note payable was cancelled. (All interest expense on this debt was recorded correctly during the year.) How did paying off the note payable change the business's financial condition?

Solve It

Condensed Balance Sheet

Cash		Operating liabilities
Receivables		Interest-bearing liabilities
Inventory		Owners' invested capital
PP&E, net		Owners' retained earnings
Assets	=	Liabilities and Owners' Equity

Concentrating on Sales

One of the most quoted sayings in business is, "Nothing happens until you sell it." (Another is, "There's no such thing as a free lunch," but I digress.) Well, there's no doubt that a business has to make sales that generate enough sales revenue to overcome its expenses and leave a residual of profit. As I'm sure you know, this is a tall task.

The effect that making a sale has on a business's financial condition depends on when cash is collected from the sale. Regarding cash collection, sales come in three flavors:

- **Cash sales:** Cash is collected when the business makes the sale and delivers the product and/or service to the customer.

- **Credit sales:** Cash isn't collected until sometime after the sale is made; the customer is given a period of time before it has to pay the business.

- **Advance payment sales:** The customer pays the business before the sale is consummated, that is, before the business delivers the product and/or service to the customer.

In short, cash may be collected at the time of the sale, after this time, or before this time.

No doubt you're familiar with cash and credit sales. However, you may be a little rusty, from an accounting point of view, on *advance payment sales*. For this type of sale, at the time of receiving an advance payment, the business does *not* record a sale; instead, it records a liability that stays on the books until the product or service is actually delivered to the customer. This specific liability is one of the business's operating liabilities.

For example, I recently sent a $500 check to *The New York Times* as advance payment for delivery of the paper every day for the coming 12 months. Similarly, if I were a rabid Denver Broncos football fan, I would buy season tickets, which require me to pay before the season starts. Do you give gift certificates to others as birthday or holiday presents? A gift certificate is another example of an advance payment sale. The liability of the advance payment sale is extinguished as papers are delivered, games are played, and gift certificates are redeemed.

Suppose I tell you that a business recorded $3,200,000 sales revenue for the year just ended. Can you tell me how its balance sheet changed as the result of that sales revenue? No, you can't — unless the business makes only cash sales. If the business makes credit sales or collects advance payments from customers for future sales, then the changes in its balance sheet caused by sales are a little more involved. Sorry, but this is a business fact of life.

Q. A business makes all three kinds of sales — cash, credit, and advance payment. For the latest year, it recorded $3,200,000 total sales revenue. Its sales caused its receivable balance to increase $75,000 during the year and its operating liabilities balance to increase $50,000 during the year. How did sales for the year change its financial condition?

A. Its sales cause the following changes in the financial condition of the business:

Condensed Balance Sheet

Cash	+$3,175,000	Operating liabilities		+$50,000
Receivables	+$75,000	Interest-bearing liabilities		
Inventory		Owners' invested capital		
PP&E, net		Owners' retained earnings		+$3,200,000
Assets	+$3,250,000 =	Liabilities and Owners' Equity	+$3,250,000	

Some important points to note in this scenario are:

- Credit sales cause receivables to increase $75,000 during the year, so the year-end balance of receivables is $75,000 higher than the start-of-year balance. Generally speaking, receivables increase when sales increase year-to-year.

- Advance payment sales cause operating liabilities to increase $50,000 during the year, so the year-end balance of the liability for advance payments from customers is $50,000 higher than the start-of-year balance. Generally speaking, this liability increases when sales increase year-to-year.

 The $3,200,000 sales revenue for the year increases owners' retained earnings. But don't forget that the business has expenses for the year. Expenses must be deducted from sales revenue to get to the net effect on owners' retained earnings, which is profit for the year. (Expenses are examined in the section "Concentrating on Expenses" later in this chapter.)

---

9. A business sells only to other businesses and makes all sales on credit; it doesn't have any cash sales or advance payment sales. During the year, the business made $35,000,000 sales. From these sales, the business collected $31,500,000 during the year, and it also collected the $3,250,000 receivables balance at the start of the year. What are the effects of these collections on the business's financial condition?

Solve It

Condensed Balance Sheet

Cash	Operating liabilities
Receivables	Interest-bearing liabilities
Inventory	Owners' invested capital
PP&E, net	Owners' retained earnings
Assets =	Liabilities and Owners' Equity

10. A business requires advance payments on all sales. In other words, it collects cash from customers before products are delivered to them later. During the year, the business received $12,500,000 in advance payments from customers. By the end of the year, the business had delivered 85 percent of products to customers for advance payments received during the year. Also, the business delivered products to customers during the year that fully discharged the $1,500,000 balance in liability for advance payments at the start of the year. What are the effects of these exchanges on the business's financial condition?

Solve It

Condensed Balance Sheet

Cash		Operating liabilities
Receivables		Interest-bearing liabilities
Inventory		Owners' invested capital
PP&E, net		Owners' retained earnings
Assets	=	Liabilities and Owners' Equity

11. During the year, a business made $3,650,000 cash sales. The business has a very liberal product return policy and therefore accepted product returns from customers and refunded $450,000 cash. What are the effects of these returns on the business's financial condition?

Solve It

Condensed Balance Sheet

Cash		Operating liabilities
Receivables		Interest-bearing liabilities
Inventory		Owners' invested capital
PP&E, net		Owners' retained earnings
Assets	=	Liabilities and Owners' Equity

12. During its first year of business, a company made $6,250,000 credit sales. The business collected $5,600,000 cash from customers during the year from these sales. Unfortunately, a few customers didn't pay despite repeated requests and threats of legal action. The business cut off credit to these "deadbeat" customers and refused to make any more credit sales to them. The business had to write off $150,000 uncollectible receivables. What are the effects of these events on its financial condition?

Solve It

Condensed Balance Sheet

Cash		Operating liabilities
Receivables		Interest-bearing liabilities
Inventory		Owners' invested capital
PP&E, net		Owners' retained earnings
Assets	=	Liabilities and Owners' Equity

Concentrating on Expenses

Just as cash is collected before, after, or at the time of sale, cash is paid before, after, or at the time that an expense is recorded. The following are some examples of cash payment for expenses:

- **Paying cash before an expense is recorded:** The expense of cost of goods (products) sold is not recorded until the sale is made. (Products are bought and paid for before they're sold to customers.) Another example is that businesses pay for insurance policies today that provide coverage for six months or more, but the insurance expense isn't recorded until time passes.

- **Paying cash after an expense is recorded:** A business records advertising expenses because the ads have already appeared on TV or in newspapers, but it may not pay the bills for these ads until next year.

- **Paying cash when an expense is recorded:** Wages and salaries expenses are generally recorded at the time employees are paid.

Most businesses invest in long-term operating assets, the cost of which is charged to *depreciation* expense over many years. Essentially, a business pays for the asset today, but the cost of the asset is recorded as expense over several future years.

Suppose I tell you that a business recorded $3,000,000 total expenses for the year just ended. Does this simply mean that cash decreased this amount? Hardly! Recording expenses involves other assets than just cash — it involves operating liabilities as well.

Q. Refer back to the business examined in the "Concentrating on Sales" to complete that business's profit accounting for the year. Expenses are now dealt with to close the profit circle. During the year just ended, the business recorded all three types of expenses — expenses recorded before, after, and at the time of paying the expense. For the year, the business recorded $3,000,000 total expenses. These expenses caused inventory to increase $50,000 during the year, PP&E, net to decrease $75,000 (because depreciation on the assets was recorded), and operating liabilities to increase $45,000. How did the company's expenses change its financial condition?

A. Here's a realistic scenario for how expenses change the financial condition of the business:

Condensed Balance Sheet

Cash	–$2,930,000	Operating liabilities	+$45,000
Receivables		Interest-bearing liabilities	
Inventory	+$50,000	Owners' invested capital	
PP&E, net	–$75,000	Owners' retained earnings	–$3,000,000
Assets	–$2,955,000 =	Liabilities and Owners' Equity	–$2,955,000

Some important points to note in this scenario are:

- The business recorded $75,000 depreciation expense for the year, so its long-term operating assets (PP&E, net) decrease this amount.

- The $50,000 *increase* in inventory may strike you as an odd effect of expenses. Keep in mind, however, that a business can purchase or manufacture more inventory than it sells during the year, in which case its inventory balance increases. That's exactly what happened in this example.

- The business has $45,000 more operating liabilities at year-end than it did at the start of the year. In other words, its unpaid expenses at the end of the year are $45,000 more than at the beginning of the year.

13. A business recorded $4,500,000 total expenses for the year. The expenses caused $100,000 increase in its operating liabilities, and a $200,000 depreciation expense was recorded in the year. There was no change in inventory during the year (which is unusual). How did expenses change the financial condition of the business?

Solve It

Condensed Balance Sheet

Cash		Operating liabilities
Receivables		Interest-bearing liabilities
Inventory		Owners' invested capital
PP&E, net		Owners' retained earnings
Assets	=	Liabilities and Owners' Equity

14. A business leases all its long-term operating assets (buildings, machines, vehicles, and so on). Thus, it has no depreciation expense. For the year just ended, the business recorded $2,450,000 total expenses. Expenses caused $75,000 increase in operating liabilities. Inventory increased $45,000 during the year. How did expenses change the financial condition of the business?

Solve It

Condensed Balance Sheet

Cash		Operating liabilities
Receivables		Interest-bearing liabilities
Inventory		Owners' invested capital
PP&E, net		Owners' retained earnings
Assets	=	Liabilities and Owners' Equity

15. A business was just about ready to prepare its financial statements for the year when a sharp-eyed bookkeeper noticed that the business had failed to accrue (record) certain liabilities for unpaid expenses at the end of the year. So, a correcting entry has to be made. The amount of these liabilities for unpaid expenses at year-end is $38,000. What changes in financial condition does recording this additional amount of expense for the year cause? (Ignore income tax effects.)

Solve It

Condensed Balance Sheet

Cash		Operating liabilities
Receivables		Interest-bearing liabilities
Inventory		Owners' invested capital
PP&E, net		Owners' retained earnings
Assets	=	Liabilities and Owners' Equity

16. A business decides to engage in accounting fraud to improve its profit performance for the year. Of course this is unethical and illegal, but the chief executive of the business is desperate, and the chief accountant agrees to conspire with the chief executive to carry out this accounting fraud. They decide that they can't manipulate sales revenue for the year, so the accounting fraud has to be done on the expense side of the ledger. The changes in financial condition caused by the actual expenses of the business for the year are given below. How might management go about misstating the expenses in order to boost profit $125,000? (*Note:* You have to think like a crook to work this problem.)

Solve It

Condensed Balance Sheet

Cash	–$4,800,000	Operating liabilities	+$275,000	
Receivables		Interest-bearing liabilities		
Inventory	+$50,000	Owners' invested capital		
PP&E, net	–$400,000	Owners' retained earnings	–$5,425,000	
Assets	–$5,150,000 =	Liabilities and Owners' Equity	–$5,150,000	

Determining the Composite Effect of Profit

To determine the profit or loss of a business for the year, it's necessary to blend sales revenue and expenses together. The equation for profit is as follows:

Profit = Sales revenue – Expenses

For example,

Sales revenue	$3,200,000
Less: Expenses	–3,000,000
Equals: Profit	$200,000

Determining the effects of profit on the year-end financial condition of a business is a little more involved than the profit computation. You merge the two summaries of changes in financial condition presented earlier in this chapter — one from revenue (see the section "Concentrating on Sales") and the second from expenses (see the section "Concentrating on Expenses") — to determine the composite effect on assets, liabilities, and owners' retained earnings.

Two kinds of balance sheet accounts aren't affected by sales and expense transactions: interest-bearing liabilities and owners' invested capital.

Q. What is the composite change in the year-end financial condition of the business caused by its profit-making activities over the year? Refer back to the financial condition changes caused by sales and expenses, which are presented earlier in the chapter (see the example questions in the sections "Concentrating on Sales" and "Concentrating on Expenses"), to answer this question.

A. Combining the changes caused from sales with the changes caused from expenses gives the following:

Condensed Balance Sheet – Composite Net Changes From Sales and Expenses

Cash	+$245,000	Operating liabilities	+$95,000	
Receivables	+$75,000	Interest-bearing liabilities		
Inventory	+$50,000	Owners' invested capital		
PP&E, net	−$75,000	Owners' retained earnings	+$200,000	
Assets	+$295,000 =	Liabilities and Owners' Equity	+$295,000	

To determine each amount of change, combine the change caused by sales and the change caused by expenses. For instance, sales increase cash $3,175,000 and expenses decrease cash $2,930,000, so the net change is $245,000 increase.

---

17. Suppose that expenses for the year caused the following changes in the company's financial condition:

Condensed Balance Sheet

Cash	−$2,880,000	Operating liabilities	+$150,000	
Receivables		Interest-bearing liabilities		
Inventory	+$25,000	Owners' invested capital		
PP&E, net	−$95,000	Owners' retained earnings	−$3,100,000	
Assets	−$2,950,000 =	Liabilities and Owners' Equity	−$2,950,000	

What is the composite effect on financial condition from the company's profit-making activities for the year? (Assume that changes in financial condition from its sales are the same.)

Solve It

Condensed Balance Sheet

Cash		Operating liabilities
Receivables		Interest-bearing liabilities
Inventory		Owners' invested capital
PP&E, net		Owners' retained earnings
Assets	=	Liabilities and Owners' Equity

18. Suppose that sales for the year caused the following changes in the company's financial condition:

Condensed Balance Sheet

Cash	+$3,000,000	Operating liabilities		−$50,000
Receivables	+$250,000	Interest-bearing liabilities		
Inventory		Owners' invested capital		
PP&E, net		Owners' retained earnings		+$3,300,000
Assets	+$3,250,000 =	Liabilities and Owners' Equity		+$3,250,000

What is the composite effect on financial condition from the company's profit-making activities for the year? (Assume that changes in financial condition from expenses are the same.)

Solve It

Condensed Balance Sheet

Cash	Operating liabilities
Receivables	Interest-bearing liabilities
Inventory	Owners' invested capital
PP&E, net	Owners' retained earnings
Assets =	Liabilities and Owners' Equity

---

19. Starting with the financial condition of the business at the beginning of the year (see "Seeing Both Sides of Business Transactions" earlier in this chapter) and the changes caused by its profit-making activities during the year (see "Concentrating on the Composite Effect of Profit and Loss" earlier in this chapter), what is its financial condition at the end of the year, ignoring other transactions that occurred during the year?

To help you work this problem, the company's financial condition at the start of the year is repeated here (from Figure 2-1):

Condensed Balance Sheet

Cash	$250,000	Operating liabilities	$350,000
Receivables	$300,000	Interest-bearing liabilities	$500,000
Inventory	$400,000	Owners' invested capital	$250,000
PP&E, net	$550,000	Owners' retained earnings	$400,000
Assets	$1,500,000 =	Liabilities and Owners' Equity	$1,500,000

Solve It

Condensed Balance Sheet

Cash	Operating liabilities
Receivables	Interest-bearing liabilities
Inventory	Owners' invested capital
PP&E, net	Owners' retained earnings
Assets =	Liabilities and Owners' Equity

20. Building on your answer to Question 19, assume that the business had other non-profit transactions during the year, as follows:

✔ Increased its interest-bearing liabilities $100,000.

✔ Paid $80,000 distribution from profit to its shareowners

Taking into account these additional transactions, what is the financial condition of the business at the end of the year?

Solve It

Condensed Balance Sheet

Cash		Operating liabilities
Receivables		Interest-bearing liabilities
Inventory		Owners' invested capital
PP&E, net		Owners' retained earnings
Assets	=	Liabilities and Owners' Equity

Answers to Problems on Financial Effects of Transactions

The following are the answers to the practice questions presented earlier in this chapter.

1 **Financing activity.** To start a business, its owners invest an initial amount of capital (usually money) and from time to time after start-up, they may invest more capital in the business.

2 **Profit-making activity.** Wages and salaries is a basic type of expense of all businesses.

3 **Profit-making activity.** The cost of utilities is a basic expense of all businesses.

4 **Set-up and follow-up transactions for sales and expenses.** This payment is the follow-up transaction that completes the previous purchase on credit.

5 **Condensed Balance Sheet**

Cash	+$950,000		Operating liabilities	
Receivables			Interest-bearing liabilities	
Inventory			Owners' invested capital	
PP&E, net			Owners' retained earnings	+$950,000
Assets	+$950,000	=	Liabilities and Owners' Equity	+$950,000

6 **Condensed Balance Sheet**

Cash	+$100,000		Operating liabilities	
Receivables			Interest-bearing liabilities	+$850,000
Inventory			Owners' invested capital	
PP&E, net	+$750,000		Owners' retained earnings	
Assets	+$850,000	=	Liabilities and Owners' Equity	+$850,000

7 **Condensed Balance Sheet**

Cash			Operating liabilities	
Receivables			Interest-bearing liabilities	
Inventory	−$175,000		Owners' invested capital	
PP&E, net			Owners' retained earnings	−$175,000
Assets	−$175,000	=	Liabilities and Owners' Equity	−$175,000

8 **Condensed Balance Sheet**

Cash	−$500,000		Operating liabilities	
Receivables			Interest-bearing liabilities	−$500,000
Inventory			Owners' invested capital	
PP&E, net			Owners' retained earnings	
Assets	−$500,000	=	Liabilities and Owners' Equity	−$500,000

9 **Condensed Balance Sheet**

Cash	+$34,750,000	Operating liabilities		
Receivables	+$250,000	Interest-bearing liabilities		
Inventory		Owners' invested capital		
PP&E, net		Owners' retained earnings	+$35,000,000	
Assets	+$35,000,000 =	Liabilities and Owners' Equity	+$35,000,000	

The business added $35,000,000 to receivables from its credit sales during the year. It collected $34,750,000 on receivables during the year ($31,500,000 + $3,250,000). Therefore, receivables increased $250,000, as you see in the balance sheet above.

10 **Condensed Balance Sheet**

Cash	+$12,500,000	Operating liabilities	+$375,000
Receivables		Interest-bearing liabilities	
Inventory		Owners' invested capital	
PP&E, net		Owners' retained earnings	+$12,125,000
Assets	+$12,500,000 =	Liabilities and Owners' Equity	+$12,500,000

The business fulfilled 85 percent of its advanced payment for sales during the year, which means it recorded $10,625,000 sales revenue. Also, the company earned $1,500,000 by delivering products to "pay off" the balance in the liability account for advance payments at the start of the year. Sales revenue is the sum of the two, or $12,125,000. The business has not delivered on 15 percent of its $12,500,000 advance payment sales during the year, which gives a $1,875,000 year-end balance in this liability. The year-end balance is $375,000 higher than the beginning balance in this liability. By the way, if you got this answer right the first time around, congratulations! This is a tough problem.

11 **Condensed Balance Sheet**

Cash	+$3,200,000	Operating liabilities	
Receivables		Interest-bearing liabilities	
Inventory		Owners' invested capital	
PP&E, net		Owners' retained earnings	+$3,200,000
Assets	+$3,200,000 =	Liabilities and Owners' Equity	+$3,200,000

12 **Condensed Balance Sheet**

Cash	+$5,600,000	Operating liabilities	
Receivables	+$500,000	Interest-bearing liabilities	
Inventory		Owners' invested capital	
PP&E, net		Owners' retained earnings	+$6,100,000
Assets	+$6,100,000 =	Liabilities and Owners' Equity	+$6,100,000

In its income statement for the year, the business reports $6,250,000 sales revenue and $150,000 bad debts expense for the receivables written-off during the year. So, the net effect on owners' retained earnings is an increase of $6,100,000.

13 **Condensed Balance Sheet**

Cash	−$4,200,000	Operating liabilities		+$100,000
Receivables		Interest-bearing liabilities		
Inventory		Owners' invested capital		
PP&E, net	−$200,000	Owners' retained earnings		−$4,500,000
Assets	−$4,400,000 =	Liabilities and Owners' Equity		−$4,400,000

14 **Condensed Balance Sheet**

Cash	−$2,420,000	Operating liabilities		+$75,000
Receivables		Interest-bearing liabilities		
Inventory	+$45,000	Owners' invested capital		
PP&E, net		Owners' retained earnings		−$2,450,000
Assets	−$2,375,000 =	Liabilities and Owners' Equity		−$2,375,000

15 **Condensed Balance Sheet**

Cash		Operating liabilities		+$38,000
Receivables		Interest-bearing liabilities		
Inventory		Owners' invested capital		
PP&E, net		Owners' retained earnings		−$38,000
Assets	=	Liabilities and Owners' Equity		

The income tax effect of recording the additional $38,000 expenses is not reflected in this answer. The additional $38,000 is deductible to figure taxable income, so the income tax expense for the year would decrease.

16 **Condensed Balance Sheet**

Cash		Operating liabilities		−$125,000
Receivables		Interest-bearing liabilities		
Inventory		Owners' invested capital		
PP&E, net		Owners' retained earnings		+$125,000
Assets	=	Liabilities and Owners' Equity		

Thinking like a crook, I probably would manipulate liabilities for unpaid expenses; I would deliberately not record $125,000 of these liabilities. The effects of this manipulation are shown in the condensed balance sheet above. As you see, operating liabilities are understated $125,000. Therefore, total expenses for the year are $125,000 lower, and net income is $125,000 higher (before income tax is taken into account). Doing accounting fraud this way may deceive auditors because there's no record of these unrecorded liabilities in the accounts. However, a sharp auditor may notice something missing if he or she looks carefully for unrecorded liabilities.

17 **Condensed Balance Sheet**

Cash	+$295,000	Operating liabilities		+$200,000
Receivables	+$75,000	Interest-bearing liabilities		
Inventory	+$25,000	Owners' invested capital		
PP&E, net	−$95,000	Owners' retained earnings		+$100,000
Assets	+$300,000 =	Liabilities and Owners' Equity		+$300,000

18 **Condensed Balance Sheet**

Cash	+$70,000	Operating liabilities		–$5,000
Receivables	+$250,000	Interest-bearing liabilities		
Inventory	+$50,000	Owners' invested capital		
PP&E, net	–$75,000	Owners' retained earnings		+$300,000
Assets	+$295,000	=	Liabilities and Owners' Equity	+$295,000

19 **Condensed Balance Sheet**

Cash	$495,000	Operating liabilities		$445,000
Receivables	$375,000	Interest-bearing liabilities		$500,000
Inventory	$450,000	Owners' invested capital		$250,000
PP&E, net	$475,000	Owners' retained earnings		$600,000
Assets	$1,795,000	=	Liabilities and Owners' Equity	$1,795,000

20 **Condensed Balance Sheet**

Cash	$515,000	Operating liabilities		$445,000
Receivables	$375,000	Interest-bearing liabilities		$600,000
Inventory	$450,000	Owners' invested capital		$250,000
PP&E, net	$475,000	Owners' retained earnings		$520,000
Assets	$1,815,000	=	Liabilities and Owners' Equity	$1,815,000

Chapter 3

Getting Started in the Bookkeeping Cycle

* *

In This Chapter
▶ Establishing a chart of accounts
▶ Recognizing the difference between real and nominal accounts
▶ Appreciating the centuries-old debits and credits method
▶ Making journal entries for business transactions

* *

The bookkeeping and recordkeeping system of a business requires an accountant to do the following:

✔ Establish the *chart of accounts* in which the transactions of the business are recorded

✔ Record *original entries* for transactions of the business as they occur day by day

✔ Use the *debits and credits* system for recording transactions in order to keep the books (accounts) of the business in balance

✔ Record additional *adjusting entries* at the end of the period to adjust revenue and expense accounts in order to make profit correct

✔ Record certain "housekeeping" entries, called *closing entries*, to bring the profit accounting process for the year to a close

This chapter explains the first three elements: the chart of accounts, original entries, and debits and credits. Chapter 4 completes the recordkeeping cycle by explaining the last two elements: adjusting entries and closing entries.

It makes no difference whether the bookkeeping process is handled by a person recording entries by hand (popularly envisioned wearing a green eyeshade and arm garters and making entries with a quill pen) or a 21st-century bookkeeper working at a computer keyboard. The recordkeeping process is fundamentally the same: Adopt a chart of accounts, make original entries using debits and credits to keep the books in balance, make adjusting entries to get profit for the period right, and close the books at the end of the year. IBM does it this way, and so does you local convenience store. The process reminds me of the saying: "The more things change, the more things stay the same."

Constructing the Chart of Accounts

Accounts are the basic building blocks of an accounting system. An account is a category of information, like a file in which a certain type of information is stored. The reason for establishing an account is that the business needs specific information pulled together in order to prepare a financial statement or some other accounting report.

The first step in setting up an accounting system is to identify the particular accounts that are needed. The financial effects of transactions are recorded as increases or decreases in accounts, and you can't make an accounting entry for a transaction without having accounts to increase or decrease. In short, no accounts mean no accounting!

Suppose you're the chief accountant of a brand new business. It's your very first day on the job. Where do you start (after finding the restroom)? Your first order of business is to establish the *chart of accounts* that will be used to record the transactions of the business. The chart of accounts becomes the official set of accounts that you use to record the effects of transactions. Unless you authorize the creation of a new account, the accounts in the chart are the only ones you use.

The need for one account in the chart of accounts, the cash account, is pretty obvious. A business needs to know how much money it has in its checking account with its bank, so it must establish a cash account and record cash receipts and disbursements in the account. Which other accounts are needed? This is the $64,000 question. To answer this question, the chief accountant looks to the information the business needs to report in its financial statements and income tax returns (the two major information demands on the accounting system of a business).

Business corporations file Form 1120, *U.S. Corporation Income Tax Return,* with the Internal Revenue Service (IRS). The first page of this income tax return requires the following revenue and income information:

- Line 1, Gross receipts or sales
- Line 1b, Less sales returns and allowances
- Line 1c, (Line 1 minus Line 1b)
- Line 2, Cost of goods sold
- Line 3, Gross profit (Line 1c minus Line 2)
- Line 4, Dividends
- Line 5, Interest
- Line 6, Gross rents
- Line 7, Gross royalties

Q. Which accounts should the business establish to provide the information required in the first part of its annual income tax return?

A. The business should establish the following accounts:

- *Sales revenue* for gross revenue from sales to customers

- *Sales returns and allowances* for returns of products and price reductions after making sales

- *Cost of goods sold expense* for the cost of products sold to customers

- *Dividend income* for income from investments in stocks of other companies

- *Interest income* for interest earned on investments and loans

- *Rental income* for income from property being leased to others

- *Royalty income* for income from mineral rights, copyrights, and so on owned by the business

The exact titles of these accounts vary from business to business. However, the account titles listed here are fairly typical. The sales returns and allowance account is a *contra account* to the sales revenue account, which means that it offsets the sales revenue account. The balance in this account is deducted from sales revenue to determine *net sales revenue,* which is reported on Line 1c in Form 1120. If a business knows that it won't have any income from dividends, interest, rents, and royalties, then it shouldn't bother to establish accounts for these sources of income. No account is needed for Line 1c or Line 3 because they're *calculated amounts,* not balances of accounts.

---

1. A business rents the building that houses its retail store, its warehouse, and its administrative offices. It pays rent in cash, so obviously the business needs a cash account. Should the business include an expense account for rent in its chart of accounts?

Solve It

2. A business borrows money from its bank. Identify the liability account and the expense account that it should include in its chart of accounts for the borrowing of money.

3. A business employs a typical range of employees — janitors, salespeople, book-keepers, truck drivers, managers, and so on. It provides a basic retirement plan and pays the premiums for employees' medical and hospital insurance. The annual income tax return filed with the IRS requires the following information: compensation of officers; salaries and wages; employee benefit program; and pension and profit-sharing plans. Should the business include a separate expense account for each of these compensation elements in its chart of accounts?

Solve It

4. The income tax Form 1120 for business corporations requires the reporting of the following assets: trade notes and accounts receivables; buildings and other depreciable assets; and loans to shareholders. Should the business include separate accounts for each of these assets in its chart of accounts? (These are only three of many items of information that the IRS requires to be reported in the balance sheet that must be included in a business's annual income tax returns.)

Solve It

Distinguishing Real and Nominal Accounts

Businesses keep two types of accounts:

- **Real accounts** are those reported in the balance sheet, which is the summary of the assets, liabilities, and owners' equities of a business.

  The label *real* refers to the continuous, permanent nature of this type of account. Real accounts are active from the first day of business to the last day. (A real account could have a temporary zero balance, in which case it's not reported in the balance sheet.) Real accounts contain the balances of assets, liabilities, and owners' equities *at a specific point in time,* such as at the close of business on the last day of the year. A real account is a record of the amount of asset, liability, or owners' equity at a precise moment in time. The balance in a real account is the *net amount* after subtracting decreases from increases in the account.

- **Nominal accounts** are those reported in the income statement, which is the summary of the revenue and expenses of a business for a period of time.

  Balances in nominal accounts are *cumulative* over a period of time. Take the balance in the sales revenue account at the end of the year, for example. This balance is the total amount of sales over the entire year. Likewise, the balance in advertising expense is the total amount of the expense over the entire year. At the end of the period, the accountant uses the balances in the nominal accounts of a business to determine its net profit or loss for the period — this is the main reason for keeping the nominal accounts.

Here's a rough analogy to help you understand the difference between real and nominal accounts: Consider the water held behind a dam at a particular point in time. The water is real because you can dip your toe in it. Compare this body of water with the total amount of water that flowed through the dam over the last year. This water isn't there because it has already gone downriver. This amount is the measure of total flow for a period of time. Assets are like the water behind the dam, and sales revenue is like the flow of water over the year.

Nominal (revenue and expense) accounts are *closed* at the end of the year. After these accounts have done their jobs accumulating amounts of sales and expenses for the year 2006, for example, their balances are closed. Their balances are reset to zero to start the year 2007. Nominal accounts are emptied out to make way for accumulating sales revenue and expenses during the following year. I cover closing entries in Chapter 4.

Q. A business has just released its financial report for the year just ended, which includes its balance sheet at year-end and its income statement for the year. You take the time to count the number of accounts in each statement and find 20 accounts in the balance sheet and 6 accounts in the income statement. These counts do *not* include calculated amounts, such as the total of assets in the balance sheet and gross profit in the income statement. How many accounts does the business need?

A. The absolute minimum number of accounts that business needs is 20 balance sheet (real) accounts and 6 income statement (nominal) accounts. Otherwise, it doesn't have enough separation of information to prepare its two financial statements. In actual practice, businesses keep many more accounts than they report in their balance sheets and income statements.

If you were to look at the chart of accounts maintained by even a relatively small business, you'd find hundreds of accounts (maybe more). For example, a business may keep a separate account for each checking account it uses but, in its balance sheet, report only one cash account, which is the combined total of all its separate cash accounts. Similarly, the business may keep different notes payable accounts, one for each note payable obligation, but combine all notes into one total liability amount in its balance sheet. Another example is a business that keeps different sales revenue accounts, broken down by product lines, sales territories, and so on. It reports only one total sales revenue account in its income statement. (Public businesses are subject to disclosure rules regarding segment reporting of sales, which is too technical to go into here.)

5. Suppose a business just opened its doors on the first day of the year. Not a single transaction has taken place yet in the new year. Which of the following accounts have balances in them, and which don't?

- Cash

- Notes payable

- Sales revenue

- Owners' equity — Invested capital

- Wages and salaries expense

- Inventory

Solve It

6. This question focuses on just two accounts taken from the chart of accounts of a business that makes credit sales. (Even a small business keeps hundreds of accounts.) The first is a real account, *accounts receivable*. The second is a nominal account, *sales revenue*. Are increases *and* decreases recorded in both accounts during the year, or are only increases recorded during the year?

Solve It

7. The following condensed balance sheet presents eight core accounts of a business. Which of the eight accounts have a high frequency of transactions recorded in them during the year, and which have a low frequency of transactions? In other words, which of these eight are busy accounts, and which are not?

Condensed Balance Sheet

Cash	$250,000		Operating liabilities	$350,000
Receivables	$300,000		Interest-bearing liabilities	$500,000
Inventory	$400,000		Owners' invested capital	$250,000
PP&E, net	$550,000		Owners' retained earnings	$400,000
Assets	$1,500,000	=	Liabilities and Owners' Equity	$1,500,000

Solve It

8. A good friend is reading the most recent financial report of your business. In the balance sheet, she comes across an account called "Owners' equity — Retained earnings." She asks you, "Is this an asset account? If it is, is it money in the bank?" How do you answer?

 Solve It

Knowing Your Debits from Your Credits

Business transactions are *economic exchanges* because something of value is given and something of value is received. By its very nature, an economic exchange is a *two-sided* transaction. For example, a business sells a product for $400. It receives the money (either immediately or later) and gives the product to the customer. In another example, a business receives $10 million from a lender and gives the lender a legal instrument called a *note* that promises to return the money at a future date and to pay interest every period starting from the date of the loan forward.

Accountants and bookkeepers use an ingenious scheme to record transactions while keeping the accounting equation constantly in balance — it's called *double-entry accounting*. This method has been in use a long time. In fact, a book published in 1494 describes the method. What do you think of that?

 Double-entry accounting records both sides of a transaction, and the accounting equation remains in balance as transactions are recorded. For example, if a transaction decreases cash $25,000, then the other side of the transaction is a $25,000 increase in some other asset, or a $25,000 decrease in a liability, or a $25,000 increase in an expense (to cite three possibilities).

To keep the accounting equation in balance as they record transactions, accountants use the system of *debits* and *credits*. The famous German philosopher Goethe is reputed to have called double-entry accounting "one of the finest inventions of the human mind." Well, I'm not sure that this bookkeeping technique deserves such high praise, but it's undeniable that the debits and credits method has been in use over six centuries.

Figure 3-1 summarizes the basic rules for debits and credits. By long-standing convention, debits are shown on the left and credits on the right. An increase in a liability, owners' equity, revenue, and income account is recorded as a credit, so the increase side is on the right. The recording of all transactions follows these rules for debits and credits.

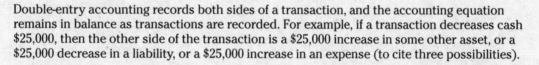

Assets		Liabilities and Owner's Equities	
Increases	Decreases	Decreases	Increases
Debits	*Credits*	*Debits*	*Credits*

Expenses and Losses		Revenue and Income	
Increases	Decreases	Decreases	Increases
Debits	*Credits*	*Debits*	*Credits*

Figure 3-1: Rules for debits and credits.

Practically everyone has trouble with the rules of debits and credit. (I certainly did!) Frankly, the rules aren't very intuitive. Learning the rules for debits and credits is a rite of passage for bookkeepers and accountants. The only way to really understand the rules is to make accounting entries — over and over again. After a while, using the rules becomes like tying your shoes — you do it without even thinking about it.

Notice the horizontal and vertical lines under the accounts in Figure 3-1. These lines form the letter "T." Although the actual accounts maintained by a business don't necessarily look like T accounts, accounts usually have one column for increases and another column for decreases. In other words, an account has a debit column and a credit column. Also an account may have a *running balance* column to continuously keep track of the account's balance.

In the following example question, the number of accounts is limited to simplify the problem; even a small business typically needs more than 100 accounts.

Q. Suppose a small business keeps just the following eight accounts.

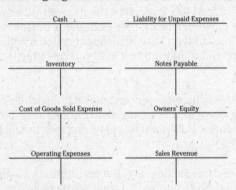

The business's transactions during the year include:

a. Made sales during the year for $2,400 (all were cash sales)

b. The cost of goods sold during the year was $1,600

c. Incurred $425 in operating expenses, which will be paid sometime later

d. Borrowed $10,000 from bank (ignore the interest expense on this note)

e. Cut a check for $275 in payment of operating expenses; these particular expenses are recorded as paid and haven't been recorded previously in a liability account

How should these transactions be recorded in the business's accounts?

A. The following figure shows how the transactions are recorded in the business's accounts. (The letters in the entries correspond to the transactions listed in the question.) In each transaction, the debit amount equals the credit amount.

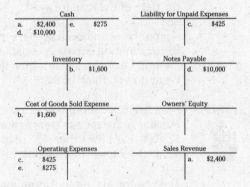

In every account, debits are on the left, and credits are on the right. And don't forget that increases in assets and expenses are recorded as debits, and increases in liabilities and sales revenue are recorded as credits. These few transactions are a very small sample of the large number of transactions the business makes over the course of one year.

Questions 9 through 12 use the same eight accounts given in the preceding example question.

9. The business purchases products for inventory and pays $3,500 cash for the purchase. How should this transaction be recorded in the accounts?

Solve It

_____|_____   _____|_____

10. The business pays the $425 liability for the operating expenses noted in the example question's transaction list. How should this transaction be recorded in the accounts?

Solve It

_____|_____   _____|_____

11. The business pays a note payable that came due in the amount of $5,000. (Ignore interest expense.) How should this transaction be recorded in the accounts?

Solve It

_____|_____   _____|_____

12. The owners invest an additional $25,000 in the business. How should this transaction be recorded in the accounts?

Solve It

_____|_____   _____|_____

Making Original Journal Entries

To explain and illustrate double-entry recordkeeping in the preceding section, I enter the effects of transactions directly into accounts. By keeping the number of accounts to a minimum, you can see the "big picture" because all assets, liabilities, owners' equity, revenue, and expenses fit on one page. Looking at accounts this way is a useful first step in understanding the rules of debits and credits.

However, with a large number of accounts, recording the effects of transactions directly in the accounts of a business isn't practical. The debit's in one account and the credit's in another account, and the accounts may be far removed from one another. A much more useful method is to record every transaction such that both sides of the transaction are in one place; keep the debit(s) and credit(s) in the entry for the transaction next to each other.

Therefore, the standard practice is to record transactions first in *journal entries* so that both sides of a transaction are contiguous. Both the debits and credits of the transaction are recorded in one place. A journal is like a diary in that it's a chronological listing of transactions. After journal entries have been recorded, the debits and credits of the transactions are recorded in the accounts of the business. The debits and credits are delivered to their proper addresses, which in accounting parlance is called *posting* to the accounts.

The journey from transactions to financial statements is as follows:

Transactions → Journal entries → Posting to accounts → Financial statements

One reason for keeping journals instead of recording the effects of transactions directly in accounts is that a business needs a chronological listing of all its transactions in one place. With journals, each transaction is stored in one place and is available for inspection and review. At a later date, a question or challenge may arise regarding how a transaction was recorded, and the journals allow direct access to original recording of the transaction, which is especially important for audit purposes.

Businesses use several specialized journals, usually one for each basic type of transaction. A typical business has a sales journal, purchases journal, cash receipts journal, cash disbursements (payments) journal, payroll journal, and perhaps other journals as well. In addition, a business needs one *general journal* in which it records low frequency and non-routine accounting entries. Adjusting and closing entries made at the end of the year (discussed in Chapter 4) are recorded in the general journal.

Today, businesses use computer-based bookkeeping/accounting systems. The days of manual journals and accounts are history. Using computerized systems, accountants do the same things that were done in traditional bookkeeping systems, including constructing a chart of accounts, recording journal entries for transactions, posting the debits and credits of journal entries in the accounts, making end-of-period adjusting entries, and using the accounts to prepare financial statements.

Q. A business makes $2,350 cash sales for the day. What is the journal entry for these sales?

A. I can't show you the process for entering the information for this sales transaction into a computer-based accounting system, so here's the hand-written journal entry:

| Cash | $2,350 |
| Sales Revenue | $2,350 |

This journal entry follows the conventional format for journal entries in that debits appear first and on the left and credits come second and are indented to the right. (This layout jibes with the rules for debits and credits shown in Figure 3-1.) In this journal entry, the cash account is debited, or increased $2,350; the sales revenue account is credited, or increased $2,350.

---

13. What is the explanation for this journal entry?

| Inventory | $48,325 |
| Accounts Payable | $48,325 |

Solve It

14. What is the explanation for this journal entry?

| Cash | $250,000 |
| Notes Payable | $250,000 |

Solve It

15. What is the explanation for this journal entry?

Rent Expense	$48,325	
Cash		$48,325

Solve It

16. What is the explanation for this journal entry?

Accounts Payable	$19,250	
Cash		$19,250

Solve It

Recording Revenue and Income

In Chapter 2, I explain that when making sales, a business receives cash at the time of making the sale, after the time of sale, or before the time of sale. What about credit card sales? As you know, individuals use credit cards for a large percent of their purchases from businesses. As far as businesses are concerned, credit card sales are virtually the same as cash sales. The business immediately transmits its credit card sales to its bank for deposit into its checking account.

A business doesn't get one hundred cents on the dollar for its credit card sales. Banks discount the credit card amounts. For example, assume a bank discounts 1.5 percent from the credit card amount. Therefore, for a $100.00 credit card sale, the bank puts only $98.50 in the business's checking account. The credit card discount rate can be higher or lower depending on several factors, but a 1.5 percent discount rate is in the ballpark for many businesses.

In addition to sales revenue, a business may have other sources of income. A prime example is *investment income.* Many businesses invest their spare cash in short-term marketable securities that pay interest. Some businesses make loans to officers and employees and charge interest on the loans, which generates interest income, of course. Legally, a business faces few restrictions on the types of investments it can make unless the business adopts formal limits on permissible investments.

Q. For a particular business, the day's sales are summarized as follows:

Cash sales	$3,500
Credit card sales	$14,800
Credit sales	$23,400

Its bank discounts 1.75 percent from credit card sales. In journal entry form, record the sales activity of the business for the day.

A. The separate journal entries for the three types of sales for the day are:

Cash	$3,500	
Sales Revenue		$3,500

Cash sales for day.

Cash	$14,541	
Credit Card Discount Expense	$259	
Sales Revenue		$14,800

Credit card sales for day, discounted by bank.

Accounts Receivable	$23,400	
Sales Revenue		$23,400

Credit sales for the day.

Here are a few things to note in these entries:

- These account titles are typical but not universal. Different businesses use slightly different account titles.

- Credit card discount expense is recorded for the credit card sales; in this case, the calculation is $14,800 face value of credit card charges × 1.75 percent discount fee charged by bank = $259. Sales revenue is recorded *gross*, or before the bank's discount is deducted.

17. For the day, a business makes $38,900 credit sales to other businesses. How should these credit sales be recorded? (Use the journal entry format shown in the preceding example answer.)

18. For the day, a business makes $48,000 credit card sales to individuals. It immediately sends the credit card information to its bank, which deducts 1.5 percent on credit card charges and puts the remainder in the business's checking account. How should these credit card sales be recorded? (Use the journal entry format shown in the preceding example answer.)

19. Over the course of a business day, a few customers return products to the business. For the day, the total of customer returns is $2,300, and the business refunds cash to these customers. How should the product returns be recorded? (Use the journal entry format shown in the preceding example answer.)

Solve It

20. A business invests in short-term government securities to earn income on excess cash that it doesn't need for its day-to-day operations. It just received a $4,500 check from the government for interest earned over the last six months. None of this income has been recorded yet. How should this income be recorded? (Use the journal entry format shown in the preceding example answer.)

Solve It

Recording Expenses and Losses

How many expense accounts should a business maintain? There's no easy answer to this question. The glib answer is "As many as it needs." To make a profit, business managers have to control expenses, and this task requires a good deal of specific information about expenses.

To get an idea of the broad range of expenses a business may have and therefore needs to account for, imagine a business with $10 million annual sales revenue. With that much revenue, you know right off that this company isn't a small, storefront operation. The business probably has more than 50 employees and hundreds or thousands of customers. It may have several locations, and it pays property taxes on its real estate. The business may manufacture the products its sells, or it may be a retailer that buys products in condition for resale. Most likely, it buys insurance coverage to protect against various risks. It also probably advertises the products its sells. For a $10 million business like this one, I would expect to find several hundred different expense accounts — even a thousand or more wouldn't surprise me.

Most businesses with $10 million annual sales revenue have total annual expenses over $9 million, or more than 90 percent of their sales revenue. Few businesses earn 10 percent or higher bottom-line profit on their sales revenue. As you may have already figured out, it takes a lot of accounts to keep track of over $9 million expenses.

Accountants record expenses by decreasing assets or increasing liabilities. Sounds straightforward enough, doesn't it? It ain't! Many different assets and liabilities are credited in making expense entries. The amounts recorded for certain expenses aren't definite or clear-cut. To complicate matters further, the liabilities used to record certain expenses are nebulous and difficult to understand. Frankly, expense accounting is a hodgepodge, so strap on your seat belt.

Figure 3-2 presents a broad overview of expenses. This summary matches expenses with the balance sheet accounts that are credited in recording the expenses. For instance, in recording cost of goods sold expense, the inventory asset account is credited. Many different expenses are recorded when cash disbursements for the expenses are made. Figure 3-2 shows that a specific expense account is recorded when a cash payment is made. The expense could be one of many in the business's chart of accounts.

Expense Account Debited	Balance Sheet Account Credited
	Assets
Many specific expenses	Cash
Bad debts expense	Accounts receivable
Cost of goods sold expense	Inventory
Several specific expenses	Prepaid expenses
Depreciation expense	Fixed Assets
	Liabilities
Many specific expenses	Account payable
Several specific expenses	Accrued expense liabilities
Income tax expense	Income tax payable
Labor cost expense	Employee's retirement liability
Income tax expense	Deferred income tax liability
	Owner's Equity
Stock option expense	Invested capital
	Retained earnings

Figure 3-2: Balance sheet accounts credited in recording expenses.

Q. A business has three expenses that it must record:

- The business issued a $45,000 check to its advertising agency for spot commercials that appeared on local television during last month; this cost has not been recorded yet.

- The accountant calculated that depreciation for the period is $306,500.

- The accountant calculated that the cost of vacation and sick pay accumulated by employees during the period just ended is $15,400; employees have taken none of this time yet.

What journal entries should be recorded for these expenses?

A. The following journal entries are recorded for the three expenses:

Advertising Expense	$45,000
Cash	$45,000

Because no expense has been recorded before the time of making cash payment, the advertising expense account is debited (increased) at the time of making payment.

Depreciation Expense	$306,500
Accumulated Depreciation	$306,500

The cost of a *long-term operating asset*, also called a *fixed asset*, is allocated over the estimated useful life of the asset, so a fraction of the cost is charged to the depreciation expense account each period. The fixed asset is credited (decreased) — not by a direct credit in the asset account but by a credit in the contra account, accumulated depreciation. The balance in this contra account is deducted from the original cost of the fixed asset.

Employees' Benefits Expense	$15,400
Accrued Expense Liability	$15,400

Some expenses accrue, or build up over time, even though the business doesn't receive a bill for the expense. A good example is vacation and sick pay accumulated by employees. Rather than waiting until individual employees actually take time off to record the expense, the creeping liability for this expense is recorded each period. When the employees are paid for vacation and sick time, the liability is debited (decreased).

21. The business's cost of goods sold for its sales during the period is $938,450. The sales revenue for these sales has been recorded. What journal entry should be made for this expense?

Solve It

22. The business just received a bill for $15,000 from the outside security firm that guards its warehouse and offices. No entry has been made for this expense yet, and the business normally waits several weeks to pay this bill. What journal entry should be made for this expense?

Solve It

23. Its actuarial firm informs the business that the cost of its employees' retirement pension benefit for the period is $565,000. According to the contract with its employees, the business decides to transfer $300,000 to the trustee of the pension plan and to defer payment of the remainder until a later time (which it has the option to do). No entry has been made for this expense yet. What journal entry should be made for this expense?

Solve It

24. Unfortunately, one of the major customers of the business declared bankruptcy. This customer owes the business $35,000. The business has already recorded the credit sale to the customer and the cost of goods sold for the sale. After careful analysis, the business comes to the conclusion that it will not collect a dime from this customer. The business doesn't record an expense caused by uncollectible receivables until it actually writes off the receivable. What journal entry should be made for this expense?

Solve It

Recording Set-Up and Follow-Up Transactions for Revenue and Expenses

Chapter 2 explains the basic types of business transactions, one of which consists of those transactions that take place before or after revenue and expenses are recorded. These *set-up* and *follow-up transactions* are supporting transactions for the profit-making activities of a business. These transactions are necessary, as you can see in the following examples:

✔ Buying products for inventory (the goods are held in inventory until they're sold and delivered to customers)

✔ Collecting receivables from customers

✔ Paying liabilities for products, supplies, and services that were bought on credit

✔ Paying certain expenses in advance, such as for insurance policies, shipping containers, and office supplies

Profit-making activities are reported in the income statement, and investing and financing activities are reported in the statement of cash flows. In contrast, set-up and follow-up transactions for revenue and expenses aren't reported in a financial statement. Nevertheless, these housekeeping activities have financial consequences and must be recorded in the accounts of a business. Although no revenue or expense account is involved in recording these activities, these transactions change assets and liabilities.

Q. A business purchases fire insurance on its building and contents. The insurance policy covers the next six months. The business writes a check for $25,000 to the insurance company. Also, the business recently purchased $328,000 of products for inventory on credit. The products were delivered to the company's warehouse, and after inspection, the company accepted the products. Record these two transactions in journal entry form.

A. The journal entries for the two transactions are as follows:

Prepaid Expenses	$25,000
Cash	$25,000

The cost of insurance policies is entered in the asset account called *prepaid expenses*. Over the six months of insurance coverage, the cost is allocated to insurance expense. The payment for the insurance policy decreases one asset (cash) and increases another asset (prepaid expenses).

Inventory	$328,000
Accounts Payable	$328,000

The purchase of products doesn't result in an expense; rather, the transaction is the acquisition of an asset called *inventory*. The cost of products remains in the asset account until the products are sold to customers, at which time the cost of goods sold expense is recorded, and the asset inventory is decreased. Because the purchase was made on credit, the liability *accounts payable* is credited (increased). When this liability is paid later, the account is debited (decreased), and cash is decreased.

25. The business buys on credit a large supply of shipping containers that should be enough for the next six months of deliveries. The bill for the purchase is $26,500, and the business will pay it in about 30 days. What journal entry should be made for this transaction?

Solve It

26. The business receives $49,000 from customers in payment for their previous purchases on credit from the business. To encourage prompt payment, the business offered its customers a 2 percent discount off the sales invoice amount if they paid within ten days of sale, and all the customers took advantage of this incentive. What journal entry should be made for this transaction?

Solve It

27. The business enters into a contract with a major supplier in which it agrees to buys a minimum amount of products every month over the next five years. Also, set prices are established in the contract. As of yet, the business hasn't made a purchase under this contract, but it expects to do so in the near future. Should a journal entry be made for entering into this contract?

Solve It

28. A few days after recording the purchase of products on credit, the business discovers that some of the products are defective. The business hasn't paid for the purchase yet, and the vendor agrees to accept return of these defective products for full credit. The products returned to the vendor cost $16,300. What journal entry should be made for this transaction?

Solve It

Recording Investing and Financing Transactions

Suppose a business recorded 10,000 transactions during the year. The large majority would be sales and expense transactions and the set-up and follow-up transactions for sales and expenses. Perhaps fewer than 100 would be *investing* and *financing transactions*. Though few in number, investing and financing transactions are very important and usually involve big chunks of money. In fact, these two types of transactions are reported in the statement of cash flows — that ought to tell you something.

Investing activities include the purchase and construction of long-term operating assets, such as land, buildings, machines, equipment, vehicles, and so on. In general, these investments are called *capital expenditures*. (The term *capital* refers to the large amounts of money invested in the assets as well as the long-term nature of these investments.) These economic resources are also called *fixed assets*. They're not held for sale in the normal course of business; rather, they're held for use in the operations of the business. When grouped together in a balance sheet, fixed assets are typically labeled *property, plant, and equipment*. Eventually, the business disposes of these assets by trading them in for new assets, selling them off for residual value, or just having the junk collector come and haul them away.

Investing transactions include acquisitions of other long-term assets, such as intangible resources (patents, for example), rental real estate, and research projects in the development stage. For example, a business could invest in a sports franchise, such as the Oakland Raiders. (Being a Denver Broncos fan, I doubt if I would buy the stock shares of a business that invested in the Oakland Raiders — just kidding!)

Financing activities basically fall into three categories:

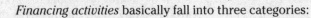

- ✔ A business borrows money on the basis of interest-bearing debt and either pays these loans at their maturity dates or renews them.

- ✔ A business raises capital (usually money) from shareowners and may return some of the invested capital to them.

- ✔ A business distributes cash to its shareowners based on its profit performance.

These are the three basic kinds of financing activities. Large public corporations engage in much more complex and sophisticated financing deals and instruments than these basic types, but those activities are beyond the scope of this book.

Q. The investing and financing activities for the year of a new, start-up business corporation are summarized as follows:

- Received $10,000,000 from a venture capital (VC) firm; in exchange, the business signed a $5 million note payable (interest-bearing, of course) to the VC firm and issued shares of stock to the VC firm equal to 10 percent of the total number of shares of stock issued by the business

- Purchased various long-term operating assets for total cash payments of $6,000,000

Make the journal entries for these investing and financing activities.

A. The journal entries for these investing and financing activities are as follows:

Cash	$10,000,000	
Notes Payable		$5,000,000
Owners' Equity — Invested Capital		$5,000,000

Property, Plant, & Equipment	$6,000,000	
Cash		$6,000,000

One-half of the money invested in the start-up business by the VC firm is secured by a note payable on which the business has to pay interest. This transaction is recorded in the notes payable liability account to indicate that the business has the legal obligation to pay interest and to pay the loan at its maturity date. The other half of the money that the VC firm put in the business is attributed to the account for capital stock shares issued by the business. The account title property, plant, and equipment is a generic title for long-term operating assets. The business would maintain more-specific accounts for each major asset purchased, such as buildings, machinery, vehicles, and so on.

29. A business corporation needed more capital to expand and grow, so it issued additional stock shares for a total of $25,000,000. What journal entry should be made for this financing transaction?

Solve It

30. A business has had a very good year; its $58,000,000 net income for the year is an all-time high. Being in a generous mood, its board of directors declares a whopping cash distribution of $30,000,000 based on the business's record-setting performance. What journal entry should be made for this financing transaction?

Solve It

Answers to Problems on the Bookkeeping Cycle

The following are the answers to the practice questions presented earlier in this chapter.

1 A business rents the building that houses its retail store, its warehouse, and its administrative offices. It pays rent in cash, so obviously the business needs a cash account. Should the business include an expense account for rent in its chart of accounts?

Sure; the business definitely needs a *rent expense* account in which to record the payments to the landlord.

2 A business borrows money from its bank. Identify the liability account and the expense account that it should include in its chart of accounts for the borrowing of money.

The business needs a *notes payable* liability account and an *interest expense* account. In fact, it needs a separate note payable liability account for each loan from the bank, although it probably needs only one interest expense account.

3 A business employs a typical range of employees — janitors, salespeople, bookkeepers, truck drivers, managers, and so on. It provides a basic retirement plan and pays the premiums for employees' medical and hospital insurance. The annual income tax return filed with the IRS requires the following information: compensation of officers; salaries and wages; employee benefit program; and pension and profit-sharing plans. Should the business include a separate expense account for each of these compensation elements in its chart of accounts?

Because the business needs to separate out information for the various components of its total cost of labor according to the categories required in its income tax return, it should set up a separate expense account for each of the categories listed in the question.

Most businesses don't disclose detailed information about their labor costs in their income statements as required in their federal income tax returns. If total labor cost is disclosed — and not all businesses disclose this expense separately — it's typically reported as one total amount. You seldom see compensation of officers reported as a separate expense in an income statement, although there's no rule against doing so.

4 The income tax Form 1120 for business corporations requires the reporting of the following assets: trade notes and accounts receivables; buildings and other depreciable assets; and loans to shareholders. Should the business include separate accounts for each of these assets in its chart of accounts? (These are only three of many items of information that the IRS requires to be reported in the balance sheet that must be included in a business's annual income tax returns.)

The fairly obvious answer is that a business should establish separate accounts for these different assets. Typical titles for these accounts are: accounts receivable; notes receivable; buildings; machinery; equipment; vehicles; and loans to offices and shareholders. Exact titles vary from business to business.

5 Suppose a business just opened its doors on the first day of the year, and not a single transaction has taken place yet in the new year. Which of the following accounts have balances in them, and which don't?

• Cash

• Notes payable

• Sales revenue

- Owners' equity — Invested capital
- Wages and salaries expense
- Inventory

The *real* accounts, which are cash, notes payable, owners' equity — invested capital, and inventory, start the year with balances.

The *nominal* accounts, which are sales revenue and wages and salaries expense, start the year with zero balances.

6 This question focuses on just two accounts taken from the chart of accounts of a business that makes credit sales. (Even a small business keeps hundreds of accounts.) The first is a real account, *accounts receivable*. The second is a nominal account, *sales revenue*. Are increases *and* decreases recorded in both accounts during the year, or are only increases recorded during the year?

Both increases and decreases are recorded in the accounts receivable asset account. Increases are recorded for sales made on credit, and decreases are recorded for collections from customers. In contrast, the sales revenue account records only increases during the year. To be more precise, some decreases may be recorded in this revenue account, but they're the exception rather than the rule. After recording sales revenue, an error may be discovered that requires a decrease in the account to correct the error.

7 The following condensed balance sheet presents eight core accounts of a business. Which of the eight accounts have a high frequency of transactions recorded in them during the year, and which have a low frequency of transactions? In other words, which of these eight are busy accounts, and which are not?

Condensed Balance Sheet

Cash	$250,000	Operating liabilities	$350,000
Receivables	$300,000	Interest-bearing liabilities	$500,000
Inventory	$400,000	Owners' invested capital	$250,000
PP&E, net	$550,000	Owners' retained earnings	$400,000
Assets	$1,500,000 =	Liabilities and Owners' equity	$1,500,000

The high frequency accounts are cash; receivables; inventory; and operating liabilities. The low frequency accounts are PP&E, net; interest-bearing liabilities; owners' invested capital; and owners' retained earnings.

8 A good friend is reading the most recent financial report of your business. In the balance sheet, she comes across an account called "Owners' equity — Retained earnings." She asks you, "Is this an asset account? If it is, is it money in the bank?" How do you answer?

No, no, no, no! Many people assume that retained earnings is an asset account and, in particular, that it's money stashed away someplace. (The title of the account may suggest this misleading interpretation.) You should stress that assets are listed under assets in the balance sheet and that assets aren't tucked under owners' equity on the other side of the balance sheet. Retained earnings is no more an asset than notes payable. Retained earnings is one of the sources of assets accounts reported on the right-hand side of the balance sheet. Basically, it says that $400,000 of the $1,500,000 total assets of the business is from the earning of profit over the years that has been retained and not distributed to its shareowners.

9 The business purchases products for inventory and pays $3,500 cash for the purchase. How should this transaction be recorded in the accounts?

| Inventory | | Cash | |
| $3,500 | | | $3,500 |

10 The business pays the $425 liability for the operating expenses noted in the example question's transaction list. How should this transaction be recorded in the accounts?

Liability for Unpaid Expenses		Cash	
$425			$425

11 The business pays a note payable that came due in the amount of $5,000. (Ignore interest expense.) How should this transaction be recorded in the accounts?

Notes payable		Cash	
$5,000			$5,000

12 The owners invest an additional $25,000 in the business. How should this transaction be recorded in the accounts?

Cash		Owners' Equity	
$25,000			$25,000

13 What is the explanation for this journal entry?

Inventory	$48,325
Accounts Payable	$48,325

This entry records purchase of products on credit.

14 What is the explanation for this journal entry?

Cash	$250,000
Notes Payable	$250,000

This entry records the borrowing of money on the basis of an interest-bearing note.

15 What is the explanation for this journal entry?

Rent Expense	$48,325
Cash	$48,325

This entry records rent payments to the landlord.

16 What is the explanation for this journal entry?

Accounts Payable	$19,250
Cash	$19,250

This entry records the payment of amounts owed for previous purchases on credit.

17 For the day, a business makes $38,900 credit sales to other businesses. How should these credit sales be recorded?

Accounts Receivable	$38,900
Sales Revenue	$38,900

18 For the day, a business makes $48,000 credit card sales to individuals. It immediately sends the credit card information to its bank, which deducts 1.5 percent on credit card charges and puts the remainder in the business's checking account. How should these credit card sales be recorded?

Cash	$47,280
Credit Card Discount Expense	$720
Sales Revenue	$48,000

19 Over the course of a business day, a few customers return products to the business. For the day, the total of customer returns is $2,300, and the business refunds cash to these customers. How should the product returns be recorded?

Sales Returns & Allowances	$2,300
Cash	$2,300

 In this scenario, the debit isn't in the sales revenue account but rather in sales returns and allowances account, which is the contra account to sales revenue. The balance in this account is deducted from sales revenue to determine net sales revenue, and the balance in sales returns and allowances is compared with the balance in sales revenue to gauge the returns against sales. (Also, I should mention that a second entry should be made to record the return of products to inventory. The question doesn't give the cost of the goods returned by customers, so you're not asked to include this entry.)

20 A business invests in short-term government securities to earn income on excess cash that it doesn't need for its day-to-day operations. It just received a $4,500 check from the government for interest earned over the last six months. None of this income has been recorded yet. How should this income be recorded?

Cash	$4,500
Investment Income	$4,500

21 The business's cost of goods sold for its sales during the period is $938,450. The sales revenue for these sales has been recorded. What journal entry should be made for this expense?

Cost of Goods Sold Expense	$938,450
Inventory	$938,450

22 The business just received a bill for $15,000 from the outside security firm that guards its warehouse and offices. No entry has been made for this expense yet, and the business normally waits several weeks to pay this bill. What journal entry should be made for this expense?

Security Guard Expense	$15,000
Accounts Payable	$15,000

23 Its actuarial firm informs the business that the cost of its employees' retirement pension benefit for the period is $565,000. According to the contract with its employees, the business decides to transfer $300,000 to the trustee of the pension plan and to defer payment of the remainder until a later time (which it has the option to do). No entry has been made for this expense yet. What journal entry should be made for this expense?

Employees' Benefit Expense	$565,000	
Cash		$300,000
Employees' Retirement Liability		$265,000

Determining the annual cost of a defined benefits pension plan is an exceedingly complex computation. The Financial Accounting Standards Board (FASB) lays down the general rules for United States businesses. You have to be a CPA to wade through all these rules, and even some CPAs find it tough going. I should mention that many business corporations defer funding of their employee pension plans. Some of these companies have gone into bankruptcy, making their ability to fully fund their pension plans doubtful.

24 Unfortunately, one of the major customers of the business declared bankruptcy. This customer owes the business $35,000. The business has already recorded the credit sale to the customer and the cost of goods sold for the sale. After careful analysis, the business comes to the conclusion that it will not collect a dime from this customer. The business doesn't record an expense caused by uncollectible receivables until it actually writes off the receivable. What journal entry should be made for this expense?

Bad Debts Expense	$35,000	
Accounts Receivable		$35,000

I deliberately made this bad debt that has to be written off as uncollectible a relatively large amount in order to call your attention to this problem. Basically, the business gave away its products for nothing. That really smarts! Of course, the business should shut off credit privileges to this customer and also consider reporting this incident to credit-rating agencies.

25 The business buys on credit a large supply of shipping containers that should be enough for the next six months of deliveries. The bill for the purchase is $26,500, and the business will pay it in about 30 days. What journal entry should be made for this transaction?

Prepaid Expenses	$26,500	
Accounts Payable		$26,500

When some of the containers are used to ship the products sold to customers, an entry is made to remove the appropriate amount from the prepaid expenses asset account and to charge this amount to an expense, such as transportation or shipping expense. The prepaid expense account may be called something more specific, such as shipping containers.

26 The business receives $49,000 from customers in payment for their previous purchases on credit from the business. To encourage prompt payment, the business offered its customers a 2 percent discount off the sales invoice amount if they paid within ten days of sale, and all the customers took advantage of this incentive. What journal entry should be made for this transaction?

Cash	$49,000	
Sales Discounts	$1,000	
Accounts Receivable		$50,000

In recording sales, you record the full amount (before any prompt payment discount) in the sales revenue account and in the accounts receivable account. Therefore, the accounts receivable account for these sales has a balance of $50,000. This amount is fully discharged when the customers take the 2 percent prompt payment discount ($50,000 × 2 percent = $1,000). The business records $1,000 in the sales discounts account, which is usually viewed as a sales revenue contra account (not an expense account).

27 The business enters into a contract with a major supplier in which it agrees to buys a minimum amount of products every month over the next five years. Also, set prices are established in the contract. As of yet, the business hasn't made a purchase under this contract, but it expects to do so in the near future. Should a journal entry be made for entering into this contract?

Even though it's an important event, no entry is made for entering into this purchase contract. However, financial reporting disclosure standards require that salient details of this contract be presented in a footnote to the financial statements. The one escape clause, or loophole, in this disclosure standard is that the business doesn't have to disclose the details of the contract if it judges that the contract isn't material, or significant in the affairs of its operations.

28 A few days after recording the purchase of products on credit, the business discovers that some of the products are defective. The business hasn't paid for the purchase yet, and the vendor agrees to accept return of these defective products for full credit. The products returned to the vendor cost $16,300. What journal entry should be made for this transaction?

Accounts Payable	$16,300
Inventory	$16,300

Some accountants argue that instead of crediting the asset inventory in a scenario such as this, a contra account called *purchase returns and allowances* should be credited. The balance in this contra account is deducted from total purchases for the year to determine net purchases. Unless purchase returns are a serious problem, I favor the entry shown above.

29 A business corporation needed more capital to expand and grow, so it issued additional stock shares for a total of $25,000,000. What journal entry should be made for this financing transaction?

Cash	$25,000,000
Owners' Equity — Invested Capital	$25,000,000

30 A business has had a very good year; its $58,000,000 net income for the year is an all-time high. Being in a generous mood, its board of directors declares a whopping cash distribution of $30,000,000 based on the business's record-setting performance. What journal entry should be made for this financing transaction?

Owners' Equity — Retained Earnings	$30,000,000
Cash	$30,000,000

Instead of directly debiting (decreasing) the retained earnings account, as shown in the entry above, some accountants favor making two entries for dividends, as follows:

Dividends	$30,000,000
Cash	$30,000,000

Owners' Equity — Retained Earnings	$30,000,000
Dividends	$30,000,000

As you can see, the end result is the same: The retained earnings account is decreased by the amount of the dividends.

Chapter 4

The Bookkeeping Cycle: Adjusting and Closing Entries

T he end of its fiscal year is a very important time for a business. Accountants prepare the business's *income statement* and *statement of cash flows* for the year as well as its *balance sheet.* The board of directors critically reviews these financial statements to assess the business's financial performance and position and to plan the future course of the business. The financial statements are sent to lenders and shareowners who make their lending and investment decisions based on these accounting reports.

In short, the annual financial statements of a business are extraordinarily important. Accordingly, the financial statements require extraordinarily good accounting; financial statements are no better than the quality of accounting behind them. As I explain in Chapter 3, good accounting demands a well-designed and reliable recordkeeping system, one that records the business's transactions during the period completely and accurately.

This chapter moves on to the additional accounting procedures done at the end of the period. An accountant can't use a business's various accounts to prepare financial statements until these end-of-period accounting steps are completed. As the saying goes, "It ain't over until the fat lady sings."

Getting Accurate with Adjusting Entries

During an accounting period, certain expenses either aren't recorded or aren't fully recorded. The accountant waits until the end of the period and records *adjusting entries* for these expenses. In addition to expenses, revenue and income accounts may also need adjusting entries at the end of the period. Adjusting entries complete the profit accounting process for the period.

The term "adjusting" doesn't mean "fiddling with." Adjusting entries aren't made to manipulate profit, such as to move profit closer to the forecast target for the period. Rather, an accountant makes adjusting entries to make profit for the period as accurate as possible. In other words, adjusting entries make revenue and expenses correct for the period, and without them, the bottom-line net income for the period would be wrong. Keep in mind that the managers, directors, lenders, and shareowners of a business rely on the profit number more than any other figure in the business's financial statements.

As you may know, businesses prepare quarterly (three-month) financial statements. In this chapter, I focus on the *annual* (twelve-month) accounting period. In the business world (and for economic analysis in general), one year is the standard time unit. One year includes the complete cycle of seasonal variations that many businesses experience. The annual income statement draws the most attention in business financial reporting, and everyone holds the annual income statement to high standards of accounting.

In broad overview, year-end adjusting entries are needed for two reasons:

- ✔ To correct errors that may have crept into the recordkeeping process
- ✔ To make final entries for the year in revenue, income, expense, and loss accounts so that the profit or loss for the year is accurate (or as accurate as possible given the inherent accounting problems of measuring profit and loss)

An accounting system involves an enormous amount of data and detail, so safeguards and procedures should be put in place to prevent bookkeeping errors. A business is well-advised to conduct a thorough search at the end of the year for bookkeeping errors that have gone undetected. In the section "Instituting Internal Controls" later in the chapter, I discuss internal accounting controls that should be put into place to minimize bookkeeping errors. Despite their best efforts, most businesses find that errors sneak into their bookkeeping systems.

Q. At year-end, the business searches for bookkeeping errors that may have gone undetected. Based on its year-end review, the business discovers that some office and computer supplies were thrown away and no entry was made. (The supplies were thrown out because they were no longer of any use, but the bookkeeping department wasn't informed that the supplies had been put in the Dumpster.) In general, at the time of purchase, the costs of office and computer supplies are entered (debited) in an asset account called *prepaid expenses*. As these supplies are used, the appropriate amount of cost is removed from the asset account and recorded to expense. The cost of the discarded supplies was $4,800. What adjusting entry should be made to correct this error?

A. The entry to correct the error of not recording the cost of supplies thrown away is:

Office and Computer Supplies Expense	$4,800
Prepaid Expenses	$4,800

You could argue that throwing away office and computer supplies causes a special type of loss that should be recorded in a separate loss account, but I think that most accountants would put the cost of discarded office and computer supplies in the regular expense account.

1. In its year-end review for errors, a business discovers that the recent bill from its law firm was entered as $6,500 instead of $5,600, which is the correct amount. The bill has not been paid yet. What adjusting entry should be made to correct this error?

Solve It

2. In its year-end review for errors, a business discovers that an order of products was shipped to a customer, and the cost of the products was correctly charged to cost of goods sold expense. However, the paperwork for this particular sales order wasn't sent to the bookkeeping department on time. Therefore, the sale hasn't been recorded. The total price for this credit sale is $36,260. What adjusting entry should be made to correct this error?

Solve It

3. The $1,500 trash collection bill for the last month of the fiscal year normally arrives before the end of the month. However, the waste management company didn't get its bills out on time, so the expense hasn't been recorded. What adjusting entry should be made to correct this error?

Solve It

4. In the hustle and bustle of the end-of-year accounting activities, the bookkeeper simply forgot to record the business's social security taxes on its last payroll in the year. As you may know, a business employer pays social security taxes equal to the amount withheld from employees' paychecks. The amount of employer's social security tax for the last pay period is $29,600. What adjusting entry should be made to correct this error?

Solve It

Breaking Down the End-of-Year Adjusting Entries

The chief accountant of a business, usually known as the *Controller,* must know which end-of-year adjusting entries should be made and should follow through to make sure that these critical entries are recorded correctly. In most businesses, the Controller takes a hands-on approach in recording adjusting entries at the end of the year. Recording year-end adjusting entries marks a dividing line between bookkeeping and accounting. Bookkeeping consists of following established rules for accounting and recordkeeping, and the chief accountant makes and enforces the rules and takes charge of the year-end adjusting entries.

Recording depreciation expense

The theory of depreciation isn't complicated. Businesses invest in long-term operating assets such as land, buildings, machines, equipment, delivery trucks and cars, fork lifts, office furniture, computers, and so on. These are called *fixed assets* because they're fixed in place, or stationary (well, trucks and cars move around of course). The term "fixed" also implies that the assets aren't held for sale (that is, not until they reach the end of their useful lives to the business). In a balance sheet, these assets typically are reported in a category called *property, plant, and equipment* (although reporting practices vary on this point).

Charging the entire cost of fixed assets to expense at the time they're bought or constructed wouldn't be very smart. The obvious thing to do is to allocate the cost of a fixed asset over the years of its useful life; this practice is called *depreciation.* Ah, but here's the rub. Can you predict the future useful life of a fixed asset? A building may stand 40 or 50 years — or more. Some machines don't really wear out; with proper maintenance and repair, they could last indefinitely. Another complicating factor is that businesses replace many fixed assets before the end of their useful lives — not because they wear out physically, but because they become obsolete and inefficient.

Congress charges the Internal Revenue Service (IRS), everyone's favorite government agency, with the responsibility of implementing income tax legislation. The income tax law and IRS rulings deal with depreciation in a practical, if not entirely correct theoretical, manner. Useful life guidelines have been established for several categories of fixed assets. Generally speaking, these estimates are shorter than the actual useful lives of fixed assets.

For example, a business building is depreciated over 39 years, even though many buildings are used longer, and trucks are depreciated over five years, even though they may be driven for more years. As a practical matter, many businesses (probably the majority) simply adopt the depreciation useful life estimates permitted under the federal income tax law, although the estimates conflict with economic reality to a certain extent.

Depreciation also raises the question of whether each year of using a fixed asset should be charged with the same amount of depreciation. Or should some years be hit with more depreciation expense than others? Generally the answer to this question boils down to a choice between the *straight-line depreciation method* (an equal amount is charged to expense each year) and an *accelerated depreciation method* (earlier years are hit with more expense than later years). I explain depreciation in-depth in Chapter 9. My purpose here is simply to illustrate the year-end adjusting entry for depreciation.

Q. A business bought new computer software for $57,750 at the start of the year. It decides to follow IRS rules for depreciation of computer software and thus will depreciate the software cost over three years. The straight-line method (equal amounts per year) is used. The business has not recorded any depreciation on this software during the year. What year-end adjusting entry is recorded for depreciation of the computer software?

A. Computer software isn't your typical depreciable fixed asset. Because it's hard to see or touch computer software, you may consider it to be an intangible asset. (I discuss intangible assets in the next section.) However, computer software is part and parcel of using computer hardware, and computer hardware isn't good for anything without software to tell it what to do.

The entry to record the annual depreciation on the computer software is:

Depreciation Expense — Computer Software	$19,250
Accumulated Depreciation — Computer Software	$19,250

In the entry, I debit a specific depreciation expense account, but this doesn't mean that this depreciation account is disclosed separately in the business's income statement. Probably it's grouped with other depreciation expense accounts, and only one total depreciation expense is reported in the income statement. A full-year depreciation amount is recorded because the business has used the asset the entire year. The calculation is $57,750 ÷ 3 years = $19,250 per year.

Instead of crediting (decreasing) the fixed asset account, the standard accounting practice is to credit *accumulated depreciation,* which is the contra account to the fixed asset account. In essence, the contra account is the credit side of the fixed asset account. It's maintained so that both the original cost of fixed assets and the cumulative depreciation amount on the fixed assets are available for reporting in the balance sheet.

5. Based on its depreciation schedules, the annual depreciation on the business's machinery is $420,000. The business uses the straight-line depreciation method. The business recorded a machinery depreciation expense at the end of each quarter during the year, but no entry has been made for the fourth and final quarter. What adjusting entry for machinery depreciation should be recorded at year-end?

Solve It

6. Rather than own the real estate, a business leases its land and buildings. The lease agreement calls for monthly rents. Does the business record depreciation on this real estate?

Solve It

7. A bookkeeper who was recently hired by a business recorded the depreciation expense on delivery trucks for the year as follows:

Depreciation Expense — Delivery Trucks	$215,000
Delivery Trucks	$215,000

Is this entry wrong?

Solve It

8. On the last day of the year, a particular piece of equipment that originally cost $87,500 many years ago was removed from the production line and put on the shipping dock. The equipment is of no further use to the business and will be hauled away to the junk heap in a few days. The asset is fully depreciated. What entry should be made for the retirement of the fixed asset?

Solve It

Recording amortization expense

In addition to tangible fixed assets, a business may invest in *intangible assets,* which can't be seen or touched. The value of an intangible asset is rooted in law. For example, a patent gives the owner the exclusive legal right to use the patent in the pursuit of profit. No one else can legally use the patent without being held liable for infringement. There are all sorts of intangible assets. For instance, a business may purchase a list consisting of thousands of names of potential customers or acquire the right to use an established trade name and logo.

The acquisition of an intangible asset is recorded as a debit (increase) in an asset account. The cost of an intangible asset usually is allocated over its predicted useful life to the business, much like depreciation (see the preceding section). Allocating the cost of an intangible asset to expense over the years of its useful life is called *amortization.*

Q. A business invests in a franchise, which gives it the right to operate under a well-known trade name and logo. The franchise contract is for ten years, and the business pays $250,000 to the franchisor. What adjusting entry should be made at the end of the first year concerning the cost of the franchise?

A. At the end of the first year, the business has used up one year of the ten-year franchise investment. Therefore, the following year-end adjusting entry is made:

Franchise Amortization Expense	$25,000
Franchise	$25,000

Generally, the straight-line amortization method is used, which means that an equal amount is charged to expense each year. The asset account is credited (decreased) in recording amortization expense. A contra account is not used to accumulate amortization.

9. A business pays the owner of a patent $500,000 for the right to use the patent for a period of five years.

   a. What entry should be made for the purchase of the patent right?

   b. What adjusting entry should be made one year later?

Solve It

10. The business signs a ten-year contract with the inventor of a secret process that it will use in its manufacturing operations. As an incentive to agree to the contract, the business immediately pays the inventor $1,000,000. In addition, the business agrees to pay the inventor a royalty equal to five percent of its sales revenue from these products over the next ten years.

   a. What entry should be made for the initial payment to the inventor?

   b. What adjusting entry should be made one year later?

Solve It

Recording other adjusting entries

Depending on the business, year-end adjusting entries are made for:

- Investment income that has been earned but not recorded

- Bad debts expense (caused by uncollectible accounts receivable)

- Inventory losses due to shrinkage and write-downs required by the lower of cost or market (LCM) accounting rule

- Losses due to asset impairments

- Buildup of liabilities for operating expenses that haven't been recorded

- Income tax liability based on the final determination of income tax for the year

- Liability for product warranty and guarantee costs

- Increases in liability for unfunded employees' retirement benefits and for post-retirement medical and healthcare benefits

This list is quite a dog's breakfast, isn't it? And I don't even list all possible adjusting entries made by businesses! This list should give you some idea of the burden on the chief accountant of a business to make sure that all its revenue and expenses are correctly recorded for the year.

0. A business makes mostly credit sales. At the end of the year, its accountant does an *aging analysis* of its accounts receivables, analyzing the receivables according to how old they are. Generally, the older a receivable is, the greater the risk of not collecting it or not collecting the entire amount owed by the customer. At the end of the year, the business has $4,538,600 total accounts receivable. This ending balance doesn't include specific accounts receivable that were written off during the period. Based on its aging analysis, the business estimates that sooner or later about $95,000 of the ending balance of its accounts receivable will not be paid by customers. What year-end adjusting entry is made?

A. There are two methods of accounting for bad debts expense. In the *direct write-off method,* no expense is recorded until specific accounts receivable are actually written off. Under this method, no adjusting entry is made at year-end because the business hasn't identified *specific* customers' accounts from its accounts receivable at year-end that should be written off. During the year, the business did write off specific receivables, and bad debts expense was debited (increased) in these entries. Only these write-offs are recorded in the bad debts expense account.

In the *allowance method,* based on the estimated amount of accounts receivable that will have to be written off in the future, the following entry is made:

Bad Debts Expense	$95,000
Allowance for Doubtful Accounts	$95,000

Allowance for doubtful accounts is the contra account to the accounts receivable asset account.

I don't discuss several bookkeeping procedures connected with the allowance method for recording bad debts expense because my goal simply is to illustrate that bad debt expense can be recorded before specific accounts receivable are actually identified and written off as uncollectible. The compelling theory of the allowance method is that the expense is recorded in the same period as the credit sales that generated the bad debts. On the other hand, estimating the amount of future write offs of accounts receivable is very tricky and is open to manipulation. As a matter of fact, the IRS doesn't permit businesses other than financial institutions to use the allowance method.

The following questions offer examples of common year-end adjusting entries made by businesses, but a particular business doesn't necessarily make every one of the following adjusting entries. For instance, consider a business that makes only cash sales and no credit sales. This business doesn't have bad debts expense from uncollectible accounts receivable, but it does have expenses from taking counterfeit currency, accepting bad checks, making mistakes in giving change to customers, and thefts from cash registers.

11. A business makes almost all credit sales. At the end of the year, the business has $485,000 total accounts receivable. This ending balance doesn't include $28,500 specific accounts receivable that were written off during the period. The business estimates that customers will not pay $6,500 of the ending balance of its accounts receivable. What year-end adjusting entry is made?

12. The business has more cash than it needs for day-to-day operations, so the excess cash is invested in short-term marketable securities that pay interest. During the year, the business receives interest checks, which it records in the interest income account. At the end of the year, $48,500 interest has been earned but not yet received. This interest will be included in the interest checks the business receives next year. The business hasn't recorded this earned interest. What adjusting entry is made at the end of the year?

Solve It

13. At the end of the year, the business owes its employees $58,300 for accumulated vacation and sick pay. This amount will be paid when employees actually take their vacations and time off for sick leave. No entry has been made for this accrued liability. What adjusting entry is made at the end of the year?

Solve It

14. Based on the final determination of its federal income tax for the year, the business owes $431,500. During the year, it made $3,978,500 total installment payments towards its income tax, which were charged (debited) to its income tax expense account. The $431,500 balance still owed to the government will be paid when the business's income tax return is filed later.

a. What adjusting entry is made at the end of the year?

b. What is the amount of income tax expense reported in its income statement for the year?

Solve It

15. At the end of the year, the business owes $10,000,000 on interest-bearing notes payable. During the year, it records interest expense as it's paid to lenders. Accordingly, the business recorded $515,400 interest expense during the year. At the close of the year, it owes $97,500 interest that hasn't yet come due for payment and that hasn't been recorded.

a. What adjusting entry is made at the end of the year?

b. What is the amount of interest expense reported in its annual income statement?

16. At the end of the year, the business counts and inspects its ending inventory of products on hand, which is stored in its warehouse and retail sales areas. Usually, employees discover some damaged and spoiled products that can't be sold. This year is no exception. The cost of spoiled and damaged products that will have to be thrown away is $26,300. What adjusting entry is made?

Closing the Books on the Year

The annual income statement of a business is prepared from its revenue, other income, expense, and loss accounts for the year. Indeed, where else could information for preparing the income statement come from? Accountants use these accounts to determine the amount of profit or loss for the year. I needn't remind you how important the annual profit number is to the managers and directors of the business as well as its lenders and shareowners.

Even a modest-size business may have 100 or so revenue accounts and 1,000 or so expense accounts. Managers need a lot of detailed information to run their businesses, so they depend on their accountants to generate regular reports that provide the detailed account information they need for decision-making and management control. In sharp contrast, relatively few lines of information are included in the *external income statement* distributed to a business's lenders and shareowners. In its external income statement, the business compresses its many revenue accounts into only one or two sales revenue lines and its many expense accounts into relatively few expense lines. (I say more about this funneling of information in Chapter 5.)

After the business has prepared its annual financial statements, the revenue and expense accounts have served their dual purpose — to provide information for preparing the income statement and to aid in determining profit or loss for the year. What happens to these revenue and expense accounts after the year is concluded? The traditional bookkeeping procedure is to make *closing entries* in the accounts. These special entries close, or shut down, the revenue and expense accounts for the year just ended. Also, the amount of profit or loss for the year is recorded in the *retained earnings* account.

In the few pages I have here to illustrate closing entries, I can't show you a hundred revenue accounts and a thousand expense accounts. So in the following example, I use just one sales revenue account and only four expense accounts. This scenario isn't realistic, but it gets the point across.

EXAMPLE

Q. At the end of the year, after all year-end adjusting entries have been made and posted, the balances in the revenue and expense accounts of the business are as follows:

Cost of Goods Sold Expense		Sales Revenue	
$2,725,000			$4,526,500

Selling & Administrative Expenses	
$1,228,500	

Interest Expense	
$175,000	

Income Tax Expense	
$138,000	

What entry is made to close the nominal accounts and enter the profit or loss for the year?

A. The journal entry to close the books is as follows:

Sales Revenue	$4,526,500
Cost of Goods Sold Expense	$2,725,000
Selling & Administrative Expenses	$1,228,500
Interest Expense	$175,000
Income Tax Expense	$138,000
Owners' Equity — Retained Earnings	$260,000

The debit to sales revenue and the credits to expenses close out these accounts. The $260,000 profit for the year (sales revenue less all expenses) is recorded in the retained earnings account, where it belongs. Are the books still in balance? In other words, is the accounting equation still in balance after making this entry? Sure. The total credit in this closing entry equals the total debit. So this entry doesn't throw the accounting equation out of balance.

17. Refer to the closing entry in the answer to the example in this section. The T accounts before the closing entry is recorded are provided here. What are the balances in the revenue and expense accounts after the closing entry is posted?

Solve It

Cost of Goods Sold Expense		Sales Revenue	
$2,725,000			$4,526,500

Selling & Administrative Expenses	
$1,228,500	

Interest Expense	
$175,000	

Income Tax Expense	
$138,000	

18. The business is organized legally as a partnership and therefore doesn't pay income tax. (A partnership's annual taxable income or loss is passed through to its partners who pick up their share of profit or loss in their individual income tax returns.) Year-end adjusting entries have been recorded and posted, and the business's revenue and expense accounts are provided here. What closing entry is recorded?

Solve It

Cost of Goods Sold Expense		Sales Revenue	
$687,500			$1,764,500

Selling & Administrative Expenses	
$674,300	

Interest Expense	
$76,500	

Instituting Internal Controls

Have you ever made an error in your checkbook or forgot to pay a bill on time? Have you ever misplaced an important document that you desperately needed but couldn't find? Have you started to fill out a loan application and realized that you don't keep records for the types of information the lender wants to know? (Trust me; you don't want to know *my* answers to these questions.) Your individual bookkeeping system may have holes in it, but you can probably get by. In contrast, a business can't get by if its bookkeeping system is full of errors and doesn't provide the information accountants need. A good accounting system is a matter of life and death for a business.

A business accounting system has many components:

- **The forms and procedures used to facilitate business transactions and activities,** such as making purchases, paying bills, depositing cash receipts in the bank, preparing payroll checks, and so on
- **The chart of accounts,** which I discuss in Chapter 3
- **The bookkeeping procedures used to record its transactions,** which should work perfectly if no errors are made

Bookkeeping errors can happen, of course. (I presume you've heard of Murphy's Law: "If something can go wrong, it will.") To counteract bookkeeping errors, a layer of *internal accounting controls* is superimposed on the recordkeeping procedures of the business. This layer of controls builds redundancy into the accounting system in that accountants take extra steps to double-check the data and information recorded in the original entries and accounts. It's like looking at your speedometer not once but twice to make sure your speed is acceptable. Businesses know that effective internal accounting controls reduce the incidence of recordkeeping errors to a minimum, and that's extremely important.

The accountant's function extends beyond establishing and policing internal accounting controls. The accounting department is assigned responsibility for designing and enforcing controls to guard against a broad range of threats facing the business. Businesses are at risk from all sorts of dishonesty, theft, and fraud. They handle a lot of cash and have valuable assets, so businesses are natural targets for people who steal and cheat. Everyone that a business deals with poses a potential risk.

Another serious problem to consider is that instead of being the victim, a business may be the perpetrator of wrongdoing. A business may cheat its employees and customers, knowingly violate laws, or resort to *accounting fraud* to make its financial statements look better than the facts support. In other words, a business may *cook its books.* You may have heard about Enron and other high profile accounting fraud scandals that led to the passage of the federal Sarbanes-Oxley Act of 2002. This legislation puts a heavy burden on the top-level executives of public companies to certify that their businesses have effective controls to prevent fraudulent financial reporting. (For more on the Sarbanes-Oxley Act, see *Sarbanes-Oxley For Dummies* by Jill Gilbert Welytok.)

The chief accountant of a business has to make sure basic internal accounting controls are in place and working effectively to minimize bookkeeping errors. In addition, he or she is responsible for establishing effective controls that prevent employee theft and embezzlement as well as fraud against the business by its customers, vendors, and the other outside parties it deals with. Furthermore, a business needs to adopt controls to prevent it from issuing fraudulent financial statements. All this is a tall order, to say the least!

Q. The business has established an internal control procedure that, for every cash disbursement $2,500 or more, a second manager must countersign the check. The manager who has authority to initiate the disbursement signs the check and then sends the check with supporting documentation to the second manager for his or her signature. What is the logic of this control?

A. The theory behind this internal control procedure is that the second manager will make a careful review and judge whether the payment is for a legitimate purpose and is reasonable in amount. If two persons have to sign off on expenditures over a certain amount, then they would have to collude to pull off a scam against the business. Even if someone were inclined to make a quick buck and didn't care how you did it, he or she probably wouldn't be in cahoots with another untrustworthy crook.

19. The purchasing manager of the business has authority to issue purchase orders. He also inspects shipments as they arrive, approves vendors' invoices for payment, and mails checks to the vendors. Do you see any potential problems here?

Solve It

20. A business doesn't bother to reconcile its monthly bank statement balance and its cash account balance, claiming that its bookkeepers have more important things to do and, besides, the bank never makes a mistake. What do you think?

Solve It

Answers to Problems on the Bookkeeping Cycle

The following are the answers to the practice questions presented earlier in this chapter.

1 In its year-end review for errors, a business discovers that the recent bill from its law firm was entered as $6,500 instead of $5,600, which is the correct amount. The bill has not been paid yet. What adjusting entry should be made to correct this error?

Accounts Payable	$900
Legal Expense	$900

This type of error is called a *transposition error* because two digits in the number are transposed, or switched. It's a common error. Experienced bookkeepers and accountants know that this type of error is divisible by nine. (The difference caused by any two digits you transpose is always divisible by nine.)

2 In its year-end review, for errors a business discovers that an order of products was shipped to a customer, and the cost of the products was correctly charged to cost of goods sold expense. However, the paperwork for this particular sales order wasn't sent to the bookkeeping department on time. Therefore, the sale hasn't been recorded. The total price for this credit sale is $36,260. What adjusting entry should be made to correct this error?

Accounts Receivable	$36,260
Sales Revenue	$36,260

The sales revenue for this sale should be recorded because the sale was completed, and the products were delivered to the customer. The sale should be recorded to match revenue and expense. If this error isn't corrected, a mismatch will occur because the expense is in this year but the revenue will be in next year.

3 The $1,500 trash collection bill for the last month of the fiscal year normally arrives before the end of the month. However, the waste management company didn't get its bills out on time, so the expense hasn't been recorded. What adjusting entry should be made to correct this error?

Trash Collection Expense	$1,500
Accounts Payable	$1,500

This entry records the 12th month of expense for the year. If this entry were not recorded, only eleven months of trash collection expense would be recorded for the year. Also, the amount owed to the trash collection company is clearly a liability of the business and should be included in its accounts payable balance at the end of the year.

4 In the hustle and bustle of the end-of-year accounting activities, the bookkeeper simply forgot to record the business's social security taxes on its last payroll in the year. As you may know, a business employer pays social security taxes equal to the amount withheld from employees' paychecks. The amount of employer's social security tax for the last pay period is $29,600. What adjusting entry should be made to correct this error?

Social Security Tax Expense	$29,600
Social Security Taxes Payable	$29,600

Most businesses put both the social security taxes withheld from employees' wages and the equal amount paid by the business in one liability account for social security taxes payable.

5   Based on its depreciation schedules, the annual depreciation on the business's machinery is $420,000. The business uses the straight-line depreciation method. The business recorded a machinery depreciation expense at the end of each quarter during the year, but no entry has been made for the fourth and final quarter. What adjusting entry for machinery depreciation should be recorded at year-end?

Machinery Depreciation	$105,000	
Accumulated Depreciation — Machinery		$105,000

Note: By the end of the year, the business had already recorded three quarters of depreciation on its machinery. In the year-end adjusting entry, only the last quarter of the total annual depreciation expense is recorded.

6   Rather than own the real estate, a business leases its land and buildings. The lease agreement calls for monthly rents. Does the business record depreciation on this real estate?

No, because there's no depreciation expense to record. As each lease payment is made, the business records rent expense, which takes the place of depreciation expense (which would be recorded if the business owned the building).

7   A bookkeeper who was recently hired by a business recorded the depreciation expense on delivery trucks for the year as follows:

Depreciation Expense — Delivery Trucks	$215,000	
Delivery Trucks		$215,000

Is this entry wrong?

The debit to depreciation expense is correct, but the wrong account is credited. The credit should be made in the Accumulated Depreciation — Delivery Trucks account, which is the contra account to the Delivery Trucks asset account.

Standard practice is to report the original cost of fixed assets in the balance sheet and to deduct the cumulative amount of depreciation from original cost. To have this information available for preparing the balance sheet, the accumulated depreciation account is credited when recording depreciation expense.

8   On the last day of the year, a particular piece of equipment that originally cost $87,500 many years ago was removed from the production line and put on the shipping dock. The equipment is of no further use to the business and will be hauled away to the junk heap in a few days. The asset is fully depreciated. What entry should be made for the retirement of the fixed asset?

Accumulated Depreciation — Equipment	$87,500	
Equipment		$87,500

When a fixed asset is retired and removed from service, its cost and accumulated depreciation should be removed from the accounts. The fixed asset is fully depreciated, so the balance in the accumulated depreciation account is equal to the original cost of the fixed asset. Not making this entry would inflate the balances of the fixed asset account and of its contra account.

9   A business pays the owner of a patent $500,000 for the right to use the patent for a period of five years.

a. What entry should be made for the purchase of the patent right?

The entry to record the purchase of the patent is:

Patent	$500,000	
Cash		$500,000

b. What adjusting entry should be made one year later?

The entry to record the first year amortization expense on the patent is:

Patent Amortization Expense	$100,000	
Patent		$100,000

The business has the right to use the patent for only five years. Therefore, it should amortize the cost of the patent right over the five-year period. Generally, the straight-line method of allocation is used for amortizing the cost of an intangible asset. So $100,000 expense (⅕ of $500,000) is recorded each year. The amortization is recorded as a direct reduction (credit) in the intangible asset account.

10 The business signs a ten-year contract with the inventor of a secret process that it will use in its manufacturing operations. As an incentive to agree to the contract, the business immediately pays the inventor $1,000,000. In addition, the business agrees to pay the inventor a royalty equal to five percent of its sales revenue from these products over the next ten years.

a. What entry should be made for the initial payment to the inventor?

The entry to record the purchase of the rights to the secret process is:

Secret Process	$1,000,000	
Cash		$1,000,000

b. What adjusting entry should be made one year later?

The entry to record the first year amortization expense on the cost of the secret process is:

Secret Process Amortization Expense	$100,000	
Secret Process		$100,000

The purpose of this question is to illustrate that the cost of the intangible asset should be amortized over the life of the contract to use the secret process. To be more accurate, however, this is a cost of production. The amortization amount should be charged to the cost of the products that are manufactured using the secret process. When these products are sold, their costs are charged to the cost of goods sold expense account. So, the amortization ends up in the cost of goods sold expense account. Likewise, depreciation on fixed assets that are used in a company's manufacturing process is charged to the cost of products manufactured.

11 A business makes almost all credit sales. At the end of the year, the business has $485,000 total accounts receivable. This ending balance doesn't include $28,500 specific accounts receivable that were written off during the period. The business estimates that customers will not pay $6,500 of the ending balance of its accounts receivable. What year-end adjusting entry is made?

If the business uses the direct write-off method, no adjusting entry is made at the end of the year. Only the receivables actually written off during the year are included in bad debts expense. So its bad debts expense for the year is $28,500.

If the business uses the allowance method, the following adjusting entry is made at the end of the year:

Bad Debts Expense	$6,500	
Allowance for Doubtful Accounts		$6,500

Its bad debts expense for the year is $35,000 ($28,500 specific accounts written off during the year + $6,500 recorded in this adjusting entry).

12 The business has more cash than it needs for day-to-day operations, so the excess cash is invested in short-term marketable securities that pay interest. During the year, the business receives interest checks, which it records in the interest income account. At the end of the year, $48,500 interest has been earned but not yet received. This interest will be included in the interest checks the business receives next year. The business hasn't recorded this earned interest. What adjusting entry is made at the end of the year?

The following year-end adjusting entry is made to pick up the additional amount of interest income that has been earned but not received:

Accrued Interest Receivable	$48,500	
Interest Income		$48,500

When the interest income checks are received next year, the bookkeeper has to remember that $48,500 interest income has already been recorded. Accordingly, when the interest income checks are received, $48,500 is entered as a credit in the accrued interest receivable asset account.

13 At the end of the year, the business owes its employees $58,300 for accumulated vacation and sick pay. This amount will be paid when employees actually take their vacations and time off for sick leave. No entry has been made for this accrued liability. What adjusting entry is made at the end of the year?

The year-end adjusting entry for the accumulation of vacation and sick pay is as follows.

Wages and Salaries Expense	$58,300	
Accrued Operating Liabilities Payable		$58,300

TIP The titles of the accounts debited and credited in this year-end entry vary from business to business. For example, a separate expense account for employees' benefits can be used instead of debiting all labor costs in one general wages and salaries expense account. And the exact title of the liability account credited may vary; separate accounts may be used for each specific liability.

14 Based on the final determination of its federal income tax for the year, the business owes $431,500. During the year, it made $3,978,500 total installment payments towards its income tax, which were charged (debited) to its income tax expense account. The $431,500 balance still owed to the government will be paid when the business's income tax return is filed later.

a. What adjusting entry is made at the end of the year?

The year-end adjusting entry to record the full amount of income tax expense for the year is as follows:

Income Tax Expense	$431,500	
Income Tax Payable		$431,500

b. What is the amount of income tax expense reported in its income statement for the year?

The amount of income tax expense reported in its income statement is $4,410,000, which the total of the installment payments made during the year plus the amount recorded in the year-end adjusting entry.

15 At the end of the year, the business owes $10,000,000 on interest-bearing notes payable. During the year, it records interest expense as it's paid to lenders. Accordingly, the business recorded $515,400 interest expense during the year. At the close of the year, it owes $97,500 interest that hasn't yet come due for payment and that hasn't been recorded.

a. What adjusting entry is made at the end of the year?

The year-end adjusting entry for unpaid interest expense is:

Interest Expense	$97,500
Accrued Interest Payable	$97,500

b. What is the amount of interest expense reported in its annual income statement?

The interest expense reported in its annual income statement for the year is $612,900, which is the total of the interest payments during the year plus the amount recorded in the year-end adjusting entry.

16 At the end of the year, the business counts and inspects its ending inventory of products on hand, which is stored in its warehouse and retail sales areas. Usually, employees discover some damaged and spoiled products that can't be sold. This year is no exception. The cost of spoiled and damaged products that will have to be thrown away is $26,300. What adjusting entry is made?

The business should make the following year-end adjusting entry:

Cost of Goods Sold Expense	$26,300
Inventory	$26,300

Some accountants may disagree about the account I debit in this adjusting entry. Some amount of spoilage and damage from handling products is unavoidable and a normal cost of receiving, moving, storing, and handling products. Therefore, I include this amount in the cost of goods sold expense. On the other hand, an unusually high percent of products could be thrown away — beyond what's normal for the business. In such a situation, I would record the excess cost as a special expense, such as loss from damaged products. Regardless of which expense account is debited, accountants definitely agree that the cost of products thrown out should be recorded to expense in the year.

17 Refer to the closing entry in the answer to the example in this section. The T accounts after the closing entry is posted are provided here. What are the balances in the revenue and expense accounts after the closing entry is posted?

Cost of Goods Sold Expense		Sales Revenue	
$2,725,000	$2,725,000	$4,526,500	$4,526,500

Selling & Administrative Expenses	
$1,228,500	$1,228,500

Interest Expense	
$175,000	$175,000

Income Tax Expense	
$138,000	$138,000

As you can see, the accounts have zero balances. They have served their purposes for the year and are shut down and made ready for next year.

18 The business is organized legally as a partnership and therefore doesn't pay income tax. (A partnership's annual taxable income or loss is passed through to its partners who pick up their share of profit or loss in their individual income tax returns.) Year-end adjusting entries have been recorded and posted, and the business's revenue and expense accounts are provided here. What closing entry is recorded?

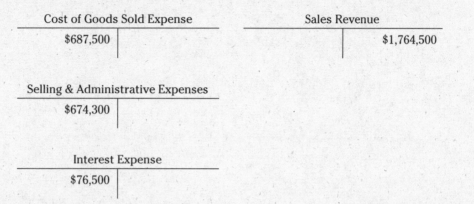

Cost of Goods Sold Expense		Sales Revenue	
$687,500			$1,764,500

Selling & Administrative Expenses	
$674,300	

Interest Expense	
$76,500	

The following closing entry is recorded.

Sales Revenue	$1,764,500
Cost of Goods Sold Expense	$687,500
Selling & Administrative Expenses	$674,300
Interest Expense	$76,500
Partners' Equity	$326,200

The annual profit of a partnership is allocated among the individual partners' equity (also called *capital*) accounts. In this entry, only one general partners' equity account is shown. Generally, partnerships don't separate between invested capital and retained earnings, as do corporations.

19 The purchasing manager of the business has authority to issue purchase orders. He also inspects shipments as they arrive, approves vendors' invoices for payment, and mails checks to the vendors. Do you see any potential problems here?

This business is asking for trouble. Assigning all these different functions to the same person violates a fundamental tenet of internal control: the *separation of duties*. Giving the purchasing manager control over the procurement process from start to finish is dangerous; ideally, a different person should be in charge of each of the steps listed in the question. For example, someone other than the purchasing manager should inspect shipments as they arrive on the receiving dock to make sure the items received match up with the items listed on the invoice from the vendor, and a different person should mail checks to vendors. If I were the boss, I'd tell the purchasing manager that his time is too valuable to do all these things and that he should focus on getting better prices.

20 A business doesn't bother to reconcile its monthly bank statement balance and its cash account balance, claiming that its bookkeepers have more important things to do and, besides, the bank never makes a mistake. What do you think?

A business should routinely reconcile its monthly bank statement balance and its cash account balance. Even if the bank "never" makes an error (hum!), the bookkeeper may make errors in recording cash receipts and payments. Also, keep in mind that the monthly bank statement reports checks from customers that have bounced (for insufficient funds) and unusual charges by the bank that the business may not have recorded as well as regular charges that the business may wait to record until it gets its monthly bank statement. In short, the bookkeeper should make time to do a monthly reconciliation.

Part II
Preparing Financial Statements

The 5th Wave — By Rich Tennant

"Have someone in accounting do a cash flow statement, a basic EPS, and finish this Sudoku puzzle for me."

In this part . . .

One main purpose of accounting is to prepare the financial statements of the business. This part explains the three primary financial statements of every business: the income statement that reports the profit-making activities of the business for the period, the balance sheet that summarizes its financial condition at the end of the profit period, and the statement of cash flows for the period.

One innovative feature in this part is Chapter 7, in which I explain the connections between sales revenue and expenses reported in the income statement with their corresponding assets and liabilities reported in the balance sheet. These couplings are very important to understand. The end result of making profit is not found in the income statement (even though profit is called the bottom line.) As you discover, the final resulting place of profit is actually in the balance sheet.

Chapter 5

The Effects and Reporting of Profit

*B*usiness is profit-motivated. As I explain in *The Fast Forward MBA in Finance* (Wiley), profit stimulates innovation; it's the reward for taking risks; it's the return on capital invested in business; it's compensation for hard work and long hours; it motivates efficiency; it weeds out products and services no longer in demand; it keeps pressure on companies to maintain their quality of customer service and products.

In short, the profit system delivers the highest standard of living in the world. Despite all this, it's no secret that many in society have a deep-seated distrust toward our profit-motivated, free-enterprise, and open-market system — and not entirely without reason.

The job of accountants is to measure profit performance, not to pass judgment on its morality. Yet, accountants shouldn't behave like the three monkeys who see no evil, speak no evil, and hear no evil. If a business is acting illegally, the last thing it wants to do is record a liability because of the likelihood of losing a major lawsuit or having to pay a huge fine because of its illegal activities. The chief accountant has to decide whether to be part of the conspiracy to conceal the illegal activities or to leave the business.

This chapter explains the effects of profit or loss on financial condition and how profit and loss performance is reported *outside* the business in the income statement. The term "income statement" generally means the *external* income statement reported by a business to its shareowners and lenders. (In Part III of this book, I discuss *internal* profit reports used by a business's managers; internal management profit reports include much more detailed and confidential information than external income statements.)

Externally reported income statements are bound by authoritative financial reporting standards for measuring and reporting profit. These rules are called *generally accepted accounting principles,* or GAAP for short. Business profit measurement and reporting shouldn't deviate from these standards in any significant respect. Otherwise, the income statement could be judged as misleading and possibly fraudulent.

Understanding the Nature of Profit

Profit doesn't have just one universal meaning or definition. One concept of profit is to buy low and sell high. This definition applies to investing in stocks and real estate, but it's not a good definition for *business* profit. Another concept of profit is an increase in the market value of an asset. Accounting for business profit ignores market value increases of operating assets. Except for investment companies, hedge funds, and mutual funds, businesses don't earn profit by holding assets that appreciate in value.

Most businesses earn profit through an ongoing process of selling products and services for prices that provide revenue higher than the expense of providing the products and services. Business profit is the residual, or the amount remaining after deducting expenses from revenue. To make profit, a business needs to raise capital (generally money) to invest in *operating assets* that are used in its profit-making activities. These assets aren't held for sale or for market value appreciation. The business's sources of capital expect a return on their capital, and interest is paid on money loaned to the business. The profit remaining after paying interest to lenders and income tax to the government accrues to the benefit of the shareowners of the business.

Of course, a business may pursue profit in many other directions — from trading in pork belly futures to real estate speculation. But this chapter focuses on making profit the old-fashioned way — making sales and controlling expenses. The income statement I discuss in this chapter is for the standard model of a business that sells products and services.

Profit is a calculated number equal to the difference between sales revenue and expenses. Sales revenue is on one side of the scale, expenses are on the other side, and profit is the measure of how much the revenue side outweighs the expense side. To locate profit, you must trace the effects of revenue and expenses.

Suppose a business collects cash for all its sales and pays cash for all its expenses during the year. You need look to only one place — its cash account — to find the business's profit. However, a business may make credit sales and not collect cash from all its sales during the year. Furthermore, the typical business doesn't pay all its expenses during the year and pays some expenses before the start of the year. In summary, sales and expenses affect several assets, including cash and liabilities.

To follow the trail of profit, keep the following in mind:

- ✔ Sales Revenue = Asset Increase or Liability Decrease
- ✔ An Expense = Asset Decrease or Liability Increase

Q. During the year, Business A's assets increase $3,000,000, and its liabilities increase $400,000 as the result of its profit-making activities. During the year, Business B's assets increase $2,700,000, and its liabilities increase $100,000 as the result of its profit-making activities. During the year, Business C's assets increase $2,000,000, and its liabilities decrease $600,000 as the result of its profit-making activities. None of these three businesses distributed any part of their annual profit to their shareowners during the year. What is the annual profit of each business?

A. All three businesses earn the same profit for the year: $2,600,000. In Chapter 1, I explain that the accounting equation can be stated as follows:

Assets – Liabilities = Owners' equity

Profit increases the owners' equity of a business, which means that the changes in assets and liabilities have the effect of increasing owners' equity. For each business in this scenario, owners' equity improves $2,600,000, which is the amount of profit for the year.

1. A business reports $346,000 net income (profit) for the year just ended. Determine two valid scenarios for changes in its assets and liabilities resulting from its profit for the year.

Solve It

2. A business reports $3,800,000 loss for the year just ended. Determine two valid scenarios for changes in its assets and liabilities resulting from its loss for the year.

Solve It

3. A business reports $5,250,000 net income for the year just ended. In its statement of cash flows for the year (see Chapter 8), the business reports that its cash flow from operating activities (from its profit for the year) is $4,650,000. In other words, its cash balance increased $4,650,000 from its profit-making activities for the year. Determine two valid scenarios for changes in assets other than cash and in liabilities that result from its profit for the year.

Solve It

4. A business reports $836,000 loss for the year just ended. In its statement of cash flows for the year (see Chapter 8), the business reports that its cash flow from operating activities (from its loss for the year) is a *negative* $675,000. In other words, its cash balance decreased $675,000 from its profit-making activities for the year. Determine two valid scenarios for changes in assets other than cash and in liabilities resulting from its loss for the year.

Solve It

Choosing the Income Statement Format

The bottom line profit (or loss) in an income statement draws the most attention, but the income statement is really about sales revenue and expenses. A business can't make profit without sales and expenses. Therefore, the income statement reports sales revenue and expenses.

An income statement reports three basic items of information, in the following order:

- ✔ Sales Revenue
- ✔ Expenses
- ✔ Profit

Income statements are reported in two basic formats:

- ✔ **Multi-step format:** This format typically presents four measures of profit — gross margin, operating earnings, earnings before income tax, and net income. One revenue line and four profit lines are presented. One purpose of this format is to disclose *gross margin,* which is a key determinant in the bottom-line profit performance of businesses that sell products. Any slippage in gross margin as a percent of sales revenue is viewed with alarm.

- ✔ **Single-step format:** In this format, all expenses are added and their total is deducted from sales revenue. Unlike the multi-step format, there's only one profit line, which is bottom-line net income.

Figure 5-1 is an illustration of the multi-step format. Reading this income statement is like walking down stairs, one step at a time.

Sales Revenue	$26,000,000
Cost of Goods Sold Expense	14,300,000
Gross Margin	$11,700,000
Selling and General Expenses	8,700,000
Operating Earnings	$3,000,000
Interest Expense	400,000
Earnings Before Income Tax	$2,600,000
Income Tax Expense	910,000
Net Income	$1,690,000

Figure 5-1: Example of multi-step income statement format.

The single-step income statement format for the same business is shown in Figure 5-2. In actual practice, you see countless variations of these two basic income statement formats.

Sales Revenue		$26,000,000
Cost of Goods Sold Expense	$14,300,000	
Selling and General Expenses	8,700,000	
Interest Expense	400,000	
Income Tax Expense	910,000	24,310,000
Net Income		$1,690,000

Figure 5-2: Example of single-step income statement format.

5. The sales revenue and expenses of a business for the year just ended are as follows:

Cost of goods sold expense	$6,358,000
Income tax expense	$458,000
Interest expense	$684,000
Selling and general expenses	$4,375,000
Sales revenue	$13,125,000

Prepare the annual income statement of the business in the multi-step format.

Solve It

6. The sales revenue and expenses of a business for the year just ended are as follows:

Cost of goods sold expense	$598,500
Income tax expense	none
Interest expense	$378,000
Selling and general expenses	$896,500
Sales revenue	$1,698,000

Prepare the annual income statement of the business in the single-step format.

Solve It

Deciding on Disclosure in the Income Statement

After a business decides on the format for reporting its income statement (multi-step or single-step; see the preceding section), the next main decision concerns how much information to disclose about its expenses. Public companies are subject to financial disclosure rules issued by the United States Securities and Exchange Commission (SEC). A publicly owned business has no choice but to abide by these rules. Otherwise, trading in its stock shares could be suspended by the SEC — the kiss of death for a public company.

Income statement disclosure standards for nonpublic businesses (that is, those not subject to the SEC's jurisdiction) are surprisingly vague and permissive. Generally accepted accounting standards (GAAP) say little about how much information should be disclosed about expenses in the income statement. Generally speaking, businesses that sell products report their cost of goods sold expenses, and almost all businesses report their interest and income tax expenses. But, it's much more difficult to generalize about the disclosure of other expenses.

Figures 5-1 and 5-2 disclose only one conglomerate operating expense: Selling and General Expenses. Some businesses disclose only this expense because they're very stingy about revealing any more detail about their operating expenses. Other businesses report five or ten operating expenses in their income statements.

In deciding how much expense disclosure should be included in income statements, businesses make three main considerations:

✔ **Confidentiality:** Many businesses don't want to reveal the compensation of the officers of the business, for example. They argue that this information is private and personal.

✔ **Materiality:** Most businesses don't see any point in reporting expense information that's relatively insignificant and would only clutter the income statement.

✔ **Practicality:** Businesses limit the income statement contents to what fits on one page. A business can put additional detail about expenses in the footnotes to its financial statements, but many argue that shareowners and lenders have only so much time to read financial statements and putting too much information in their financial reports is counterproductive.

Q. Assume that you are one of the major shareowners of the private business whose annual income statement is shown in Figure 5-1. You aren't a manager of the business or on its board of directors, but as an outside investor, you're vitally interested in how the business is doing financially. So you carefully read the business's financial statements, especially its income statement. You depend on the business making a profit in order to pay dividends from profit to its shareowners. Are you satisfied with the extent of expense disclosure in the income statement? Do you want the income statement to report one or more of the following expenses?

• Compensation of officers

• Salaries and wages of employees

• Repairs and maintenance

• Bad debts

• Rents

• Taxes and licenses

• Depreciation

• Advertising

• Pension and profit-sharing plans

• Employee benefit plans

A. In all likelihood, the business keeps accounts for these expenses because they have to be reported in its annual federal income tax return. So the information is available and could be reported in the business's income statement. When I served on the board of directors of a local bank and reviewed loan applications from our business customers, I saw income statements that reported all these expenses. On the other hand, I saw many income statements that didn't disclose these expenses.

If I were a major outside shareowner in this business, I would request that, either in the income statement itself or in the footnotes to the financial statements, information be reported about four expenses: repairs and maintenance, advertising, pension and profit-sharing plans, and employee benefit plans. Why these four? Repairs and maintenance expense can be manipulated by management to push profit up or down for the year. Advertising is a very discretionary expense that I'd want to compare to sales revenue. Pension and profit-sharing plans and employee benefit plans can be very large encumbrances on a business.

7. A business's income statement doesn't disclose its advertising expenses for the year. Give an argument for not disclosing this expense, and give an argument for disclosing this expense.

Solve It

8. Some years ago, businesses in the cosmetic industry did *not* report sales revenue and cost of goods sold expense. Their income statements started with the gross margin line, and their gross margins were a very large percent of sales revenue (over 70 percent). The companies argued that if their customers found out that their gross margins were so fat, many would refuse to pay such high prices for lipstick, rouge, and so on. Is this a legitimate reason for a business with high gross profit margins to not report sales revenue and cost of goods sold expense?

Solve It

Examining How Sales and Expenses Change Assets and Liabilities

In a financial report, the income statement may seem like a tub standing on its own feet, disconnected from the balance sheet and the statement of cash flows. Nothing is further from the truth. The three financial statements are interdependent and interconnected. For example, if sales revenue or one of the expenses had been just $10 different than the amount reported in the income statement, a $10 difference would appear somewhere in the balance sheet and statement of cash flows.

As you know, an income statement reports sales revenue, expenses, and profit or loss. But an income statement doesn't report how sales revenue and expenses change the financial condition of the business. For example, in Figure 5-1, $26,000,000 sales revenue is reported in the annual income statement of a business. The business also reports $24,310,000 total expenses for the year. How did the sales revenue and expenses change its financial condition? The income statement doesn't say.

Business managers rely on their accountants to explain how sales and expenses change the assets and liabilities of their businesses. Business lenders and shareowners also need to understand these effects in order to make sense of financial statements.

Suppose you're the chief accountant of the business whose income statement is presented in Figure 5-1. The president asks you to explain the financial effects of sales revenue and expenses reported in its latest annual income statement at the next meeting of its board of directors. To help organize your thoughts for the presentation, you decide to prepare summary sales revenue and expense journal entries for the year. Based on your analysis, you prepare the following summary journal entries for sales revenue and for each of the four expenses reported in the income statement.

Sales Revenue:

Cash	$25,000,000
Accounts Receivable	$1,000,000
Sales Revenue	$26,000,000

The business makes credit sales. When recording a credit sale, the asset account *accounts receivable* is debited. When the customer pays, accounts receivable is credited. The business collected $25,000,000 from customers. Therefore, its accounts receivable balance increased $1,000,000.

Cost of Goods Sold Expense:

Cost of Goods Sold Expense	$14,300,000
Inventory	$2,000,000
Cash	$14,500,000
Accounts Payable	$1,800,000

The business purchases $16,300,000 of products during the year, and its cost of goods sold was $14,300,000. So, its inventory increased $2,000,000. It didn't pay for all its $16,300,000 of purchases. Its accounts payable for inventory purchases increased $1,800,000. Therefore, cash outlay for products during the year was $14,500,000.

Selling and General Expenses:

Selling and General Expenses	$8,700,000
Prepaid Expenses	$300,000
Cash	$6,900,000
Accounts Payable	$850,000
Accrued Expenses Payable	$725,000
Accumulated Depreciation	$525,000

Selling and General Expenses is a somewhat complicated entry because operating expenses involve several balance sheet accounts. The business added $300,000 to its prepaid expenses balance during the year. It recorded $525,000 depreciation expense for the year, as you see in the credit to accumulated depreciation. (Depreciation expense is included in the selling and general expenses amount reported in its income statement.) Not all expenses were paid for by the end of the year; unpaid expenses caused $850,000 increase in accounts payable and $725,000 increase in accrued expenses payable.

Interest Expense:

Interest Expense	$400,000
Cash	$350,000
Accrued Expenses Payable	$50,000

The business paid $350,000 interest during the year. The amount of unpaid interest at year-end increased $50,000. A general liability account for accrued expenses is shown in this entry. (The business may credit a more specific account, such as accrued interest payable.)

Income Tax Expense:

Income Tax Expense	$910,000	
Cash		$830,000
Accrued Expenses Payable		$80,000

At the end of last year, the business didn't owe any income tax. During the year, it made $830,000 installment payments toward its estimated income tax (as required by law). Based on the final determination of its income tax for the year, the business still owes $80,000, which will be paid when its return is filed. The general liability account for accrued expenses is shown in this entry. (The business may credit a more specific account, such as income tax payable.)

These five summary entries aren't actual journal entries recorded by a business; they simply help summarize the effects of sales and expenses on the assets and liabilities of the business. Also, I should point out that to develop the information for these entries, the accountant has to analyze the balance sheet accounts affected by sales and expenses, which takes time.

Q. From the five summary journal entries for sales revenue and expenses for the year, can you determine the cash flow from profit (that is, the net cash increase or decrease from its profit-making activities for the year)?

A. Yes, indeed you can. Each of the summary entries involves a debit (increase) or credit (decrease) to the cash account. The net effect on cash from its sales revenue and expenses for the year is summarized as follows:

Sales revenue	$25,000,000
Cost of Goods Sold Expense	($14,500,000)
Selling and General Expenses	($6,900,000)
Interest Expense	($350,000)
Income Tax Expense	($830,000)
Net Cash Increase	$2,420,000

Note: The $2,420,000 net cash increase is labeled "cash flow from operating activities" in the statement of cash flows. (For more on this financial statement see Chapter 8.)

9. Refer to the summary sales revenue entry earlier in this section. Assume that accounts receivable increased $500,000 instead of the $1,000,000 increase in that entry. Prepare the summary journal entry for sales revenue.

Solve It

10. Refer to the summary cost of goods sold expense entry earlier in this section. Assume that inventory *decreased* $500,000 during the year because the business sold more products than it purchased. And assume that accounts payable *decreased* $250,000 during the year because the business paid more of its purchase liabilities than it bought on credit. Prepare the summary journal entry for cost of goods sold expense.

Solve It

11. Refer to the summary selling and general expenses entry earlier in this section. Assume that prepaid expenses didn't change during the year. The amounts for depreciation expense and the increases in accounts payable and accrued expenses payable are the same as in the summary journal entry. Selling and general expenses are $8,700,000, the same as in the example. Prepare the summary journal entry for selling and general expenses.

12. Refer to the summary income tax expense entry earlier in this section. Assume that the business overpaid its income tax for the year; the total of installment payments during the year was $50,000 more than its $910,000 income tax for the year. The overpayment will be refunded to the business. Prepare the summary journal entry for income tax expense.

Solve It

Summing Up the Manifold Effects of Profit

Making sales and incurring expenses cause a multitude of effects on the assets and liabilities of a business. In other words, making profit causes many changes in the financial condition of a business. It would be convenient if a $1 profit caused a $1 cash increase and nothing more, but the effects of making profit are much broader and reach throughout the balance sheet.

The journal entries in the preceding section summarize the effects of sales and expenses on a business's assets and liabilities. Figure 5-3 shows these changes in T accounts for the assets and liabilities. As you probably know, T accounts aren't the official, formal accounts of a business. Rather, T accounts are like scratch paper that accountants use to analyze and "think out" the effects of transactions. A T account has two columns: debits are always put in the left column and credits in the right column. The rules for debits and credits are explained in Chapter 3.

In Figure 5-3, I use seven asset and liability accounts to illustrate the recording of sales revenue and expenses for the year. Even a relatively small business keeps 100 or more asset and liability accounts. However, the seven asset and liability accounts in the example are sufficient to illustrate the effects of sales revenue and expenses on the financial condition of a business.

Cash		Accounts Payable	
$25,000,000	$14,500,000		$1,800,000
	$6,900,000		$850,000
	$350,000		
	$830,000	Accrued Expenses Payable	
			$725,000
Accounts Receivable			$50,000
$1,000,000			$80,000

Figure 5-3: Changes in assets and liabilities caused by sales and expenses.

Inventory		Accumulated Depreciation	
$2,000,000			$525,000
Prepaid Expenses			
$300,000			

In order to help you understand what profit consists of, I collapse the changes in assets and liabilities caused by sales and expenses shown in Figure 5-3 into one comprehensive journal entry that shows the diverse effects of making profit. In this entry, the $1,690,000 profit for the year is shown as an increase in the retained earnings owners' equity account.

Comprehensive Journal Entry that Summarizes Changes in Assets and Liabilities from Profit-Making Activities During the Year

Cash	$2,420,000
Accounts Receivable	$1,000,000
Inventory	$2,000,000
Prepaid Expenses	$300,000
Accounts Payable	$2,650,000
Accrued Expenses Payable	$855,000
Accumulated Depreciation	$525,000
Owners' Equity — Retained Earnings	$1,690,000

Q. This comprehensive journal entry for the asset and liability effects of making profit "speaks" to an accountant, who's familiar with journal entries and debits and credits. Translate this journal entry into plain English, giving an explanation that non-accounting business managers, lenders, and investors can understand.

A. A good way of explaining the diverse effects of profit on assets and liabilities is to prepare a summary of the changes in balance sheet accounts affected.

Summary of Asset and Liability Changes from Making Profit

Cash	$2,420,000
Accounts Receivable	$1,000,000
Inventory	$2,000,000
Prepaid Expenses	$300,000
Fixed Assets (Depreciation)	($525,000)
Net Increase of Assets	$5,195,000
Accounts Payable	$2,650,000
Accrued Expenses Payable	$855,000
Increase of Liabilities	$3,505,000
Net Worth Increase From Profit	$1,690,000

Profit improves the *net worth* of a business. Net worth, another name for the owners' equity, equals total assets minus total liabilities. In this example, the business makes a profit, and the effect on the balance sheet is that assets increase more than liabilities, which is the typical profit effect. On the other hand, assets could remain relatively flat and liabilities could decrease. (Although it isn't very common, profit could consist of a decrease in liabilities more than the decrease in assets.)

13. The effects from sales and expenses for the year just ended for a business were as follows:

Sales revenue was $15,700,000; the business collected $13,900,000 cash from customers, and accounts receivable increased $1,800,000.

The cost of products sold during the year was $9,800,000, and the business added $500,000 of products to inventory. It didn't pay for all $10,300,000 in purchases. Its accounts payable for inventory purchases increased $250,000.

Selling and general expenses were $4,860,000. The business added $125,000 to its prepaid expenses balance during the year. It recorded a $145,000 depreciation expense for the year. (Depreciation is included in the selling and general expenses amount reported in its income statement.) Not all expenses were paid for by the end of the year; unpaid expenses caused a $150,000 increase in accounts payable and a $225,000 increase in accrued expenses payable.

The business paid $200,000 interest during the year. The amount of unpaid interest at year-end increased $25,000. (Use the general liability account *accrued expenses payable*.)

The business is organized legally as a limited liability company (LLC) and has elected not to pay income tax. Its taxable income for the year is passed through to its shareowners, who include their respective portions of the business's taxable income in their individual income tax returns.

a. Prepare the annual income statement of the business in single-step form.

b. Prepare a summary journal entry for the sales and for each expense of the business for the year.

c. Prepare a comprehensive entry showing the changes in assets and liabilities from profit for the year.

14. The comprehensive entry for this business summarizing the changes in assets and liabilities from its sales and expenses for the year is as follows:

Cash	$280,000
Accounts Receivable	$825,000
Inventory	$375,000
Prepaid Expenses	$25,000
Accounts Payable	$955,000
Accrued Expenses Payable	$475,000
Accumulated Depreciation	$390,000
Owners' Equity — Retained Earnings	$875,000

For the business's board of directors, prepare a schedule of changes in assets and liabilities that summarizes the effects on the business's financial condition from its profit for the year.

Solve It

Answers to Problems on the Effects and Reporting of Profit

The following are the answers to the practice questions presented earlier in this chapter.

1 A business reports $346,000 net income (profit) for the year just ended. Determine two valid scenarios for changes in its assets and liabilities resulting from its profit for the year.

The simplest scenario is that assets increase $346,000 and liabilities remain the same (zero change). Another valid scenario is a situation in which assets increase $346,000 more than liabilities increase; for example, assets increase $846,000 and liabilities increase $500,000. An unusual but valid scenario would be that assets remain the same (zero change) and liabilities decrease $346,000. The key point is that if profit is $346,000, then *net worth* (assets minus liabilities) increases $346,000.

2 A business reports $3,800,000 loss for the year just ended. Determine two valid scenarios for changes in its assets and liabilities resulting from its loss for the year.

The simplest scenario is that assets decrease $3,800,000 and liabilities remain the same (zero change). Another valid scenario is a situation in which assets decrease $3,800,000 more than liabilities decrease; for example, assets decrease $6,800,000 and liabilities decrease $3,000,000. An unusual but valid scenario would be that assets remain the same (zero change) and liabilities increase $3,800,000. The key point is that if loss is $3,800,000, then *net worth* (assets minus liabilities) decreases $3,800,000.

3 A business reports $5,250,000 net income for the year just ended. In its statement of cash flows for the year, the business reports that its cash flow from operating activities (from its profit for the year) is $4,650,000. In other words, its cash balance increased $4,650,000 from its profit-making activities for the year. Determine two valid scenarios for changes in assets other than cash and in liabilities that result from its profit for the year.

$5,250,000 profit less the $4,650,000 cash increase from profit leaves $600,000 to be explained. One asset (cash) increased $4,650,000, so you have to figure out what happened to other assets and to liabilities. One valid scenario is that assets other than cash increased $1,600,000 and liabilities increased $1,000,000. If liabilities remained the same (zero change), then assets other than cash would have increased $600,000. It's possible, though not very likely, that assets other than cash remained the same (zero change) and liabilities decreased $600,000.

4 A business reports $836,000 loss for the year just ended. In its statement of cash flows for the year, the business reports that its cash flow from operating activities (from its loss for the year) is a *negative* $675,000. In other words, its cash balance decreased $675,000 from its profit-making activities for the year. Determine two valid scenarios for changes in assets other than cash and in liabilities resulting from its loss for the year.

Not all the loss is accounted for by the cash decrease. The $836,000 loss compared with the $675,000 cash decrease leaves $161,000 to be explained. The simplest scenario is that liabilities remained the same (zero change) and assets other than cash decreased $161,000. The reverse of this scenario is that assets other than cash remained the same (zero change) and liabilities increased $161,000. I wouldn't be surprised if assets other than cash increased even though the business suffered a loss for the year, in which case liabilities would have increased $161,000 more than assets other than cash.

5 The sales revenue and expenses of a business for the year just ended are as follows:

Cost of goods sold expense	$6,358,000
Income tax expense	$458,000
Interest expense	$684,000
Selling and general expenses	$4,375,000
Sales revenue	$13,125,000

Prepare the annual income statement of the business in the multi-step format.

The annual income statement in multi-step form is

Sales Revenue	$13,125,000
Cost of Goods Sold Expense	6,358,000
Gross Margin	$6,767,000
Selling and General Expenses	4,375,000
Operating Earnings	$2,392,000
Interest Expense	684,000
Earnings Before Income Tax	$1,708,000
Income Tax Expense	458,000
Net Income	$1,250,000

6 The sales revenue and expenses of a business for the year just ended are as follows:

Cost of goods sold expense	$598,500
Income tax expense	none
Interest expense	$378,000
Selling and general expenses	$896,500
Sales revenue	$1,698,000

Prepare the annual income statement of the business in the single-step format.

The annual income statement in single-step form is:

Sales Revenue		$1,698,000
Cost of Goods Sold Expense	$598,500	
Selling and General Expenses	896,500	
Interest Expense	378,000	$1,873,000
Net Income (Loss)		($175,000)

7 A business's income statement doesn't disclose its advertising expenses for the year. Give an argument for not disclosing this expense, and give an argument for disclosing this expense.

The main argument for not disclosing advertising expense is that the business may give up a competitive advantage by doing so. The thinking is that it's best if a business's competitors don't know how much it spends on advertising. (Of course, a business may not know how much its competitors spend on advertising, either.) Another argument rests on the general grounds of confidentiality; many private businesses believe that they have rights of privacy about their financial affairs.

One main argument in favor of disclosing an advertising expense is that this particular expense is very discretionary and arbitrary in nature. A business could be spending far too much on advertising with little payoff. Conversely, a business could be spending very little on advertising with the result that its sales are anemic. Many lenders and investors argue that they need to know how much a business spends on advertising so they can compare this expense against sales revenue. Also, how much a business spends on advertising says a lot about its general aggressiveness and strategy. This expense is considered a good indicator of a business's competitive strategy.

8 Some years ago businesses in the cosmetic industry did *not* report sales revenue and cost of goods sold expense. Their income statements started with the gross margin line, and their gross margins were a very large percent of sales revenue (over 70 percent). The companies argued that if their customers found out that their gross margins were so fat, many would refuse to pay such high prices for lipstick, rouge, and so on. Is this a legitimate reason for a business with high gross profit margins to not report sales revenue and cost of goods sold expense?

I remember reading these income statements many years ago and being truly shocked. Today, financial reporting standards for businesses that sell products require that they report sales revenue, cost of goods sold expense, and gross profit (margin) in their income statements. In contrast, many businesses don't sell products, or the products they sell are incidental and secondary to the sale of services, which is the main source of their sales revenue. Airlines and movie theaters are examples of such businesses. Service-oriented businesses generally don't report cost of goods sold expense and, therefore, don't report gross profit. Many report a "cost of sales" expense in their income statements, but this expense usually isn't deducted from sales revenue, and gross profit isn't reported.

9 Refer to the summary sales revenue entry in the section "Examining How Sales and Expenses Change Assets and Liabilities." Assume that accounts receivable increased $500,000 instead of the $1,000,000 increase in that entry. Prepare the summary journal entry for sales revenue.

The summary sales revenue entry for this scenario is:

Cash	$25,500,000
Accounts Receivable	$500,000
Sales Revenue	$26,000,000

10 Refer to the summary cost of goods sold expense entry in the section "Examining How Sales and Expenses Change Assets and Liabilities." Assume that inventory *decreased* $500,000 during the year because the business sold more products than it purchased during the year. And assume that accounts payable *decreased* $250,000 during the year because the business paid more of its purchase liabilities than it bought on credit. Prepare the summary journal entry for cost of goods sold expense.

The summary cost of goods sold expense entry for this scenario is:

Cost of Goods Sold Expense	$14,300,000
Inventory	$500,000
Cash	$14,050,000
Accounts Payable	$250,000

In the summary entry for cost of goods sold expense in the example, cash decreased $14,500,000, whereas in this scenario cash decreased $14,050,000, which is a $450,000 smaller cash outlay for the year. Why? Instead of adding to inventory, which required more purchases of goods than the goods that were sold, the business allowed its inventory to fall, which meant that its purchases were less than the goods sold and produced a $2,500,000 reduction in cash outlay. In the example, accounts payable increased $1,800,000, but in this scenario, this liability was decreased $250,000. This difference means additional cash outlay of $2,050,000. The net cash difference, therefore, is $450,000. The inventory difference reduced cash outlay $2,500,000, and the accounts payable difference increased cash outlay $2,050,000.

11 Refer to the summary selling and general expenses entry in the section "Examining How Sales and Expenses Change Assets and Liabilities." Assume that prepaid expenses didn't change during the year. The amounts for depreciation expense and the increases in accounts payable and accrued expenses payable are the same as in the summary journal entry. Selling and general expenses are $8,700,000, the same as in the example. Prepare the summary journal entry for selling and general expenses.

The summary selling and general expenses entry for this scenario is:

Selling and General Expenses	$8,700,000
Cash	$6,600,000
Accounts Payable	$850,000
Accrued Expenses Payable	$725,000
Accumulated Depreciation	$525,000

This entry doesn't have any debit or credit to prepaid expenses (an asset account) because its balance didn't change in this scenario. In the example, the business increased its prepaid expenses $300,000, so in this scenario, cash outlay is $300,000 lower because the business didn't increase its prepaid expenses.

12 Refer to the summary income tax expense entry for the business example in the section "Examining How Sales and Expenses Change Assets and Liabilities." Assume that the business overpaid its income tax for the year. The total of installment payments during the year was $50,000 more than its $910,000 income tax for the year. The overpayment will be refunded to the business. Prepare the summary journal entry for income tax expense.

The summary income tax expense entry for this scenario is:

Income Tax Expense	$910,000
Income Tax Refund Receivable	$50,000
Cash	$960,000

 A business may overestimate its income tax for the year and pay more than the amount owed, but businesses try to avoid this practice because they would rather have the use of the money during the year.

13 The effects from sales and expenses for the year just ended of a business were as follows:

Sales revenue was $15,700,000; the business collected $13,900,000 cash from customers, and accounts receivable increased $1,800,000.

The cost of products sold during the year was $9,800,000, and the business added $500,000 of products to inventory. It didn't pay for $10,300,000 in purchases. Its accounts payable for inventory purchases increased $250,000.

Selling and general expenses were $4,860,000. The business added $125,000 to its prepaid expenses balance during the year. It recorded a $145,000 depreciation expense for the year. (Depreciation is included in the selling and general expenses amount reported in its income statement.) Not all expenses were paid for by the end of the year. Unpaid expenses caused a $150,000 increase in accounts payable and a $225,000 increase in accrued expenses payable.

The business paid $200,000 interest during the year. The amount of unpaid interest at year-end increased $25,000. (Use the general liability account *accrued expenses payable*.)

The business is organized legally as a limited liability company (LLC) and has elected not to pay income tax. Its taxable income for the year is passed through to its shareowners, who include their respective portions of the business's taxable income in their individual income tax returns.

a. Prepare the annual income statement of the business in single-step form.

The income statement in single-step form is:

Sales Revenue		$15,700,000
Cost of Goods Sold Expense	$9,800,000	
Selling and General Expenses	4,860,000	
Interest Expense	225,000	$14,885,000
Net Income		$815,000

b. Prepare a summary journal entry for the sales and for each expense of the business for the year.

The summary entries are as follows:

Sales Revenue:

Cash	$13,900,000
Accounts Receivable	$1,800,000
Sales Revenue	$15,700,000

Cost of Goods Sold Expense:

Cost of Goods Sold Expense	$9,800,000
Inventory	$500,000
Cash	$10,050,000
Accounts Payable	$250,000

Selling and General Expenses:

Selling and General Expenses	$4,860,000
Prepaid Expenses	$125,000
Cash	$4,465,000
Accounts Payable	$150,000
Accrued Expenses Payable	$225,000
Accumulated Depreciation	$145,000

Interest Expense:

Interest Expense	$225,000
Cash	$200,000
Accrued Expenses Payable	$25,000

c. Prepare a comprehensive entry showing the changes in assets and liabilities from profit for the year.

The comprehensive entry summarizing the changes in assets and liabilities caused by sales and expenses during the year is as follows:

Cash	$815,000
Accounts Receivable	$1,800,000
Inventory	$500,000
Prepaid Expenses	$125,000
Accounts Payable	$400,000
Accrued Expenses Payable	$250,000
Accumulated Depreciation	$145,000
Owners' Equity — Retained Earnings	$815,000

You may notice that cash decreases in this scenario. In other words, the sales and expenses of the business result in an $815,000 cash decrease even though the business earned $815,000. The fact that the cash decrease and profit are the same amounts is purely coincidental.

14 The comprehensive entry for this business summarizing the changes in assets and liabilities from its sales and expenses for the year is as follows:

Cash	$280,000
Accounts Receivable	$825,000
Inventory	$375,000
Prepaid Expenses	$25,000
Accounts Payable	$955,000
Accrued Expenses Payable	$475,000
Accumulated Depreciation	$390,000
Owners' Equity — Retained Earnings	$875,000

Prepare a schedule of changes in assets and liabilities for its board of directors that summarizes the effects on the business's financial condition from its profit for the year.

Summary of Asset and Liability Changes From Making Profit

Cash	($280,000)
Accounts Receivable	$825,000
Inventory	$375,000
Prepaid Expenses	$25,000
Fixed Assets (Depreciation)	($390,000)
Net Increase of Assets	$555,000
Accounts Payable	$955,000
Accrued Expenses Payable	$475,000
Increase of Liabilities	$1,430,000
Net Worth Decrease From Loss	$875,000

In this scenario, net worth decreased $875,000 because liabilities increased $1,430,000 and assets increased only $555,000. This unfavorable difference is the essence of a loss. Notice that even though the business suffered a loss for the year, its cash balance decreased far less than the amount of loss. The cash decrease is relatively low because the business avoided cash payments due to the relatively large increases in its accounts payable and accrued expenses payable.

Chapter 6

Reporting Financial Condition in the Balance Sheet

Your rich aunt just left you a small fortune, and you've always wanted to own and manage a business. Well, wouldn't you know? The owners of a reputable business in your hometown want to sell out. It's a privately owned corporation, and the shareowners offer to sell all their stock shares to you. You ask to see the business's latest annual financial report, but before the present owners hand over this information, they ask you to sign a *confidentiality agreement*. This contract requires that if you decide not to buy the business, you must keep confidential all the information in the financial report. You may not divulge anything you learn from the financial report. You agree and sign the agreement.

The annual financial report of a business includes four essential elements:

✔ **Income statement** for the year just ended

✔ **Balance sheet** at the close of business on the last day of the year

✔ **Statement of cash flows** for the year just ended

✔ **Footnotes** that supplement and are an integral part of the financial statements

The financial statements of a private business may or may not be audited by an independent CPA. An audit opinion adds credibility to the financial statements but doesn't come cheap.

So you study the annual income statement of the business you're interested in purchasing. All the examples and questions in this chapter are based on the following information for this business: The company reports $12,000,000 sales revenue and $11,400,000 total expenses for the year, which equal 95 percent of sales revenue. So net income is $600,000 for the year, or 5 percent of sales revenue. In your opinion, its profit performance is satisfactory for a company in this line of business. You now turn your attention to its *balance sheet,* which is a summary of the business's assets and liabilities and, as such, provides a comprehensive picture of the business's financial condition.

Getting Started on the Balance Sheet

Satisfactory profit performance doesn't guarantee that the financial condition of the business is satisfactory. In fact, the business could have serious financial problems even though it's earning profit. It may have too little cash and assets that can be converted into cash soon enough to pay its short-term liabilities. It could be operating at the mercy of its creditors. Conversely, the business may be sitting on a hoard of cash. You have to look in the balance sheet to find out what's really going on financially.

The balance sheet is also called the *statement of financial condition,* which better indicates its nature and purposes. This financial statement presents a summary of the assets and the liabilities of a business. *Liabilities* are claims against the assets of the business; they arise from unpaid purchases and expenses and from borrowing money. The readers of a balance sheet compare the liabilities of the business against its assets and judge whether the business will be able to pay its liabilities on time.

The total assets of a business should be more than its total liabilities, of course. The excess of assets over liabilities equals the *owners' equity* of the business. Liabilities have definite due dates for payment, but owners have no such claims on the business. Owners' equity is in the business for the long haul. By majority vote, the owners can decide to dissolve the business, liquidate all its assets, pay off all liabilities, and return what's left to the owners. But individual owners can't call up the business and ask for some of their equity to be paid out to them. In short, owners' equity is the permanent capital base of the business.

A business *corporation* reports two sources of owners' equity:

- ✔ The total amount of capital its owners invested in the business
- ✔ The accumulated amount of profit earned and retained by the business

In contrast, business partnerships, limited liability companies, and sole proprietorships typically report just one total amount for owners' equity.

Assets, liabilities, and owners' equity accounts aren't intermingled in the balance sheet. Assets are presented in one grouping, liabilities in another, and owners' equity in a third. Balance sheets typically report five to ten assets, five to ten liabilities, and two, three, or four owners' equity accounts. (These are rough averages, I should mention.)

The balance sheet of the business you're thinking of buying reports these three basic groups: total assets equal $8,000,000, total liabilities equal $4,800,000, and total owners' equity equals $3,200,000 at the end of its most recent year. Using printing option terminology that appears in almost all programs, the most common format, or layout, of the balance sheet is landscape (horizontal). The following is the company's balance sheet presented in the landscape layout:

		$4,800,000 Liabilities
$8,000,000 Assets	=	+
		$3,200,000 Owners' Equity

Many businesses use the portrait (vertical) format instead of the landscape (horizontal) format. One advantage of the portrait format is that it allows a business to keep its balance sheet on one page in its financial report, whereas the landscape format may require a business to put its balance sheet on two facing pages in its annual financial report. The following is the company's balance sheet presented in the portrait format:

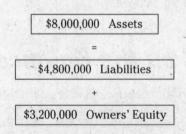

Q. The large majority of businesses use either the horizontal or vertical formats for reporting their balance sheets. However, now and then, you see a third format in which total liabilities are subtracted from total assets to determine owners' equity. The following shows this alternative format for the business example:

$8,000,000 Assets

–

$4,800,000 Liabilities

=

$3,200,000 Owners' Equity

What is the rationale for this third balance sheet format?

A. Personally, I like this third format because it makes clear that liabilities have a first, or senior, claim on the assets of the business and that owners get what's left over. After paying liabilities, the owners of a business could end up holding an empty bag.

1. A business has $2,500,000 total assets and $1,000,000 total liabilities. Present three balance sheet formats for the business.

Solve It

2. A business has $4,800,000 total liabilities and $6,500,000 total owners' equity. Present three balance sheet formats for the business.

Solve It

3. A business has $3,600,000 total assets and $4,600,000 total liabilities. Present three balance sheet formats for the business.

Solve It

4. A business has $725,000 total assets and $425,000 total owners' equity. Present three balance sheet formats for the business.

Solve It

Building a Balance Sheet

A brand-spanking-new business starts with a blank balance sheet. It builds up its balance sheet over time with three basic types of transactions:

- ✔ **Financing activities:** Includes the investment of capital in the business by its owners, the return of some capital to owners (which may happen from time to time), and distributions from profit (if the business decides to make such distributions)

- ✔ **Investing activities:** Includes the purchase and construction of long-lived assets used in the operations of the business, the purchase of intangible assets used in manufacturing and making sales, and the disposal of operating assets when they're no longer needed or are replaced

- ✔ **Operating activities:** Includes the profit-making activities of the business, including sales, expenses, and other income and losses

In Chapter 5, I explain how sales and expenses change the financial condition of the business. In fact, a good part of its balance sheet is driven by the profit-making transactions of the business. Before a business begins its profit-making activities, it needs to raise capital and invest capital in long-term operating assets. These financing and investing activities are the place to start in building a balance sheet.

EXAMPLE

Q. Several investors come together to start a new business. They raise $1,000,000 and invest this sum in the business. The business issues 10,000 shares of capital stock to them. The business borrows $1,500,000 from a bank on the basis of a long-term interest-bearing note payable. The business purchases various long-term operating assets (fixed assets) for a total cost of $2,000,000. It's now ready to begin hiring employees, manufacturing products, and making sales. Prepare the company's balance sheet after these initial financing and investing activities. Use the landscape (horizontal) format for the balance sheet.

A. The company's balance sheet after its initial financing and investing activities is as follows:

Assets		Liabilities & Owners' Equity	
Cash	$500,000	Long-term Notes Payable	$1,500,000
Property, Plant, & Equipment	$2,000,000	Owners Equity: Capital Stock (10,000 shares)	$1,000,000
Total Assets	$2,500,000	Total Liabilities & Owners' Equity	$2,500,000

The business hasn't yet started manufacturing products, making sales, and incurring expenses. Therefore, its balance sheet doesn't yet include certain other assets and liabilities that are generated by the profit-making process.

EXAMPLE

Q. After its initial financing and investing activities, the business manufactures its first batch of products. The total cost of this production run is $800,000. No sales have been made yet, but the business is poised to send out its sales force to call on customers. Its balance sheet after the first production run is as follows:

Assets		Liabilities & Owners' Equity	
Cash	$440,000	Accounts Payable	$225,000
Inventory	$800,000	Short-term Notes Payable	$500,000
Property, Plant, & Equipment	$2,000,000	Long-term Notes Payable	$1,500,000
Accumulated Depreciation	($15,000)	Owners Equity:	
Cost less Depreciation	$1,985,000	Capital Stock (10,000 shares)	$1,000,000
Total Assets	$3,225,000	Total Liabilities & Owners' Equity	$3,225,000

Explain the changes in the company's balance sheet, starting with its balance sheet immediately after its initial financing and investing transactions (see the preceding example question).

A. The changes in its balance sheet caused by manufacturing the first batch of products are summarized in the following journal entry:

Balance Sheet Changes Caused By Manufacturing First Batch of Products

Cash	$60,000
Inventory	$800,000
Accounts Payable	$225,000
Short-term Note Payable	$500,000
Accumulated Depreciation	$15,000

Read this entry as follows. The $800,000 cost of manufacturing the first batch of products was provided by borrowing $500,000, by purchasing $225,000 raw materials on credit, by $15,000 depreciation, and by spending down cash $60,000.

The business realized that it didn't have enough cash to pay for its first production run, so it borrowed an additional $500,000 from its bank on the basis of a short-term note payable. Because it made purchases on credit for the raw materials needed for manufacturing products, accounts payable has a balance of $225,000. The cash balance is $60,000 lower compared with its balance immediately after the initial financing and investing transactions ($500,000 balance before – $440,000 balance after = $60,000 decrease).

REMEMBER

To have products available for sale, the business had to first manufacture the products. The cost of manufacturing its first batch of products was $800,000, which is in the inventory asset account. The business recorded depreciation on its fixed assets (property, plant, and equipment) because these resources were used in the manufacturing process. The business recorded $15,000 depreciation, which is included in the cost of products manufactured.

5. Instead of the initial financing and investing transactions presented in the preceding example questions, assume the business issued 100,000 capital stock shares for $1,500,000, borrowed $2,000,000 on a long-term note payable, and invested $2,800,000 in fixed assets. Using the landscape (horizontal) format, prepare its balance sheet after these initial financing and investing transactions.

Solve It

6. Following its initial financing and investing transactions in Question 5, the business manufactured its first batch of products. The cost of products manufactured was $650,000, depreciation was $20,000, and accounts payable increased $185,000. To provide additional cash, the business borrowed $250,000 and signed a short-term note payable. Using the landscape (horizontal) format, prepare its balance sheet after its first production run. Start with the balance sheet after the initial financing and investing transactions in your answer to Question 5.

Solve It

7. A new business has just been organized. A group of investors put $5,000,000 in the business and the business issued 5,000,000 shares of capital stock to them. The business borrowed $2,500,000 from a local bank on the basis of a long-term note payable. (Several of the investors had to guarantee this note, or the bank would not have loaned the money to the business.) The business negotiated the purchase of land and buildings that cost $1,250,000. It also paid $5,250,000 for machinery, production equipment, delivery vehicles, and office equipment and furniture. Using the landscape (horizontal) format, prepare the balance sheet of the business immediately after these initial financing and investing activities.

Solve It

8. The business introduced in Question 7 manufactured its first batch of products. It has not yet sold any of these products. The balance sheet changes caused by the first production run are summarized in the following journal entry:

Cash	$665,000
Inventory	$2,000,000
Accounts Payable	$550,000
Short-term Note Payable	$750,000
Accumulated Depreciation	$35,000

Using the portrait format, prepare its balance sheet after giving effect to the first production run. Start with your balance sheet answer to Question 7.

Solve It

Fleshing Out the Balance Sheet

The most recent balance sheet of the business you're considering buying is presented in Figure 6-1. The first few transactions of the business that I explain earlier in the chapter (see the example question in the section "Building a Balance Sheet") took place some years ago. Since then, the business has grown and prospered.

Assets		Liabilities & Owners' Equity	
Cash	$1,500,000	Accounts Payable	$700,000
Accounts Receivable	$1,000,000	Accrued Expenses Payable	$600,000
Inventory	$1,800,000	Short-term Notes Payable	$1,500,000
Prepaid Expenses	$300,000	Total Current Liabilities	$2,800,000
Total Current Assets	$4,600,000		
		Long-term Notes Payable	$2,000,000
Property, Plant, & Equipment	$4,800,000		
Accumulated Depreciation	($1,400,000)	Owners Equity:	
Cost Less Depreciation	$3,400,000	Capital Stock (10,000 shares)	$1,000,000
		Retained Earnings	$2,200,000
		Total Owners' Equity	$3,200,000
Total Assets	$8,000,000	Total Liabilities & Owners' Equity	$8,000,000

Figure 6-1: The most recent balance sheet of the business in question.

What does the balance sheet in Figure 6-1 tell you about the business? In fact, it tells you a lot. You know that the business sells on credit because it reports the accounts receivable asset, and you know that it sells products, the cost of which is reported in the inventory asset. Because it reports prepaid expenses, you know that the business pays some of its expenses in advance, and the report of accrued expenses payable liability indicates that it delays paying some expenses. Also, you can tell that the business buys on credit because it reports the accounts payable liability.

The balance sheet reveals that the business borrows money, which is evident in its short-term and long-term notes payable liabilities. It has invested $4,800,000 in long-term operating assets, and over the years, it has depreciated $1,400,000 of the cost of these assets. According to the balance sheet, the owners invested $1,000,000 in the business for which they received 10,000 shares of capital stock. And the business has retained $2,200,000 of its cumulative net income over the years. Did you get all that from reading the balance sheet? If not, read it again!

EXAMPLE

Q. Does the balance sheet shown in Figure 6-1 report the current replacement costs of the business's fixed assets (which are labeled "Property, Plant & Equipment" in the balance sheet)? Also, does the balance sheet indicate which depreciation methods the business uses to depreciate its fixed assets?

A. The short answer to the first question is no, balance sheets don't report current replacement cost values of fixed assets. Indeed, the business probably hasn't taken the time and troubles to estimate these replacement costs because it isn't planning to replace its fixed assets. The answer to the second question is a little more involved. This business, like most businesses, doesn't disclose its depreciation methods in the balance sheet itself, but it discloses depreciation methods in the footnotes to the financial statements. (You have to take my word for it because this example doesn't present the footnotes to the business's financial statements.)

The following questions are based on the balance sheet details outlined earlier in this section.

9. Suppose the business didn't make credit sales and made only cash sales. Which account(s) would you not expect to see in its balance sheet?

Solve It

10. Suppose the business didn't own any of its fixed assets (long-term operating assets). Instead, it entered into long-term leases for all these assets (buildings, machinery, equipment, trucks, and so on). Which account(s) would you not expect to see in its balance sheet?

Solve It

11. Suppose the business was very conservative and didn't borrow money. Which account(s) would you not expect to see in its balance sheet?

12. Suppose the business sold only services and not products. Which account(s) would you not expect to see in its balance sheet?

Solve It

The balance sheet in Figure 6-1 separates *current assets* from other assets and separates *current liabilities* from other liabilities. Financial reporting standards require this classification of assets and liabilities.

✔ **Current assets** are cash and assets that will be converted into cash during one *operating cycle,* which is the time it takes to manufacture products, to hold the products until they're sold, and to collect the receivables from sales. (Prepaid expenses are also included in current assets because the business uses cash to prepay these costs.) This "from cash back to cash" cycle can be very short, such as a month or so, or it may be relatively long, such as six months or more. Retailers generally have short operating cycles, and manufacturers have long operating cycles.

✔ **Current liabilities** include those that will be paid within one operating cycle, which mainly are accounts payable and accrued expenses payable. Also, notes payable and any other liabilities that will be paid within one year from the balance sheet date are included in current liabilities. The subtotals of current assets and current liabilities appear in a balance sheet so that the reader can compare these two amounts. Dividing current assets by current liabilities gives the *current ratio.*

Traditionally, it has been assumed that the current ratio should be at least 2.00 to 1.00, although this minimum has never become a hard-and-fast rule. But if the current ratio dips below 1.00 to 1.00, alarm bells are certain to go off. In fact, many argue that the ratio of cash and cash equivalents (such as short-term marketable investments) divided by current liabilities should be at least 1.00 to 1.00. This is called the *quick ratio.*

Q. Referring to the balance sheet in Figure 6-1, how would you assess the *short-run solvency* of the business? (Solvency refers to the ability of a business to pay its liabilities on time.)

A. The current ratio of the business is 1.64 to 1.00 ($4,600,000 current assets ÷ $2,800,000 current liabilities = 1.64). In other words, for $1.00 of current liabilities, the business has $1.64 of current assets. The question is whether this ratio is high enough to "guarantee" the short-run solvency of the business, or whether there is a serious risk that the business may not be able to pay its short-term (current) liabilities when they come due for payment.

I doubt if the company's bank or shareowners would be upset about its 1.64 to 1.00 current ratio. The business's quick ratio is only .54 to 1.00 ($1,500,000 cash ÷ $2,800,000 current liabilities = .54 to 1.00). The company's lender (its bank) will decide whether or not this is a major impediment when it comes time to renew its short-term loan to the business. Although the business's "credit score" (as measured by its current and quick ratios) isn't on the high side, I think that its creditors wouldn't be worried about the solvency of the business in this example. On the other hand, the creditors probably would keep a close eye on the business to make sure that things don't take a turn for the worse.

The following questions draw on the business whose balance sheet appears in Figure 6-1.

13. Suppose that just before the end of the year, the business paid an additional $400,000 of its accounts payable. Normally, it would not have accelerated payments of accounts payable, but the order to do so came down from "on high," and the payments were made. Why do you think the business may have done this?

Solve It

14. Suppose the business held its books open for several days into the next year. It recorded an additional $200,000 of payments from customers as if they had been received on December 31 (the last day of its fiscal year) even though the money wasn't actually received and deposited in its bank account until after the end of the year. Why do think the business may have done this?

Solve It

This chapter focuses on the balance sheet of a business that sells products (see Figure 6-1). I make only a fleeting comment early in the chapter about the annual sales revenue and profit of the business, which, as you know, are reported in its income statement. To recap, its sales revenue for the year just ended is $12,000,000, and the business earned $600,000 bottom-line profit for the year. At this point, you can compare the revenue size of the business with its asset size.

The ratio of annual sales revenue to total assets, called the *asset turnover ratio,* varies from industry to industry. Many businesses are *capital intensive,* which means that they need a lot of assets to make sales. For example, companies that sell electricity make huge investments in electric power generating plants. Similarly, airlines make large investments in aircraft, and auto manufacturers invest heavily in production plants and equipment. These types of businesses have relatively low asset turnover ratios. Many other retailers have high asset turnover ratios because they don't need to make large investments in long-lived operating assets.

Q. Referring to Figure 6-1, determine whether the size of the business's balance sheet is consistent with the size of its income statement.

A. The business has $8,000,000 total assets (see Figure 6-1), and its annual sales revenue is $12,000,000; therefore, its annual sales revenue is 1.5 times total assets (this is its asset turnover ratio). The question asks whether this ratio is consistent with the average asset turnover for industry or not, and in order to answer that, you need to understand that businesses in most industries join trade associations. One of the functions of these trade groups is to collect information from their members and publish norms for the industry. So I look at the trade association information to judge whether the business is significantly above or below the norm for the industry. Generally speaking, an asset turnover ratio of 1.5 to 1.00 is on the low side. On the other hand, the business is fairly capital-intensive (meaning that its fixed assets represent a relatively large percent of its total assets). Therefore, its 1.5 to 1.00 asset turnover ratio may be reasonable.

15. Suppose the average asset turnover ratio for businesses in the industry is 2.0 to 1.0. The asset turnover ratio of the business you're considering buying is 1.5 to 1.0; ($12,000,000 annual sales revenue ÷ $8,000,000 total assets = 1.5). What may explain the deviation of the business's asset turnover ratio from the average ratio for the industry?

Solve It

16. Does the balance sheet presented in Figure 6-1 give any indication of how old the company is, or how many years it has been in business? Are there any particular accounts or other items in the balance sheet that indicate whether the company is fairly new or has been around for many years?

Solve It

Clarifying the Values of Assets in Balance Sheets

The evidence is pretty strong that readers of financial reports aren't entirely clear about the dollar amounts reported for assets in a balance sheet. Other than cash — the value of which is clear enough — the amounts reported for assets in a balance sheet aren't at all obvious to non-accountants. Balance sheets don't include reminders or annotations for the valuation basis of each asset. Accountants presume that balance sheet readers understand, or should understand, the asset values that are reported. Accountants are presumptuous, in my opinion.

Of course, accountants should be certain about the valuation of every asset reported in the balance sheet. In preparing a year-end balance sheet, an accountant should do a valuation check on every asset. Recent authoritative pronouncements on financial accounting standards have been moving in this direction. For example, accountants now must check at the end of the accounting year to see whether the value of any asset has been *impaired* (diminished in economic value to the business), and if so, the book value of the asset should be written down.

Except for short-term investments in marketable securities that are held for sale, the recorded values of assets aren't written up to recognize appreciation in the replacement or market values of the assets. For example, the current market value of the land and buildings owned by a business may be considerably higher than the cost paid for the real estate many years ago. Or the current replacement value of machinery and equipment owned by a business could be more than the depreciated book value of the assets. These assets are used in the operations of the business and aren't held for sale. Moreover the assets may not be replaced for many years. Therefore, appreciation in the market and replacement values of these assets aren't recorded. The business makes profit not by holding these assets for sale but rather by using them in the selling of products and services.

The dollar amounts reported for assets in a balance sheet are the amounts that were recorded in the original journal entries made when recording the asset transactions. These journal entries could have been recorded last week, last month, last year, or 20 years ago for some assets. For example,

- ✔ The balance of the asset accounts receivable is from amounts entered in the asset account when credit sales were recorded. These sales are recent, probably within the few weeks before the end of the year.

- ✔ The balance in the inventory asset account is from the costs of manufacturing or purchasing products. These costs could be from the last two or three months.

- ✔ The costs of fixed assets reported in the property, plant, and equipment asset account in the balance sheet may go back five, ten, or more years — these economic resources are used a long time.

Accountants have devised different ways to record several expenses. The choice of accounting methods affects the balances of several assets, including accounts receivable, inventory, and accumulated depreciation. (I explain these expense accounting methods in Chapter 9.) The reported values of these assets depend on which accounting methods a business adopts to record its expenses. The differences between accounting methods create yet another maddening factor in understanding the dollar amounts reported for assets. No wonder financial report readers are confused about the values reported for assets in balance sheets!

Although I don't discuss accounting fraud in this chapter (see Chapter 1), I should point out that, when reading a financial report, you should be alert for any red flags that indicate something may not be right in the financial statements. This vigilance is especially important when you're considering buying or making a major investment in a business. Not to cast aspersions on the present shareowners of the business, but they know you're considering buying the business, and it's conceivable that they may have "suggested" that the chief accountant massage the numbers or even to cook the books to make the financial statements look as good as possible.

Q. Refer to the company's most recent balance sheet in Figure 6-1. The business uses the straight-line depreciation method, by which an equal amount of depreciation is allocated to each year of a fixed asset's estimated useful life. If the business had used accelerated depreciation for its fixed assets instead, the balance in the accumulated depreciation account would be $2,100,000. How would its balance sheet be different if the business had used accelerated depreciation? (Ignore income tax effects in your answer.)

A. Accumulated depreciation would be $700,000 higher, so depreciation expense over the years would be $700,000 higher. The higher amounts of deprecation expenses would reduce cumulative net income $700,000 (before income tax). Thus, retained earnings would be $700,000 lower. The following shows what the balance sheet of the business would be. *Note:* In the following balance sheet, I've shaded the accounts, sub-totals, and totals that differ from amounts reported in Figure 6-1.

Assets		Liabilities & Owners' Equity	
Cash	$1,500,000	Accounts Payable	$700,000
Accounts Receivable	$1,000,000	Accrued Expenses Payable	$600,000
Inventory	$1,800,000	Short-term Notes Payable	$1,500,000
Prepaid Expenses	$300,000	Total Current Liabilities	$2,800,000
Total Current Assets	$4,600,000		
		Long-term Notes Payable	$2,000,000
Property, Plant, &			
Equipment	$4,800,000	Owners' Equity:	
Accumulated Depreciation	($2,100,000)	Capital Stock (10,000 shares)	$1,000,000
Cost less Depreciation	$2,700,000	Retained Earnings	$1,500,000
		Total Owners' Equity	$2,500,000
Total Assets	$7,300,000	Total Liabilities & Owners' Equity	$7,300,000

Using accelerated depreciation makes the business look considerably smaller, doesn't it? With that method, total assets are $7,300,000, compared with $8,000,000 total assets by using straight-line depreciation (see Figure 6-1).

17. Refer to the company's most recent balance sheet in Figure 6-1. The business uses very conservative accounting methods for certain expenses, but it could have used more liberal accounting methods for these expenses. (I explain alternative accounting methods in Chapter 9.) The more liberal accounting methods would have caused the following results:

• Accounts receivable balance would have been $50,000 higher

• Inventory would have been $225,000 higher

• Accumulated depreciation would have been $300,000 lower

Using the landscape format, prepare a revised balance sheet for the business giving effect to these differences. (Ignore income tax effects.)

18. Do you see anything suspicious in the balance sheet in Figure 6-1 that may indicate accounting fraud?

Using the Balance Sheet in Business Valuation

How much would you pay for a business? Frankly, no accountant could tell you what a business is worth because it's not really an accounting question. Accountants prepare financial statements; they don't put a value on the business and report this value in its financial report. Not in their wildest dreams would accountants think of doing this.

There's some argument surrounding the question of whether determining the market value of a going business is rocket science or not. One school of thought is that business valuation should be based on a complicated, multi-factor, formula-driven model. The opposite camp argues that in buying a business you're buying a future stream of earnings but forecasting future earnings is notoriously difficult and unreliable. Their argument is that you're just as well off using a simple method. What does this have to do with a balance sheet? Well, both sides agree on one thing: The profit performance track record of the business (reported in its recent income statements) and its present financial condition (reported in its latest balance sheet) are absolutely critical information for the valuation of a business. The debate concerns how you should analyze and use that information.

The owners' equity amount of a business is roughly like you telling me how much you paid for your house some years ago and how much additional money you spent over the years on home improvements. This cost isn't very relevant to the current market value of your home. When have you ever seen a home for sale advertisement that mentions the cost paid by its present owners? In a similar manner, the "cost" of the owners' equity reported in a balance sheet usually isn't very relevant in putting a value on the business.

Although not a dominant factor in setting the market value of a business, the owners' equity reported in the balance sheet isn't completely irrelevant. Owners' equity equals the book (recorded) value of assets less the liabilities of the business, and it's not often that a business sells for less than its owners' equity amount. Owners' equity tends to be a floor, or minimum value, for a business.

Q. In reading the company's latest balance sheet (Figure 6-1), you see that $3,200,000 is reported for owners' equity. Is this book value of owners' equity a good guide for putting a value on the business?

A. In answering this question, the first thing to mention is that its balance sheet is the historical financial record of the business, meaning that it looks backward. In contrast, putting a value on a business is forward-looking. The $3,200,000 balance in owners' equity is a measure of the financial sacrifice the owners have made to get the business to its present point. From Figure 6-1, you discover that the shareowners invested $1,000,000 in the business some years ago and that the business has retained $2,200,000 of its profits over the year instead of paying cash dividends to its shareowners. This amount of cumulative profit has been "plowed back" into the business. The book value (historical-based) of owners' equity isn't a bad point of departure for putting a current value on a business. However, business valuation looks at other factors as well, including the current replacement values of the business's assets, its future earnings and cash flow prospects, and so on. Factoring in these other factors in a business valuation equation often yields a current market value that's considerably higher than the book value of owners' equity reported in the business's balance sheet.

19. One simple business valuation approach doesn't look at the balance sheet, at least not in putting a numerical value on the business. (The potential buyer of a business would scour the balance sheet to see whether there may be solvency problems.) This business valuation approach is called the *earnings multiple method*. For example, the $600,000 annual income of the business could be multiplied by 8 to get $4,800,000 value for the business. Suppose you and the present shareowners agree to this price, and you buy all the capital stock shares for this price. What happens to the difference between the $4,800,000 price you paid and the $3,200,000 owners' equity reported in the balance sheet?

Solve It

20. Suppose you agree to pay $4,800,000 for all the capital stock shares of the business. At the eleventh hour, the owners ask you to make one concession: They want to take out $500,000 from the business as a cash dividend but are still asking $4,800,000 for their shares. Would this make a difference in the price you're willing to pay for the business?

Solve It

Answers to Problems on Reporting Financial Condition in the Balance Sheet

The following are the answers to the practice questions presented earlier in this chapter.

1 A business has $2,500,000 total assets and $1,000,000 total liabilities. Present three balance sheet formats for the business.

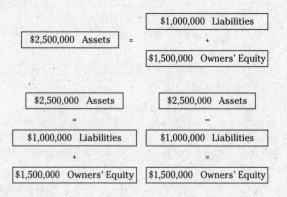

2 A business has $4,800,000 total liabilities and $6,500,000 total owners' equity. Present three balance sheet formats for the business.

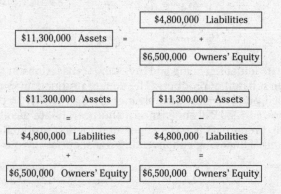

3 A business has $3,600,000 total assets and $4,600,000 total liabilities. Present three balance sheet formats for the business.

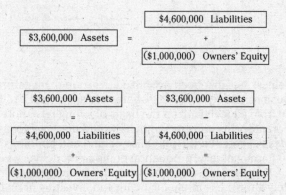

4   A business has $725,000 total assets and $425,000 total owners' equity. Present three balance sheet formats for the business.

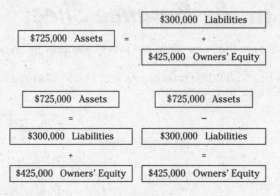

5   Instead of the initial financing and investing transactions presented in the preceding example questions, assume the business issued 100,000 capital stock shares for $1,500,000, borrowed $2,000,000 on a long-term note payable, and invested $2,800,000 in fixed assets. Using the landscape (horizontal) format, prepare its balance sheet after these initial financing and investing transactions.

Assets		Liabilities & Owners' Equity	
Cash	$700,000	Long-term Notes Payable	$2,000,000
Property, Plant, &		Owners Equity:	
Equipment	$2,800,000	Capital Stock (100,000 shares)	$1,500,000
		Total Liabilities &	
Total Assets	$3,500,000	Owners' Equity	$3,500,000

6   Following its initial financing and investing transactions in Question 5, the business manufactured its first batch of products. The cost of products manufactured was $650,000, depreciation was $20,000, and accounts payable increased $185,000. To provide additional cash, the business borrowed $250,000 and signed a short-term note payable. Using the landscape (horizontal) format, prepare its balance sheet after its first production run. Start with the balance sheet after the initial financing and investing transactions in your answer to Question 5.

Assets		Liabilities & Owners' Equity	
Cash	$700,000	Long-term Notes Payable	$2,000,000
Property, Plant, &		Owners Equity:	
Equipment	$2,800,000	Capital Stock (100,000 shares)	$1,500,000
		Total Liabilities &	
Total Assets	$3,500,000	Owners' Equity	$3,500,000

7   A new business has just been organized. A group of investors put $5,000,000 in the business and the business issued 5,000,000 shares of capital stock to them. The business borrowed $2,500,000 from a local bank on the basis of a long-term note payable. (Several of the investors had to guarantee this note, or the bank would not have loaned the money to the business.) The business negotiated the purchase of land and buildings that cost $1,250,000. It also paid $5,250,000 for machinery, production equipment, delivery vehicles, and office equipment and furniture. Using the landscape (horizontal) format, prepare the balance sheet of the business immediately after these initial financing and investing activities.

Assets		Liabilities & Owners' Equity	
Cash	$1,000,000	Long-term Notes Payable	$2,500,000
Property, Plant, &		Owners' Equity:	
Equipment	$6,500,000	Capital Stock (5,000,000 shares)	$5,000,000
		Total Liabilities &	
Total Assets	$7,500,000	Owners' Equity	$7,500,000

8 The business introduced in Question 7 manufactured its first batch of products. It has not yet sold any of these products. The balance sheet changes caused by the first production run are summarized in the following journal entry:

Cash	$665,000
Inventory	$2,000,000
Accounts Payable	$550,000
Short-term Note Payable	$750,000
Accumulated Depreciation	$35,000

Using the landscape format, prepare its balance sheet after giving effect to the first production run. Start with your balance sheet answer to Question 7.

Assets		Liabilities & Owners' Equity	
Cash	$335,000	Accounts Payable	$550,000
Inventory	$2,000,000	Short-term Notes Payable	$750,000
Property, Plant, &		Long-term Notes Payable	$2,500,000
Equipment	$6,500,000		
Accumulated Depreciation	($35,000)	Owners' Equity:	
Cost less Depreciation	$6,465,000	Capital Stock (5,000,000 shares)	$5,000,000
Total Assets	$8,800,000	Total Liabilities & Owners' Equity	$8,800,000

9 Suppose the business didn't make credit sales and made only cash sales. Which account(s) would you not expect to see in its balance sheet?

The business wouldn't have an accounts receivable asset account because the balance in this asset account comes from credit sales, which the business didn't make. Also, the business wouldn't have a bad debts expense account. This expense comes from uncollectible accounts receivable that are written off; however, a business that sells only for cash has other frustrating expenses, including accepting bad checks from customers, making the wrong change to customers, and accepting counterfeit currency.

10 Suppose the business didn't own any of its fixed assets (long-term operating assets). Instead, it entered into long-term leases for all these assets (buildings, machinery, equipment, trucks, and so on). Which account(s) would you not expect to see in its balance sheet?

In this situation, the business wouldn't have any fixed asset accounts, such as land, buildings, machinery, equipment, vehicles, computers, office furniture, and so on. Also, the business wouldn't have the accumulated depreciation accounts for fixed asset accounts. Instead of depreciation expense, the business would record rent (or lease) expense.

 Accountants should examine long-term leases to see whether a lease, in substance, is an installment purchase of the asset. Depending on the terms of the lease and the purchase options at the end of the lease, it may be accounted for as a purchase of the asset. If so, the accountant records the fixed asset and records depreciation over the estimated useful life of the fixed asset.

11 Suppose the business was very conservative and didn't borrow money. Which account(s) would you not expect to see in its balance sheet?

In this unusual situation, the business wouldn't have interest-bearing liability accounts such as notes payable or bonds payable. It wouldn't have an interest expense account, either. The business would have normal operating liability accounts, such as accounts payable and accrued expenses payable, because these operating liabilities don't bear interest.

12 Suppose the business sold only services and not products. Which account(s) would you not expect to see in its balance sheet?

The business wouldn't have an inventory asset account or a cost of goods sold expense account. Also, its accounts payable liability balance would be relatively low compared with a business that sells products. For a company that sells products, a good part of its accounts payable liability balance consists of products purchased on credit (or raw materials used in the manufacturing process that are purchased on credit). In contrast, a business that sells only services doesn't buy products or raw materials on credit.

13 Suppose that just before the end of the year, the business paid an additional $400,000 of its accounts payable. Normally, it would not have accelerated payments of accounts payable, but the order to do so came down from "on high," and the payments were made. Why do you think the business may have done this?

In order to answer this question, you need to look at the business's year-end balance sheet:

Assets		Liabilities & Owners' Equity	
Cash	$1,100,000	Accounts Payable	$300,000
Accounts Receivable	$1,000,000	Accrued Expenses Payable	$600,000
Inventory	$1,800,000	Short-term Notes Payable	$1,500,000
Prepaid Expenses	$300,000	Total Current Liabilities	$2,400,000
Total Current Assets	$4,200,000		
		Long-term Notes Payable	$2,000,000
Property, Plant, &			
Equipment	$4,800,000	Owners' Equity:	
Accumulated Depreciation	($1,400,000)	Capital Stock (10,000 shares)	$1,000,000
Cost less Depreciation	$3,400,000	Retained Earnings	$2,200,000
		Total Owners' Equity	$3,200,000
Total Assets	$7,600,000	Total Liabilities & Owners' Equity	$7,600,000

Pay attention to the current ratio: $4,200,000 current assets ÷ $2,400,000 current liabilities = 1.75 current ratio. By making pay downs on accounts payable very late in the year (perhaps on the very last day of the year), the business improved its current ratio to 1.75 from the 1.64 current ratio in the original scenario (see Figure 6-1). In many cases, a business is under pressure to keep its current ratio as high as possible. What the business in this question did isn't illegal, but the payment should arouse some uneasiness in the accountant. The accountant should make a judgment on the *materiality* of this action that improves the current ratio from 1.64 to 1.75. Is this a material difference, that is, is it one that could mislead the balance sheet readers? This is a tough question to answer.

The effect on the current ratio isn't material, so nothing would be said about it in the financial statements of the business. If the effect is judged to be material, then the accountant should consider calling it to the attention of the audit committee of the business or another high-level financial officer in the business. The business's financial statements may be audited by an independent CPA firm. The auditors should catch this manipulation of the current ratio, and if they judge it to be material, the CPA firm should bring it to the attention of the audit committee or the board of directors.

14 Suppose the business held its books open for several days into the next year. It recorded an additional $200,000 of payments from customers as if they had been received on December 31 (the last day of its fiscal year) even though the money wasn't actually received and deposited in its bank account until after the end of the year. Why do think the business may have done this?

This maneuver is called *window dressing;* it's done to improve the cash balance reported in the balance sheet and to improve the quick ratio. In order to answer this question, you need to look at the business's year-end balance sheet:

Assets		Liabilities & Owners' Equity	
Cash	$1,700,000	Accounts Payable	$700,000
Accounts Receivable	$800,000	Accrued Expenses Payable	$600,000
Inventory	$1,800,000	Short-term Notes Payable	$1,500,000
Prepaid Expenses	$300,000	Total Current Liabilities	$2,800,000
Total Current Assets	$4,600,000		
		Long-term Notes Payable	$2,000,000
Property, Plant, &			
Equipment	$4,800,000	Owners' Equity:	
Accumulated Depreciation	($1,400,000)	Capital Stock (10,000 shares)	$1,000,000
Cost less Depreciation	$3,400,000	Retained Earnings	$2,200,000
		Total Owners' Equity	$3,200,000
Total Assets	$8,000,000	Total Liabilities & Owners' Equity	$8,000,000

In the original scenario, the quick ratio is .54 to 1.00, which is lower than the manipulated ratio ($1,700,000 cash ÷ $2,800,000 current liabilities = .61 to 1.00 quick ratio). When I was in public accounting years ago, many of our audit clients employed window dressing. I must admit that we (the CPA auditors) tolerated holding the books open for a few days in order to allow the business to report a higher cash balance and a better quick ratio. Current assets and current liabilities don't change, so holding the books open doesn't change the current ratio.

15 Suppose the average asset turnover ratio for businesses in the industry is 2.0 to 1.0. The asset turnover ratio of the business you're considering buying is 1.5 to 1.0; ($12,000,000 annual sales revenue ÷ $8,000,000 total assets = 1.5). What may explain the deviation of the business's asset turnover ratio from the average ratio for the industry?

The business's total assets are too high relative to its annual sales revenue; looking at it another way, its annual sales revenue is too low relative to its total assets. One reason may be that the business has *excess capacity,* meaning that it may be over-invested in its fixed assets. For example, its building may be too large or it may have more trucks than it needs to make deliveries. Excess capacity is a good place to start, but fixed assets may not be the main reason for a below-normal asset turnover ratio. You should examine all assets to see whether their balances are too big.

The business may have allowed the size of its inventory to get out of control. Perhaps its accounts receivable balance is too high because of lax collection efforts, or it's possible that the business has too much cash relative to its day-to-day operating needs. It could be that the business had a sudden and unexpected dip in sales towards the end of the year. Perhaps it hasn't had time to downsize its assets and adjust to the lower sales level. The business may think that the drop in sales is only temporary and, therefore, it wants to keep its assets at their present levels to support the predicted bounce back in sales next year.

16 Does the balance sheet presented in Figure 6-1 give any indication of how old the company is, or how many years it has been in business? Are there any particular accounts or other items in the balance sheet that indicate whether the company is fairly new or has been around for many years?

One clue regarding the age of the business is the balance in its accumulated depreciation account as a percent of the cost of the fixed assets being depreciated. The higher the percentage, the older the business is likely to be. But this is really just guesswork. Financial statements don't report the age of a business. However, financial reports may include a historical summary of key data (such as annual sales, annual net income, total assets, and so on), which often go back to the first year of business.

17 Refer to the company's most recent balance sheet in Figure 6-1. The business uses very conservative accounting methods for certain expenses, but it could have used more liberal accounting methods for these expenses. (I explain alternative accounting methods in Chapter 9.) The more liberal accounting methods would have caused the following results:

- Accounts receivable balance would have been $50,000 higher

- Inventory would have been $225,000 higher

- Accumulated depreciation would have been $300,000 lower

Using the landscape format, prepare a revised balance sheet for the business giving effect to these differences. (Ignore income tax effects.)

The year-end balance sheet of the business would have been as follows:

Assets		Liabilities & Owners' Equity	
Cash	$1,500,000	Accounts Payable	$700,000
Accounts Receivable	$1,050,000	Accrued Expenses Payable	$600,000
Inventory	$2,025,000	Short-term Notes Payable	$1,500,000
Prepaid Expenses	$300,000	Total Current Liabilities	$2,800,000
Total Current Assets	$4,875,000		
		Long-term Notes Payable	$2,000,000
Property, Plant, &			
Equipment	$4,800,000	Owners' Equity:	
Accumulated Depreciation	($1,100,000)	Capital Stock (10,000 shares)	$1,000,000
Cost less Depreciation	$3,700,000	Retained Earnings	$2,775,000
		Total Owners' Equity	$3,775,000
Total Assets	$8,575,000	Total Liabilities & Owners' Equity	$8,575,000

The expenses of the business over the years would have been $575,000 lower; ($50,000 lower bad debts expense + $225,000 lower cost of goods sold expense + $300,000 lower depreciation expense = $575,000 lower expenses in total). Therefore, cumulative net income would have been $575,000 higher (before income tax), and the balance of retained earnings would have been $575,000 higher. (Adding the $575,000 increase in cumulative net income to the $2,200,000 retained earnings balance in Figure 6-1 equals the $2,775,000 retained earnings balance shown in this answer.)

18 Do you see anything suspicious in the balance sheet in Figure 6-1 that may indicate accounting fraud?

I don't see anything suspicious in the balance sheet that may indicate that some accounting hanky-panky is going on, but you never know. A good con artist will try to make everything look right. So, who knows for sure? The first rule of an auditor is to be skeptical. I'm an old "old auditor" at heart, and I've seen too many fraudulent financial statements in my time. As they say in politics, "Trust, but verify." The problem is that financial report users may not be able to verify the information presented in financial statements. Furthermore, CPA auditors don't necessarily catch accounting fraud in financial statements. Unfortunately, the risk of accounting fraud is always present.

19 One simple business valuation approach doesn't look at the balance sheet, at least not in putting a numerical value on the business. (The potential buyer of a business would scour the balance sheet to see whether there may be solvency problems.) This business valuation approach is called the *earnings multiple method.* For example, the $600,000 annual profit of the business could be multiplied by 8 to get $4,800,000 value for the business. Suppose you and the present shareowners agree to this price, and you buy all the capital stock shares for this price. What happens to the difference between the $4,800,000 price you paid and the $3,200,000 owners' equity reported in the balance sheet?

This question goes back to a point I mention in Chapter 1: The starting point in accounting is to identify the *entity* being accounted for. The business is one entity and your investment in the business is another entity. They're two distinct entities. Accounting for the financial activities of a business does *not* involve keeping track of the investment activities of its individual shareowners.

One shareowner may sell his or her capital stock shares to another person, but this exchange of shares isn't a transaction of the business. The business didn't receive the $4,800,000 you paid for the shares you bought; the individuals that sold their shares to you received the $4,800,000. The same number of capital stock shares remains in the hands of shareowners, and the business makes no accounting entry for the exchange of stock shares among its shareowners. In the accounting for your individual investment, you should record the $4,800,000 cost of your investment, but this is your private affair and as such isn't recorded by the business.

20 Suppose you agree to pay $4,800,000 for all the capital stock shares of the business. At the eleventh hour, the owners ask you to make one concession: They want to take out $500,000 from the business as a cash dividend but are still asking $4,800,000 for their shares. Would this make a difference in the price you're willing to pay for the business?

The market valuation of a business usually doesn't consist of adding up the market values of every asset and deducting the liabilities of the business. In most cases, the forecast of its future earnings is the dominant factor in setting a value on a business. The fact that the business would have $500,000 less cash may not affect its future earnings performance; the business would still have $1,000,000 cash to operate with, and this balance may be adequate. Yet, this last-minute tactic by the present owners isn't good because it takes $500,000 out of the business, which means that you (the new owner) have $500,000 less cash to work with for growth and expansion of the business.

Chapter 7

Coupling the Income Statement and Balance Sheet

*E*very time an accountant records a sale or expense entry using double-entry accounting, he or she sees the interconnections between the income statement and balance sheet. (I explain the rules for debits and credits in Chapter 3.) A sale increases an asset or decreases a liability, and an expense decreases an asset or increases a liability. Therefore, one side of every sales and expense entry is in the income statement, and the other side is in the balance sheet. You can't record a sale or an expense without affecting the balance sheet. The income statement and balance sheet are inseparable, but they aren't reported this way!

To properly interpret financial statements — the income statement, the balance sheet, and the statement of cash flows — you need to understand the links between the three statements, but, unfortunately, the links aren't easy to see. Each financial statement appears on a separate page in the annual financial report, and the threads of connection between the financial statements aren't referred to. In reading financial reports, non-accountants — and even accountants — usually don't spot these connections.

I explain the income statement in Chapter 5 and the balance sheet in Chapter 6. In this chapter, I stitch these two financial statements together and mark the trails of connections between sales revenue and expenses (in the income statement) and their corresponding assets and liabilities (in the balance sheet). In Chapter 8, I explain the connections between the amounts reported in the statement of cash flows and the other two financial statements.

Rejoining the Income Statement and Balance Sheet

Figure 7-1 shows the lines of connection between income statement accounts and balance sheet accounts. When reading financial statements, in your mind's eye, you should "see" these lines of connection. Because financial reports don't offer a clue about these connections, it may help to actually draw the lines of connection, like you would if you were highlighting lines in a textbook.

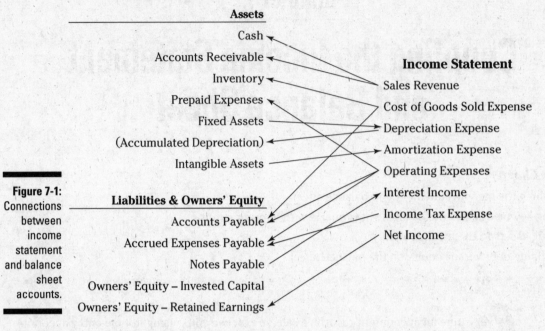

Figure 7-1:
Connections between income statement and balance sheet accounts.

Here's a quick summary explaining the lines of connection in Figure 7-1, starting from the top and working down to the bottom:

✔ Making sales (and incurring expenses for making sales) requires a business to maintain a working cash balance.

✔ Making sales on credit generates accounts receivable.

✔ Selling products requires the business to carry an inventory (stock) of products.

✔ Acquiring products involves purchases on credit that generate accounts payable.

✔ Depreciation expense is recorded for the use of fixed assets (long-term operating resources).

✔ Depreciation is recorded in the accumulated depreciation contra account (instead decreasing the fixed asset account).

✔ Amortization expense is recorded for limited-life intangible assets.

✔ Operating expenses is a broad category of costs encompassing selling, administrative, and general expenses:

  • Some of these operating costs are prepaid before the expense is recorded, and until the expense is recorded, the cost stays in the prepaid expenses asset account.

  • Some of these operating costs involve purchases on credit that generate accounts payable.

  • Some of these operating costs are from recording unpaid expenses in the accrued expenses payable liability.

✔ Borrowing money on notes payable causes interest expense.

✔ A portion (usually relatively small) of income tax expense for the year is unpaid at year-end, which is recorded in the accrued expenses payable liability.

✔ Earning net income increases retained earnings.

Q. For the year just ended, a business reports $5,200,000 sales revenue. All its sales are made on credit (to other businesses). Historically, its year-end accounts receivable balance equals about five weeks of annual sales revenue; in other words, an amount equal to five weeks of annual sales revenue is not yet collected at the end of the year. Sales are level throughout the year. What amount of accounts receivable would you expect in the business's year-end balance sheet?

A. Dividing $5,200,000 annual sales revenue by 52 weeks gives $100,000 average sales per week. Based on its past experience, the ending balance of accounts receivables should be about $500,000, which equals five weeks of annual sales revenue.

1. The business in the example question has an annual cost of goods sold expense of $3,120,000. Historically, its ending inventory balance equals about 13 weeks of annual sales. What amount of inventory would you expect in its year-end balance sheet?

Solve It

2. The business in the example question has an annual cost of goods sold expense of $3,120,000. Historically, the business's accounts payable for inventory purchases equals about four weeks of annual cost of goods sold. What amount of accounts payable for inventory purchases would you expect in its year-end balance sheet? (***Note:*** The accounts payable balance also includes an amount from purchases of supplies and services on credit; this question concerns only the amount of accounts payable from inventory purchases.)

Solve It

3. The business in the example question has an annual operating expenses amount of $1,378,000 (which excludes depreciation, amortization, interest, and income tax expenses). Historically, its year-end balance of accrued expenses payable equals about six weeks of its annual operating expenses. Ignoring accrued interest payable and income tax payable, what amount of accrued expenses payable would you expect in its year-end balance sheet?

Solve It

4. For the business in the example question, the average amount borrowed on notes payable during the year was $1,500,000. The average annual interest rate on these notes was 6.5 percent. What amount of interest expense would you find in the business's income statement for the year?

Solve It

Filling in Key Pieces of the Balance Sheet from the Income Statement

Laying the foundation for the balance sheet of a business using its normative *operating ratios* is very instructive. An operating ratio expresses the size of an asset or liability on the basis of sales revenue or an expense in the annual income statement. A *normative* operating ratio refers to how large an asset or liability *should be* relative to sales revenue or its related expense in the annual income statement.

Suppose a business, Company X, makes all its sales on credit and offers its customers one month to pay. Very few customers pay early, and some customers are chronic late-payers. To encourage repeat sales, the business tolerates these late-payers, and as a result, its accounts receivable equals five weeks of annual sales revenue. Thus, its normative operating ratio of accounts receivable to annual sales revenue is 5 to 52.

The *actual* ratio of the year-end accounts receivable balance to annual sales revenue is unlikely to be precisely 5 to 52, which equals 9.615 percent of sales revenue. The 5 to 52 operating ratio is the normative ratio between accounts receivable and annual sales revenue; it's based on the sales credit policies of the business and how aggressive the business is in collecting receivables when customers don't pay on time. The 5 to 52 ratio is a benchmark, in other words. Minor deviations are harmless, but significant variances deserve serious management attention and follow-up.

In Chapter 6, I build the balance sheet based on actual transactions of the business, starting with its initial financing and investing activities and moving to the manufacturing of its first batch of products. Of course, actual balance sheets are the result of recording actual transactions. In this section, in contrast, I start with the normative operating ratios for a business.

Based on these critical metrics for the business, I determine the balances for certain of its assets and liabilities. These amounts are what the balances would be if the results of the business's transactions came in right on the money so that every operating ratio ended up being exactly what it should be.

The annual income statement of Company X is presented in Figure 7-2. From the sales revenue and expenses reported in the income statement, I determine the balances of several assets and liabilities using the normative operating ratios for the business.

Sales Revenue	$5,200,000
Cost of Goods Sold Expense	(3,120,000)
Gross Margin	$2,080,000
Selling and General Expenses	(1,430,000)
Depreciation Expense	(160,000)
Operating Earnings	$490,000
Interest Expense	(97,500)
Earnings Before Income Tax	$392,500
Income Tax Expense	(137,375)
Net Income	$255,125

Figure 7-2: Income statement of a business for the year just ended.

Operating ratios can be expressed in terms of weeks of the 52 weeks year (or they can be expressed as percentages of annual sales revenue or annual expense). I use weeks of the year in this example. The normative operating ratios for the business whose income statement is presented in Figure 7-2 are as follows:

- Cash equals seven weeks of annual sales revenue.
- Accounts receivable equals five weeks of annual sales revenue.
- Inventory equals 13 weeks of annual cost of goods sold.
- The prepaid expenses asset balance equals four weeks of annual selling and general expenses.
- Accounts payable for inventory acquisitions equals four weeks of annual cost of goods sold.
- Accounts payable for supplies and services bought on credit equals four weeks of annual selling and general expenses.
- Accrued expenses payable for operating expenses equals six weeks of annual selling and general expenses.

The business doesn't own intangible assets and therefore doesn't have amortization expense. I don't include accrued interest payable and income tax payable in the example for two reasons: First, these year-end liabilities typically are relatively small amounts compared with the major assets and liabilities of a business. Second, the expenses that drive these liabilities aren't *operating* expenses. The year-end balance of accrued interest payable depends on the terms for paying interest on the business's debt. Income tax expense, as you know, depends on the income tax status of the business and its policies regarding making installment payments toward its annual income tax during the year. In short, it's not possible to apply operating ratios for these two liabilities.

The ratio of annual depreciation expense to the original cost of fixed assets can't be normalized. Different fixed assets are depreciated over different estimated useful life spans. Some fixed assets are depreciated according to the straight-line method and others according to an accelerated depreciation method. (I explain these depreciation methods in Chapter 9.) The annual depreciation expense should be a reasonable fraction of original cost. It would be unusual, and even suspicious, in fact, if depreciation expense were more than 15 percent or so of the total original cost of fixed assets.

Q. Using the operating ratios for Company X, whose income statement appears in Figure 7-2, determine the balances for the assets and liabilities driven by its sales revenue and expenses.

A. The asset and liability balances derived from applying the normative operating ratios to the sales revenue and expenses presented in the company's income statement (Figure 7-2) are as follows:

Assets		Computation Using Normative Operating Ratios
Cash	$700,000	7/52 x $5,200,000 sales revenue
Accounts Receivable	$500,000	5/52 x $5,200,000 sales revenue
Inventory	$780,000	13/52 x $3,120,000 cost of goods sold
Prepaid Expenses	$110,000	4/52 x $1,430,000 selling and general expenses
Liabilities		
Accounts Payable	$350,000	(4/52 x $3,120,000 cost of goods sold) +
		(4/52 x $1,430,000 selling and general expenses)
Accrued Expenses Payable	$165,000	6/52 x $1,430,000 selling and general expenses

These asset and liability balances are normative, not the actual balances that would be reported in the business's balance sheet. The balances provide a useful benchmark against which the actual balances can be compared. Unusual deviations indicate that something has gotten out of control or that the business has made a fundamental shift in its operating polices and needs to revise its operating ratio yardsticks.

In Figure 7-3, you can see a *partial* balance sheet that presents only the assets and liabilities determined in the preceding example question. Later in the chapter, I fill in the remainder of the balance sheet, including fixed assets, interest-bearing debt, and owners' equity.

Figure 7-3:
Partial balance sheet showing Company X's asset and liability balances based on normative operating ratios.

Assets		Liabilities	
Cash	$700,000	Accounts Payable	$350,000
Accounts Receivable	$500,000	Accrued Expenses Payable	$165,000
Inventory	$780,000		
Prepaid Expenses	$110,000		
Total Current Assets	$2,090,000		

Questions 5 through 10 are based on the following income statement for a new business example that I call Company Y.

Sales Revenue	$15,400,000
Cost of Goods Sold Expense	(8,470,000)
Gross Margin	$6,930,000
Selling and General Expenses	(4,368,000)
Depreciation Expense	(425,000)
Operating Earnings	$2,137,000
Interest Expense	(260,000)
Earnings Before Income Tax	$1,877,000
Income Tax Expense	(656,950)
Net Income	$1,220,050

The normative operating ratios of Company Y are as follows. Note that these operating ratios are expressed as percents of annual sales revenue and expenses rather than as weeks of the year.

- ✔ Cash equals 15 percent of annual sales revenue.

- ✔ Accounts receivable equals 12 percent of annual sales revenue.

- ✔ Inventory equals 20 percent of annual cost of goods sold.

- ✔ The prepaid expenses asset balance equals 8 percent of annual selling and general expenses.

- ✔ Accounts payable for inventory acquisitions equals 8 percent of annual cost of goods sold.

- ✔ Accounts payable for supplies and services bought on credit equals 8 percent of annual selling and general expenses.

- ✔ Accrued expenses payable for operating expenses equals 15 percent of annual selling and general expenses.

---

5. Determine the balance of cash based on the normative operating ratio for this asset account. (Refer to the preceding list of normative operating ratios for Company Y.)

Solve It

6. Determine the balance of accounts receivable based on the normative operating ratio for this asset account. (Refer to the preceding list of normative operating ratios for Company Y.)

Solve It

7. Determine the balance of inventory based on the normative operating ratio for this asset account. (Refer to the preceding list of normative operating ratios for Company Y.)

Solve It

8. Determine the balance of prepaid expenses based on the normative operating ratio for this asset account. (Refer to the preceding list of normative operating ratios for Company Y.)

Solve It

9. Determine the balance of accounts payable based on the normative operating ratios for this liability account. (Refer to the preceding list of normative operating ratios for Company Y.)

Solve It

10. Determine the balance of accrued expenses payable based on the normative operating ratio for this liability account. (Refer to the preceding list of normative operating ratios for Company Y.)

Solve It

Putting Fixed Assets in the Picture

One asset is obviously missing in the partial balance sheet shown in Figure 7-3: the *fixed assets* of the business. Virtually every business needs these long-lived economic resources to carry on its profit-making activities.

TIP

The cost and accumulated depreciation of a business's fixed assets depends on when the assets were bought (recently or many years ago?), the sort of long-term operating assets the business needs, and whether the business leases or owns these assets. I can't offer you a ratio for the original cost of fixed assets and annual sales revenue because it's very difficult to generalize about the cost of fixed assets relative to annual sales revenue. If I had to hazard a ballpark estimate for this ratio, I would say that annual sales revenue of a business is generally between two to four times the total cost of its fixed assets. But please take this estimation with a grain of salt. The ratio varies widely from industry to industry, and even within the same industry, the ratio can vary from company to company. Generally speaking, retailers have a higher ratio of sales to fixed assets than heavy equipment manufacturers and transportation companies (airlines, truckers, and so on).

In Figure 7-4, you can see my educated guess for the fixed assets' cost and the accumulated depreciation on the fixed assets. The partial balance sheet shown in Figure 7-4 tells an interesting story: Company X has $3,855,000 total assets, but where did it get that $3,855,000? Its two operating liabilities provided $515,000 of the total assets; ($350,000 accounts payable + $165,000 accrued expenses payable = $515,000). So where did the remaining $3,340,000 come from?

$3,855,000 total assets – $515,000 short-term operating liabilities = $3,340,000 needed from sources of business capital

Assets		Liabilities & Owners' Equity	
Cash	$700,000	Accounts Payable	$350,000
Accounts Receivable	$500,000	Accrued Expenses Payable	$165,000
Inventory	$780,000		
Prepaid Expenses	$110,000		
Total Current Assets	$2,090,000		
		($3,855,000 total assets – $515,000 short-term operating liabilities) = $3,340,000 capital provided by debt and equity sources	
Property, Plant, & Equipment	$2,450,000		
Accumulated Depreciation	($685,000)		
Cost Less Depreciation	$1,765,000		
Total Assets	$3,855,000		

Figure 7-4: Company X's balance sheet that includes assets and short-term operating liabilities.

11. Instead of the amounts shown in Figure 7-4, suppose that the cost of Company X's fixed assets was $3,850,000 and that accumulated depreciation was $958,000. Determine the amount of capital the business would have had to raise in this scenario.

12. Assume that the balances of assets, accounts payable, and accrued expenses payable were the same as shown in Figure 7-4. However, the balance of accumulated depreciation was $400,000. In this scenario, would Company X have had to raise more capital?

Completing the Balance Sheet with Debt and Equity

If you owned Company X, whose balance sheet is depicted in Figure 7-4, how should you have raised the $3,340,000 capital? You can debate this question until the cows come home because there's no right or best answer. The two basic sources of business capital are interest-bearing debt and equity (more precisely, owners' equity). Where to secure capital is really a business financial management question, not an accounting question per se. As a practical matter, many businesses borrow as much as they can and use owners' equity for the rest of the capital they need.

Most businesses use debt for part of their capital needs, and this practice makes sense as long as the business doesn't overextend its debt obligations. Because this isn't a book on business finance, a debate concerning debt versus equity isn't in order. Instead, I move on to the complete balance sheet of the business.

Figure 7-5 presents the complete balance sheet for Company X, including its debt and owners' equity accounts. These are the final pieces of the balance sheet puzzle (if you started at the beginning of this chapter, this is what you've been working toward). The business has borrowed $500,000 on short-term notes payable (due in one year or less) and $1,000,000 on long-term notes payable. Balance sheets may or may not report the annual interest rates on their notes (and bonds) payable. If not reported in the balance sheet proper, interest rates and other relevant details of debt contracts are disclosed in the *footnotes* to the financial statements. For example, *debt covenants* (conditions prescribed by the debt contract) may limit the amount of cash dividends the business can pay to its shareowners.

The shareowners in Company X invested $750,000, for which they received 10,000 capital stock shares. Even relatively simple-looking business corporation ownership structures can be more complex than they appear. Typically, a footnote is necessary to fully explain the ownership structure of a business corporation. (If you don't believe me, read the shareowners' equity footnotes of any business.) As a general rule, private business corporations don't have to disclose who owns how many of their capital stock shares in their financial statements. In contrast, *public* business corporations are subject to many disclosure rules regarding the stock ownership, stock options, and other stock-based compensation benefits of their officers and top-level managers.

Assets		Liabilities & Owners' Equity	
Cash	$700,000	Accounts Payable	$350,000
Accounts Receivable	$500,000	Accrued Expenses Payable	$165,000
Inventory	$780,000	Short-term Notes Payable	$500,000
Prepaid Expenses	$110,000	Total Current Liabilities	$1,015,000
Total Current Assets	$2,090,000		
		Long-term Notes Payable	$1,000,000
Property, Plant, & Equipment	$2,450,000		
Accumulated Depreciation	($685,000)	Owners' Equity:	
Cost Less Depreciation	$1,765,000	Capital Stock (10,000 shares)	$750,000
		Retained Earnings	$1,090,000
		Total Owners' Equity	$1,840,000
Total Assets	$3,855,000	Total Liabilities & Owners' Equity	$3,855,000

Figure 7-5:
Complete balance sheet of Company X.

Over the years, the business in this scenario retained $1,090,000 of its yearly profits (see retained earnings in Figure 7-5). You can't tell from the balance sheet how much of this cumulative total is from any one year. Nor can you tell from the income statement or the balance sheet how much of its $255,125 profit for the year (see Figure 7-2) was distributed as a cash dividend to shareowners during the year just ended. One purpose of the statement of cash flows (which I explain in Chapter 8) is to report the cash dividends paid from net income to shareowners during the year.

Questions 13 through 16 are based on the following income statement and balance sheet of a new business example that I call Company Z. You're asked to determine certain operating ratios for the business based on the information in its income statement and balance sheet.

Sales Revenue	$23,530,000
Cost of Goods Sold Expense	(14,118,000)
Gross Margin	$9,412,000
Selling and General Expenses	(7,722,000)
Depreciating Expense	(826,500)
Operating Earnings	$863,500
Interest Expense	(245,000)
Earnings Before Income Tax	$618,500
Income Tax Expense	(185,550)
Net Income	$432,950

Assets		Liabilities & Owners' Equity	
Cash	$1,357,500	Accounts Payable	$2,100,000
Accounts Receivable	$2,715,000	Accrued Expenses Payable	$742,500
Inventory	$2,172,000	Short-term Notes Payable	$750,000
Prepaid Expenses	$519,750	Total Current Liabilities	$3,592,500
Total Current Assets	$6,764,250		
		Long-term Notes Payable	$2,000,000
Property, Plant, &			
Equipment	$4,575,000	Owners' Equity:	
Accumulated Depreciation	($1,385,000)	Capital Stock (10,000 shares)	$1,500,000
Cost less Depreciation	$3,190,000	Retained Earnings	$2,861,750
		Total Owners' Equity	$4,361,750
Total Assets	$9,954,250	Total Liabilities & Owners' Equity	$9,954,250

13. Based on Company Z's income statement and balance sheet, determine the business's accounts receivable operating ratio. Express the ratio in weeks rather than as a percentage.

14. Based on Company Z's income statement and balance sheet, determine the business's inventory operating ratio. Express the ratio in weeks rather than as a percentage.

15. Based on Company Z's income statement and balance sheet, determine the business's accrued expenses payable operating ratio. Express the ratio in weeks rather than as a percentage.

Solve It

16. Based on Company Z's income statement and balance sheet, determine the business's prepaid expenses operating ratio. Express the ratio in weeks rather than as a percentage.

Solve It

Answers to Problems on Coupling the Income Statement and Balance Sheet

The following are the answers to the practice questions presented earlier in this chapter.

1 The business in the example question has an annual cost of goods sold expense of $3,120,000. Historically, its ending inventory balance equals about 13 weeks of annual sales. What amount of inventory would you expect in its year-end balance sheet?

$3,120,000 ÷ 52 weeks = $60,000 average cost of goods sold per week × 13 weeks operating ratio = $780,000 inventory balance in its year-end balance sheet

2 The business in the example question has an annual cost of goods sold expense of $3,120,000. Historically, the business's accounts payable for inventory purchases equals about four weeks of annual cost of goods sold. What amount of accounts payable for inventory purchases would you expect in its year-end balance sheet? (***Note:*** The accounts payable balance also includes an amount from purchases of supplies and services on credit; this question concerns only the amount of accounts payable from inventory purchases.)

$3,120,000 ÷ 52 weeks = $60,000 average cost of goods sold per week × 4 weeks operating ratio = $240,000 accounts payable for inventory purchases balance in its year-end balance sheet

3 The business in the example question has an annual operating expenses amount of $1,378,000 (which excludes depreciation, amortization, interest, and income tax expenses). Historically, its year-end balance of accrued expenses payable equals about six weeks of its annual operating expenses. Ignoring accrued interest payable and income tax payable, what amount of accrued expenses payable would you expect in its year-end balance sheet?

$1,378,000 ÷ 52 weeks = $26,500 average operating expenses per week × 6 weeks operating ratio = $159,000 accrued expenses payable balance in its year-end balance sheet

4 For the business in the example question, the average amount borrowed on notes payable during the year was $1,500,000. The average annual interest rate on these notes was 6.5 percent. What amount of interest expense would you find in the business's income statement for the year?

$1,500,000 average notes payable × 6.5 percent interest rate = $97,500 annual interest expense

5 Determine the balance of cash based on the normative operating ratio for this asset account. (Refer to the list of normative operating ratios for Company Y.)

$15,400,000 annual sales revenue × 15 percent operating ratio = $2,310,000 cash balance

6 Determine the balance of accounts receivable based on the normative operating ratio for this asset account. (Refer to the list of normative operating ratios for Company Y.)

$15,400,000 annual sales revenue × 12 percent operating ratio = $1,848,000 accounts receivable balance

7 Determine the balance of inventory based on the normative operating ratio for this asset account. (Refer to the list of normative operating ratios for Company Y.)

$8,470,000 annual cost of goods sold × 20 percent operating ratio = $1,694,000 inventory balance

8 Determine the balance of prepaid expenses based on the normative operating ratio for this asset account. (Refer to the list of normative operating ratios for Company Y.)

$4,368,000 annual selling and general expenses × 8 percent operating ratio = $349,440 prepaid expenses balance

9 Determine the balance of accounts payable based on the normative operating ratios for this liability account. (Refer to the list of normative operating ratios for Company Y.)

$8,470,000 annual cost of goods sold × 8 percent operating ratio = $677,600 accounts payable for inventory purchases

$4,368,000 annual selling and general expenses × 8 percent operating ratio = $349,440 accounts payable for selling and general expenses

$677,600 + $349,440 = $1,027,040 accounts payable balance

10 Determine the balance of accrued expenses payable based on the normative operating ratio for this liability account. (Refer to the list of normative operating ratios for Company Y.)

$4,368,000 annual selling and general expenses × 15 percent operating ratio = $655,200 accrued expenses payable balance

11 Instead of the amounts shown in Figure 7-4, suppose that the cost of Company X's fixed assets was $3,850,000 and that accumulated depreciation was $958,000. Determine the amount of capital the business would have had to raise in this scenario.

Based on the higher amount invested in fixed assets, and taking into account the larger amount of accumulated depreciation, Company X would have had to raise $4,467,000 total capital (see the following balance sheet for the business). This is $1,127,000 more compared to the example in Figure 7-4 ($4,467,000 capital raised in this scenario – $3,340,000 capital raised in Figure 7-4 = $1,127,000 additional capital).

Assets		Liabilities & Owners' Equity	
Cash	$700,000	Accounts Payable	$350,000
Accounts Receivable	$500,000	Accrued Expenses Payable	$165,000
Inventory	$780,000		
Prepaid Expenses	$110,000		
Total Current Assets	$2,090,000	($4,982,000 total assets – $515,000 short-term operating liabilities) = $4,467,000 capital provided by debt and equity sources	
Property, Plant, & Equipment	$3,850,000		
Accumulated Depreciation	($958,000)		
Cost less Depreciation	$2,892,000		
Total Assets	$4,982,000		

12 Assume that the balances of assets, accounts payable, and accrued expenses payable were the same as shown in Figure 7-4. However, the balance of accumulated depreciation was $400,000. In this scenario, would Company X have had to raise more capital?

Based on the smaller balance of accumulated depreciation, Company X would have had to raise $3,625,000 total capital (see the following balance sheet for the business). This is $285,000 more compared with the example in Figure 7-4 ($3,625,000 capital raised in this scenario – $3,340,000 capital raised in Figure 7-4 = $285,000 additional capital).

Assets		Liabilities & Owners' Equity	
Cash	$700,000	Accounts Payable	$350,000
Accounts Receivable	$500,000	Accrued Expenses Payable	$165,000
Inventory	$780,000		
Prepaid Expenses	$110,000		
Total Current Assets	$2,090,000	($4,140,000 total assets – $515,000 short-term operating liabilities) = $3,625,000 capital provided by debt and equity sources	
Property, Plant, & Equipment	$2,450,000		
Accumulated Depreciation	($400,000)		
Cost less Depreciation	$2,050,000		
Total Assets	$4,140,000		

Company X recorded $285,000 less depreciation in this scenario than in Figure 7-4 ($685,000 accumulated depreciation in Figure 7-4 – $400,000 accumulated depreciation in this scenario = $285,000 less accumulated depreciation). Therefore, the retained earnings balance of the business is $285,000 higher (before income tax). Retained earnings is part of owners' equity, so the owners' equity source of capital is $285,000 higher in this scenario than in the scenario depicted in Figure 7-4.

13 Based on Company Z's income statement and balance sheet, determine the business's accounts receivable operating ratio. Express the ratio in weeks rather than as a percentage.

$23,530,000 annual sales revenue ÷ 52 weeks = $452,500 sales revenue per week

$2,715,000 accounts receivable balance ÷ $452,500 sales revenue per week = 6 weeks operating ratio

14 Based on Company Z's income statement and balance sheet, determine the business's inventory operating ratio. Express the ratio in weeks rather than a as percentage.

$14,118,000 annual cost of goods sold ÷ 52 weeks = $271,500 cost of goods sold per week

$2,172,000 inventory balance ÷ $271,500 cost of goods sold per week = 8 weeks operating ratio

15 Based on Company Z's income statement and balance sheet, determine the business's accrued expenses payable operating ratio. Express the ratio in weeks rather than as a percentage.

$7,722,000 annual selling and general expenses ÷ 52 weeks = $148,500 selling and general expenses per week

$742,500 accrued expenses payable balance ÷ $148,500 selling and general expenses per week = 5 weeks operating ratio

16 Based on Company Z's income statement and balance sheet, determine the business's prepaid expenses operating ratio. Express the ratio in weeks rather than as a percentage.

$7,722,000 annual selling and general expenses ÷ 52 weeks = $148,500 selling and general expenses per week

$519,750 prepaid expenses balance ÷ $148,500 selling and general expenses per week = 3.5 weeks operating ratio

Chapter 8

Reporting Cash Flows and Changes in Owners' Equity

T he financial report of a business consists of three primary financial statements: the *income statement* for the period, the *balance sheet* at the end of the period, and the *statement of cash flows* for the period. This chapter examines the statement of cash flows, which is the most recent financial statement to be required in business financial reports.

The history of the statement of cash flows is complex; despite repeated calls from the investment community for cash-flow information in financial reports — and after a rather inept experiment with reporting a funds flow statement — in 1987, the accounting profession finally required that a statement of cash flows be included in financial reports. The cash-flow statement has been included in financial reports for about two decades now, and it's likely to remain a permanent fixture in business financial reporting.

In my opinion, the statement of cash flows is the most difficult of the three financial statements to understand and interpret. This statement reports a company's sources and uses of cash, and that seems pretty straightforward. However, many cash-flow statements present tangled cash-flow threads that are very difficult to follow. Accountants are partly to blame for this mess, in my opinion; if I were a paranoid investor, I may think that businesses deliberately make their statements of cash flows difficult to read.

 This chapter carries a disclaimer: The following discussion doesn't adhere to the party line. It's not the standard textbook approach to understanding cash flows. I think it's better. Of course, I might be a wee bit biased.

Figuring Profit from the Balance Sheet

Suppose you're the accountant for a business that suffers a terrible fire that destroys virtually everything, including its accounting records. (In hindsight, the business should have had stored back-up accounting records off-premises, but it didn't.) When escaping the burning building, the bookkeeper managed to grab one piece of smoldering paper. The bottom part of the page had already burned away, but the bookkeeper thought that this scrap of paper might be helpful, and he was right. The paper contains the business's balance sheets at the end of its two most recent years, minus the last few lines that burned away.

Figure 8-1 presents the balance sheets of the business at the end of its two most recent years. The changes between the year-end balances are included, and the balance sheet is presented in the portrait, or vertical format, which accountants sometimes refer to as the *report form*. (The term "report form" is not a very descriptive term, in my opinion).

Balance Sheets at Year-Ends 2006 and 2007

Assets	2006	2007	Changes
Cash	$700,000	$901,000	$201,000
Accounts Receivable	$500,000	$535,000	$35,000
Inventory	$780,000	$825,000	$45,000
Prepaid Expenses	$110,000	$125,000	$15,000
Current Assets	$2,090,000	$2,386,000	
Property, Plant, & Equipment	$2,450,000	$2,875,000	$425,000
Accumulated Depreciation	($685,000)	($876,000)	($191,000)
Cost Less Depreciation	$1,765,000	$1,999,000	
Total Assets	$3,855,000	$4,385,000	
Liabilities & Owners' Equity			
Accounts Payable	$350,000	$385,000	$35,000
Accrued Expenses Payable	$165,000	$205,000	$40,000
Short-term Notes Payable	$500,000	$625,000	$125,000
Current Liabilities	$1,015,000	$1,215,000	
Long-term Notes Payable	$1,000,000	$1,125,000	$125,000
Owners Equity:			
Capital			

Figure 8-1: Incomplete comparative balance sheet of the business.

Unfortunately, the 2007 income statement was lost in the fire. The president wants to know the net income for the year and asks whether you can determine profit from the information in Figure 8-1. Yes, you can determine profit by comparing the net worth of the business at year-end 2007 against its net worth at the end of 2006.

	2006	2007
Total Assets	$3,855,000	$4,385,000
Current Liabilities	($1,015,000)	($1,215,000)
Long-term Notes Payable	($1,000,000)	($1,125,000)
Net Worth at Year-end	$1,840,000	$2,045,000
		($1,840,000)
Tentative Net Income for 2007*		$205,000

* Depends on whether cash dividends were paid and whether the business issued additional capital stock shares for cash.

The *net worth* of a business equals its total assets minus its total liabilities. Earning net income increases the net worth of the business. The net worth of the business in this example increases $205,000 from year-end 2006 to year-end 2007, so the net income of the business for 2007 is $205,000. Well, maybe net income is $201,000 or maybe not; read on.

The net income amount for this business depends on two other factors, and you need to answer the following questions before you can reach a final answer regarding net income:

✔ **Did the shareowners invest additional capital in the business?** An infusion of new ownership capital in the business increases the net worth of the business. Any amount of net worth increase from owners putting additional capital into the business is deducted from the change in net worth in determining net income for the year.

✔ **Did the business distribute cash dividends to its shareowners during the year?** Cash dividends from profit decrease the net worth of the business. Therefore, the amount of cash dividends is added to the change in net worth in determining net income for the year.

Q. The president of the business also serves as the chair of its board of directors. After you have determined net income for 2007 based on the balance sheet in Figure 8-1, the president tells you that he thinks $200,000 cash dividends were paid to shareowners during 2007. Based on this additional information about cash dividends, what amount of net income did the business earn in 2007?

A. The net worth of the business increased $205,000 during the year, as explained earlier in this section. The $200,000 amount of cash dividends to stockholders decreased net worth because $200,000 of owners' equity is taken out of the business. The $200,000 amount of cash dividends is added to the $205,000 net worth increase to get $405,000 net income for the year. In other words, even after the $200,000 cash dividends, net worth still increased $205,000. Net income had to increase net worth $405,000 for this to happen.

1. After you revise your net income answer (see the example question in this section), the president tells you that he has since talked with other directors of the business and realized that he was wrong about the cash dividends. Now he's fairly certain that $250,000 cash dividends were paid to shareowners during 2007 and that the business issued additional capital stock shares for $50,000. Based on this additional information, what amount of net income did the business earn in 2007?

Solve It

2. A business reports $500,000 net loss for the year just ended. It didn't issue or retire any capital stock shares during the year, and it didn't pay cash dividends because of its loss in the year. Did its net worth decrease $500,000 during the year? Did its cash balance decrease $500,000 during the year because of its loss?

3. Can the net worth of a business go negative? If so, explain briefly how this may happen and if it means that the business would have a negative cash balance.

Reporting the Statement of Changes in Stockholders' Equity

From information about the company's annual profit performance, dividends, and capital invested by or returned to shareowners, the accountant prepares a *statement of changes in stockholders' equity*. This statement is included in the annual financial report of the business. It is called a "statement," but it's really more of a *schedule* of changes in the owners' equity accounts. Because the primary audience of the financial report is the business's shareowners (the stockholders of a business corporation), they're very interested in the changes in their accounts.

Figure 8-2 presents the basic structure of a statement of changes in stockholders' equity for the business example introduced in Figure 8-1. Note that the statement covers two years. The statement of changes in stockholders' equity illustrated in Figure 8-2 is actually a fairly simple example. A business may have a complicated capital structure, in which case this schedule includes much more detail than shown in Figure 8-2; the number of shares for each class of stock issued by the business would be reported, but that number isn't important for the task at hand in this section, so I don't bother to include this data in Figure 8-2.

Statement of Changes in Stockholders' Equity

	Capital Stock	Retained Earning	Total Owners' Equity
Balance at end of 2005	$750,000	$922,000	$1,672,000
Net Income – 2006		$318,000	
Cash Dividends – 2006		($150,000)	
Balance at end of 2006	$750,000	$1,090,000	$1,840,000
Capital Stock Issue	$50,000		
Net Income – 2007		$405,000	
Cash Dividends – 2007		($250,000)	
Balance at end of 2007	$800,000	$1,245,000	$2,045,000

Figure 8-2:
Statement (schedule) of changes in stockholders' equity.

In Figure 8-2, total owners' equity equals $1,840,000 at the end of 2006 ($750,000 capital stock + $1,090,000 retained earnings = $1,840,000). And at the end of 2007, total owners' equity equals $2,045,000 ($800,000 capital stock + $1,245,000 retained earnings = $2,045,000). These two owners' equity amounts are the same as the net worth amounts used in determining profit by the comparative net worth method (see the preceding section). In short, net worth equals owners' equity and net income increases owners' equity.

4. Please refer to Figure 8-1 that presents the comparative balance sheet of the business and to Figure 8-2 that presents its statement of changes in stockholders' equity. Suppose the business had paid $175,000 cash dividends (instead of $250,000) to stockholders in 2007. In this scenario, which dollar amounts in the business's comparative balance sheet would be different as the result of this one change?

Solve It

5. Suppose the business in the example (see Figure 8-2) did not issue additional shares of capital stock in 2007 and did not distribute dividends to its stockholders in either 2006 or 2007. In this scenario, is the statement of changes in stockholders' equity needed? Should it be presented in the company's 2007 annual financial report?

Solve It

Determining Cash Effect from Making Profit

Someone has to be in charge of managing the cash flows and cash balance of a business. In mid-size and large businesses, the person with this heavy responsibility is probably the treasurer, vice president of finance, or chief financial officer. In smaller businesses, the president may manage cash flows in addition to all his or her other functions. Simply put, if cash isn't managed carefully, the business could run out of cash, and that would be a disaster. (One major consequence is that employees wouldn't be paid on time.) Managing cash flow is a top priority of every business, and this management starts with cash flow from profit.

Borrowing money and gaining owner investments in the business increase its cash balance. But *cash flow from profit* doesn't refer to these two sources of cash. The term refers to the net cash result from the sales and expenses of the business during the period. Sales and expenses are also called *operating activities* or *profit-making activities*. In the statement of cash flows the increase or decrease of cash during the period from the business's profit-making activities is called *cash flow from operating activities.* This is a rather technical term that is not all that clear in my opinion. For brevity and clarity I prefer the term *cash flow from profit*, which I use throughout this chapter – except where I have to use the formal term cash flow from operating activities in the statement of cash flows.

Q. Continuing the example scenario created earlier in this chapter, the president asks you to determine cash flow from profit (net income) in 2007. In other words, he wants to know how much the business's cash balance increased from making profit in the year. Based on the information in its comparative balance sheet (Figure 8-1) and its statement of changes in stockholders equity (Figure 8-2), determine the business's cash flow from profit for 2007. Did its cash balance increase $405,000, the same amount as net income? Or, did cash increase a different amount? Did cash *decrease* as the result of the company's profit-making activities? (It's possible.)

A. During the year, the business increased its cash $250,000 from borrowing (see the increases in short-term and long-term notes payable in Figure 8-1). The business issued additional capital stock shares for $50,000 and paid $250,000 cash dividends to shareowners during the year (see Figure 8-2). Therefore, the net cash increase from its *financing activities* was $50,000: ($250,000 increase in debt + $50,000 issue of stock shares - $250,000 dividends = $50,000 cash increase). The business spent $425,000 cash for additions and replacements to its property, plant, and equipment (see the increase in this fixed asset account in Figure 8-1). These cash outlays are classified as *investing activities.* Last, note that the company's cash balance increased $201,000 during the year (see Figure 8-1).

This question asks you to determine the business's cash flow from operating activities (cash flow from profit) for the year. It does not ask you to prepare the formal statement of cash flows for the year (which I explain in the next section). Since the objective is to get cash flow from profit, I favor the method explained in Chapter 1. The four components of cash flow from profit are assembled in the following summary for the business example:

Summary of Cash Flows For the Year

Cash flow from operating activities	????
Cash flow from investing activities	($425,000)
Cash flow from financing activities	$50,000
Increase in cash during the year	$201,000

Solving for the unknown factor, cash flow from profit is $576,000 for the year. The $576,000 cash flow from profit plus the $50,000 net cash increase from financing activities provided the business $626,000 cash. It used $425,000 for capital expenditures. So its cash balance increased $201,000.

This analysis method (solving for the unknown factor) is a "backdoor" approach for determining cash flow from profit. First, you determine the net change in cash caused by the investing and financing activities. Then you compare this amount to the change in cash during the year. The rest of the change in cash during the year must equal the cash flow from profit. This method is an expedient and practical way to answer the question.

If all you need to know is the final amount of cash flow from profit for the period, the analysis method just demonstrated gives you the correct answer. But I should remind you that the statement of cash flows provides information about several determinants of cash flow from operating activities, as well as the final amount. These determinants of cash flow from profit are explained in the next section.

6. Figure 8-3 presents a business's comparative balance sheet that's missing the information for owners' equity. Assume that the company didn't issue additional capital stock shares during the year and didn't pay cash dividends to its shareowners during the year. Determine its net income for the year 2007.

Balance Sheets at Year-Ends 2006 and 2007

Assets	2006	2007	Changes
Cash	$456,000	$425,000	($31,000)
Accounts Receivable	$386,000	$340,000	($46,000)
Inventory	$518,000	$576,000	$58,000
Prepaid Expenses	$46,000	$52,000	$6,000
Current Assets	$1,406,000	$1,393,000	
Property, Plant, & Equipment	$897,000	$1,060,000	$163,000
Accumulated Depreciation	($257,000)	($318,000)	($61,000)
Cost Less Depreciation	$640,000	$742,000	
Total Assets	$2,046,000	$2,135,000	

Liabilities & Owners' Equity	2006	2007	Changes
Accounts Payable	$246,000	$230,000	($16,000)
Accrued Expenses Payable	$204,000	$215,000	$11,000
Short-term Notes Payable	$350,000	$300,000	($50,000)
Current Liabilities	$800,000	$745,000	
Long-term Notes Payable	$400,000	$525,000	$125,000

Figure 8-3:
Comparative balance sheet without owners' equity accounts.

Solve It

7. From the information presented in Figure 8-3, determine the company's cash flow from profit (operating activities) for 2007.

Solve It

8. A company's net worth decreased $425,000 during the year just ended. It didn't pay cash dividends during the year, and it didn't issue or retire capital stock during the year. Determine its profit or loss for the year.

Solve It

9. A company's net worth decreased $585,000 during the year just ended. It didn't pay cash dividends during the year, but it issued additional capital stock shares during the year for $150,000. Determine its profit or loss for the year.

Solve It

Presenting the Statement of Cash Flows

A business's accountant prepares the income statement from its sales revenue and expense accounts and prepares the balance sheet from its asset, liability, and owners' equity accounts. However, there are no cash flow accounts from which to prepare the statement of cash flows.

How does an accountant prepare the statement of cash flows without ready-made accounts with cash flow balances? This is an interesting question, well, interesting to accountants I should say. I doubt that non-accountants care a fig about how the accountants do their work in preparing financial statements. Accountants use different techniques for gathering and analyzing the information needed to prepare the statement of cash flows.

Theoretically, an accountant could analyze and classify all the entries in the cash account during the year to collect the information needed to prepare the statement of cash flows. However, going back and looking at the large number of entries in the cash account during the year isn't a very practical method for pulling together the information needed to prepare the statement of cash flows.

Today, businesses use computers in their accounting systems, as you know. It's conceivable that a company could design its data entry procedures and computer programs such that at the end of the year the computer would spit out exactly the information needed to prepare the statement of cash flows. Evidently this is not done by many businesses. In most businesses this financial statement is assembled the old fashion way — the accountant sits down and organizes the information pretty much by hand. The information can be put into a spreadsheet program to do the tedious computations and groupings.

Reporting Cash Flows

Regardless of how the accountant goes about organizing the information needed to prepare it, the statement of cash flows is fundamentally the same for every business. Figure 8-4 presents the business's statement of cash flows for 2007. The format of this financial statement is in accordance with the official standard governing reporting cash flows. Figure 8-4 presents cash flows for only one year, but most public companies present a two- or three-year comparative statement of cash flows. Their financial reporting practices are heavily influenced by the requirements of the Securities and Exchange Commission (SEC). (Financial reports of private businesses aren't in the public domain, so it's hard to generalize about their reporting practices in this respect.)

Statement of Cash Flows for 2007

Cash Flow from Operating Activities		
Net Income	$405,000	
Accounts receivable increase	($35,000)	
Inventory increase	($45,000)	
Prepaid expenses increase	($15,000)	
Depreciation expense	$191,000	
Accounts payable increase	$35,000	
Accrued expenses payable increase	$40,000	$576,000
Cash Flow from Investing Activities		
Capital expenditures		($425,000)
Cash Flow from Financing Activities		
Short-term notes payable increase	$125,000	
Long-term notes payable increase	$125,000	
Issue of capital stock	$50,000	
Cash dividends to shareowners	($250,000)	$50,000
Increase in cash during year		$201,000
Beginning cash balance		$700,000
Ending cash balance		$901,000

Figure 8-4: Statement of cash flows for the business.

In the statement of cash flows, transactions are grouped into three types (see Figure 8-4):

- **Operating activities:** The section reports the determinants of the cash increase or decrease attributable to the profit-making operations of the business during the period, and the final amount of cash flow from operating activities for the period — a positive $576,000 in the example.

- **Investing activities:** This section includes expenditures for long-term operating assets and proceeds from the disposal of these assets (if any), and the net cash increase or decrease from these activities for the period — a negative $425,000 in the example.

- **Financing activities:** This section includes the cash flows from borrowing and paying debt, owners investing capital in the business and return of capital to them, and cash dividends to owners, and the net cash increase or decrease from these activities for the period — a positive $50,000 in the example.

The "bottom line" of the statement is the net cash increase or decrease from the three types of activities reported in the statement — a positive $201,000 in the example. As you see in Figure 8-4, this $201,000 increase is not the bottom line in the literal sense, because the beginning cash balance is added to the net cash increase during the year to arrive at the ending balance of cash. The $201,000 increase in cash during the year is the bottom line in the sense that the three main types of activities caused cash to increase this amount during the year.

Financial statement readers definitely want to know whether the company's cash balance increased or decreased during the year, and they want to know the principal reasons for the increase or decrease. These are the reasons for reporting the statement of cash flows.

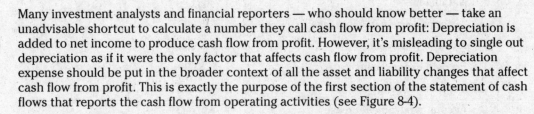

Many investment analysts and financial reporters — who should know better — take an unadvisable shortcut to calculate a number they call cash flow from profit: Depreciation is added to net income to produce cash flow from profit. However, it's misleading to single out depreciation as if it were the only factor that affects cash flow from profit. Depreciation expense should be put in the broader context of all the asset and liability changes that affect cash flow from profit. This is exactly the purpose of the first section of the statement of cash flows that reports the cash flow from operating activities (see Figure 8-4).

Depreciation often is the largest factor for the difference between cash flow and net income, as it is in the example shown in Figure 8-4. But changes in other assets and liabilities also affect cash flow from profit. In some situations, these other changes overwhelm depreciation and are the main reasons for the difference between cash flow and profit. For instance, a business may lease all its fixed assets and have no depreciation expense.

A business needs to generate sufficient cash flow from profit to pay cash dividends to shareowners. In Figure 8-4, the business generated $576,000 cash flow from profit for the year and it paid out $250,000 cash dividends to its stockholders. This comparison is one of many the reader of the statement of cash flows can make to judge the cash flow policies and decisions of the business. Given that the business needed $425,000 for investments in fixed assets during the year, should it have paid out such a large portion of its cash flow from profit? This is just one of many important issues that creditors and shareowners should ponder in reading a statement of cash flows.

Connecting Balance Sheet Changes with Cash Flows

As I have said more than once in this book, the three primary financial statements of a business are intertwined and interdependent. The numbers in the statement of cash flows are derived from the changes in the business's balance sheet accounts during the year. Changes in the balance sheet accounts drive the amounts reported in the statement of cash flows.

The lines of connection between changes in the business's balance sheet accounts during the year and the information reported in the statement of cash flows are shown in Figure 8-5. Note that the $155,000 net increase in retained earnings is separated between the $405,000 net income for the year and the $250,000 cash dividends for the year: ($405,000 net income – $250,000 dividends = $155,000 net increase in retained earnings).

Balance Sheets Changes from Year-End 2006 to Year-End 2007

Assets		Cash Flow from Operating Activities	
Cash	$201,000	Net Income	$405,000
Accounts Receivable	$35,000	Accounts receivable increase	($35,000)
Inventory	$45,000	Inventory increase	($45,000)
Prepaid Expenses	$15,000	Prepaid expenses increase	($15,000)
		Depreciation expense	$191,000
Property, Plant, & Equipment	$425,000	Accounts payable increase	$35,000
Accumulated Depreciation	($191,000)	Accrued expenses payable increase	$40,000
			$576,000
Liabilities & Owners' Equity		Cash Flow from Investing Activities	
Accounts Payable	$35,000	Capital expenditures	($425,000)
Accrued Expenses Payable	$40,000		
Short-term Notes Payable	$125,000	Cash Flow from Financing Activities	
		Short-term notes payable increase	$125,000
Long-term Notes Payable	$125,000	Long-term notes payable increase	$125,000
		Issue of capital stock	$50,000
Owners' Equity:		Cash dividends to shareowners	($250,000)
Capital Stock	$50,000		$50,000
Retained Earnings	$155,000	Increase in cash during year	$201,000
		Beginning cash balance	$700,000
		Ending cash balance	$901,000

Figure 8-5: Connections between the balance sheet changes and the statement of cash flows.

Balance sheet account changes, such as those shown in Figure 8-5, are the basic building blocks for preparing a statement of cash flows. These changes in assets, liabilities, and owners' equity accounts are the amounts reported in the statement of cash flows (as shown in Figure 8-5), or the changes are used to determine the cash flow amounts (as in the case of the change in retained earnings, which is separated into its net income component and its dividends component).

Note in the cash flow from operating activities section in Figure 8-5 that net income is listed first, then several adjustments are made to net income to determine the amount of cash flow from operating activities. The assets and liabilities included in this section are those that are part and parcel of the profit-making activity of a business. For example, the accounts receivable asset is increased (debited) when sales are made on credit. The inventory asset account is decreased (credited) when recording cost of goods sold expense. The accounts payable account is increased (credited) when recording expenses that haven't been paid. And so on.

The rules for cash flow adjustments to net income are:

- ✔ An asset increase during the period decreases cash flow from profit
- ✔ A liability decrease during the period decreases cash flow from profit
- ✔ An asset decrease during the period increases cash flow from profit
- ✔ A liability increase during the period increases cash flow from profit

Following the third listed rule, the $191,000 depreciation expense for the year is a positive adjustment, or add-back to net income — see Figure 8-4. Recording depreciation expense reduces the book value of the fixed assets being depreciated. Well, to be more precise, recording depreciation increases the balance of the accumulated depreciation contra account that is deducted from the original cost of fixed assets. Recording depreciation does not involve a cash outlay. The cash outlay occurred when the business bought the assets being depreciated, which could be years ago.

This format of the cash flow from operating activities section shown in Figure 8-4 is referred to as the *indirect method* (a rather technical term). The large majority of public businesses use this method to report their cash flow from operating activities. However, the authoritative accounting standard on this matter permits an alternative method for reporting cash flow from operating activities, which is called the *direct method* (not that this term is any clearer than the other). Very few businesses elect this alternative format, and I do not explain it here. But you should know that a business has this option for reporting cash flow from operating activities.

10. The comparative balance sheet for a business (without its owners' equity accounts) is presented in Figure 8-3. (Note that this is a different business example than the main example in the chapter.) The company didn't issue additional capital stock shares during the year and didn't pay cash dividends to its shareowners. Please refer to your answers to Questions 6 and 7. You need to know the net income of the business for the year, and you should use your answer to Question 7 as a check in answering this question. Prepare the company's statement of cash flows for 2007.

11. The beginning and ending balances of certain accounts in a company's balance sheet are as follows:

	Beginning Balance	Ending Balance	Changes
Accounts Receivable	$500,000	$465,000	($35,000)
Inventory	$780,000	$860,000	$80,000
Prepaid Expenses	$110,000	$105,000	($5,000)
Accounts Payable	$350,000	$325,000	($25,000)
Accrued Expenses Payable	$165,000	$175,000	$10,000

The business records $145,000 depreciation expense for the year and its net income is $258,000 for the year. Determine its cash flow from operating activities for the year. Present your answer in the indirect format for cash flow from operating activities in the statement of cash flows.

Solve It

12. Referring to the scenario in Question 11, assume that the facts remain the same except that the business doesn't record depreciation expense in the year. Instead, it leases all its fixed assets and pays rent. The rent expense for the year is $145,000. (Note that the rent expense is the same amount as depreciation expense in Question 11.) Determine its cash flow from operating activities for the year. Present your answer for reporting cash flow from operating activities according to the indirect format (as illustrated in Figure 8-4).

Solve It

Answers for Problems on Reporting Cash Flows and Changes in Owners' Equity

The following are the answers to the practice questions presented earlier in this chapter.

1   After you revise your net income answer (see the example question), the president tells you that he has since talked with other directors of the business and realized that he was wrong about the cash dividends. Now he's fairly certain that $250,000 cash dividends were paid to shareowners during 2007 and that the business issued additional capital stock shares for $50,000. Based on this additional information, what amount of net income did the business earn in 2007?

Net income is $405,000. The net effect on owners' equity is the same as in the example question; the capital stock issue increases net worth $50,000 and the cash dividend decreases net worth $250,000.

2   A business reports $500,000 net loss for the year just ended. It didn't issue or retire any capital stock shares during the year, and it didn't pay cash dividends because of its loss in the year. Did its net worth decrease $500,000 during the year? Did its cash balance decrease $500,000 during the year because of its loss?

Yes, net loss decreased net worth (owners' equity) $500,000. There were no other transactions that affected owners' equity during the year (no capital stock issue and no cash dividends).

To determine whether its cash balance decreased $500,000 because of the business's loss, you need to know the changes in the assets and liabilities of the business that are affected by its sales and expenses. You can't answer this cash flow question without this information. If the business didn't record any depreciation expense in the year, and if the balances of the various assets and liabilities affected by sales and expenses remained absolutely flat during the year, then and only then would the loss decrease cash $500,000 during the year. But this is a highly unlikely scenario for the business.

3   Can the net worth of a business go negative? If so, explain briefly how this may happen and if it means that the business would have a negative cash balance.

Yes, the net worth of a business can go negative. A large enough loss in the year could wipe out all owners' equity and more, or repeated losses year after year could drive owners' equity into the negative column. Remember that a loss decreases the retained earnings balance of a business. The loss for the year or cumulative losses over time can push retained earnings into a large negative balance. The negative balance of retained earnings can become more than the balance in the owners' equity invested capital account. In this case, owners' equity would be negative.

Regarding the second question, you have to put your finger on what a negative cash balance is. Usually, a negative cash balance refers to an overdrawn bank checking account balance in which the business has written checks for more than exists in its account. Banks don't typically allow overdraws to happen and refuse to honor checks after the checking account balance is drawn down to zero. However, a bank may tolerate a temporary negative balance for a good customer, but a business with a negative owners' equity hardly qualifies as a good customer. Generally speaking, the cash balance of a business can't go below zero (or, it can't go negative).

4   Please refer to Figure 8-1 that presents the comparative balance sheet of the business and to Figure 8-2 that presents its statement of changes in stockholders' equity. Suppose the business had paid $175,000 cash dividends (instead of $250,000) to stockholders in 2007. In this scenario, which dollar amounts in the business's comparative balance sheet would be different as the result of this one change?

Just one relatively small difference, like the one in this problem, causes several changes in the balance sheet. In the following answer, the amounts that are different are shaded so that you can easily identify them.

Balance Sheets at Year-ends 2006 and 2007

Assets	2006	2007	Changes
Cash	$700,000	$976,000	$276,000
Accounts Receivable	$500,000	$535,000	$35,000
Inventory	$780,000	$825,000	$45,000
Prepaid Expenses	$110,000	$125,000	$15,000
Current Assets	$2,090,000	$2,461,000	
Property, Plant, & Equipment	$2,450,000	$2,875,000	$425,000
Accumulated Depreciation	($685,000)	($876,000)	($191,000)
Cost Less Depreciation	$1,765,000	$1,999,000	
Total Assets	$3,855,000	$4,460,000	

Liabilities & Owners' Equity			
Accounts Payable	$350,000	$385,000	$35,000
Accrued Expenses Payable	$165,000	$205,000	$40,000
Short-term Notes Payable	$500,000	$625,000	$125,000
Current Liabilities	$1,015,000	$1,215,000	
Long-term Notes Payable	$1,000,000	$1,125,000	$125,000
Owners Equity:			
Capital Stock	$750,000	$800,000	$50,000
Retained Earnings	$1,090,000	$1,320,000	$230,000
Total Owners' Equity	$1,840,000	$2,120,000	
Total Liabilities & Owners' Equity	$3,855,000	$4,460,000	

5 Suppose the business in the example (see Figure 8-2) did not issue additional shares of capital stock in 2007 and did not distribute dividends to its stockholders in either 2006 or 2007. In this scenario, is the statement of changes in stockholders' equity needed? Should it be presented in the company's 2007 annual financial report?

Well, if the business did prepare and report this statement it would look as follows:

Statement of Changes in Stockholders' Equity

	Capital Stock	Retained Earnings
Balance at end of 2005	$750,000	$922,000
Net Income - 2006		$318,000
Balance at end of 2006	$750,000	$1,240,000
Net Income - 2007		$405,000
Balance at end of 2007	$750,000	$1,645,000

You can make a good case that there's no need for presenting the statement of changes in stockholders' equity in the company's annual report because it contains so little information in addition to what's already in the comparative balance sheet. The statement does report that net income is added to the retained earnings balance each year, but most financial statement readers should understand this point.

On the other hand, one could argue that showing no dividends and no issue of capital stock either year sends a message that the company is conserving its cash and presumably has a need for the cash. On balance, therefore, most businesses would go ahead and report a statement of changes in stockholders' equity. If a reader isn't interested enough to read the statement, he or she can skip it. You never know; some business investors and creditors read every financial statement and every footnote, and these people expect to see the statement of changes in stockholders' equity in the financial report.

6   Figure 8-3 presents a business's comparative balance sheet that's missing the information for owners' equity. Assume that the company didn't issue additional capital stock shares during the year and didn't pay cash dividends to its shareowners during the year. Determine its net income for the year 2007.

The company's net income for 2007 is determined as follows:

	2006	2007
Total Assets	$2,046,000	$2,135,000
Current Liabilities	($800,000)	($745,000)
Long-term Notes Payable	($400,000)	($525,000)
Net Worth at Year-end	$846,000	$865,000
		($846,000)
Net Income for 2007		$19,000

The business didn't issue capital stock and didn't pay dividends during the year, so $19,000 is its net income. In other words, the increase in net worth consists entirely of the increase in retained earnings caused by net income for the year.

You may think the net income in this scenario is a rather paltry amount, and you'd be right. Generally, a business expects to earn annual net income equal to 10 to 15 percent or more of its owners' equity. Owners' equity is the investment by the owners in the business, and the owners expect to earn a return on their investment. Based on the $846,000 balance of owners' equity at the start of 2007, a 15 percent return on investment would require about $127,000 net income. The company had better improve its profit performance, or else.

7   From the information presented in Figure 8-3, determine the company's cash flow from profit (operating activities) for 2007.

Using the method of solving for the unknown factor you set up the problem as follows:

Summary of Cash Flows For the Year

Cash flow from operating activities	????
Cash flow from investing activities	($163,000)
Cash flow from financing activities	$75,000
Decrease in cash during the year	($31,000)

Solving for the unknown factor, cash flow from profit is $57,000 for the year. In Figure 8-3, you can see that the company increased cash $75,000 from its notes payable transactions during the year ($125,000 increase in long-term notes payable – $50,000 pay down on short-term notes payable = $75,000 net increase). The business didn't raise money by issuing capital stock during the year and didn't pay cash dividends during the year. So the net cash increase from its financing activities is $75,000. It spent $163,000 on property, plant and equipment (see Figure 8-3). Therefore, cash flow from profit must have increased cash $57,000: ($57,000 cash increase from profit – $163,000 capital expenditures + $75,000 cash from financing activities = $31,000 decrease in cash during year). Did you follow all this? I hope so. Cash flow analysis isn't for sissies, is it?

8 A company's net worth decreased $425,000 during the year just ended. It didn't pay cash dividends during the year, and it didn't issue or retire capital stock during the year. Determine its profit or loss for the year.

All the decrease in net worth in this scenario must be due to the loss for the year. So, the bottom-line is that the business suffered a $425,000 loss for the year.

Does this loss mean that bankruptcy is just around the corner? A loss doesn't necessarily mean that the business is out of cash and unable to pay its debts on time. The business could have plenty of cash to buy time enough to correct its problems and move into the black. Then again, if this is the tenth straight year of losses, the business may be hanging on by a thread and may have to declare bankruptcy.

9 A company's net worth decreased $585,000 during the year just ended. It didn't pay cash dividends during the year, but it issued additional capital stock shares during the year for $150,000. Determine its profit or loss for the year.

The company's net worth increased $150,000 from the issue of capital stock. If the business had experienced a break-even year (sales revenue - expenses = zero), its net worth would have increased $150,000. But, its net worth actually decreased $585,000 during the year. Therefore, the company must have reported a $735,000 loss for the year.

10 The comparative balance sheet for a business (without its owners' equity accounts) is presented in Figure 8-3. (Note that this is a different business example than the main example in the chapter.) The company didn't issue additional capital stock shares during the year and didn't pay cash dividends to its shareowners. Please refer to your answers to Questions 6 and 7. You need to know the net income of the business for the year, and you should use your answer to Question 7 as a check in answering this question. Prepare the company's statement of cash flows for 2007.

Statement of Cash Flows for 2007

Cash Flow from Operating Activities

Net Income	$19,000	
Accounts receivable decrease	$46,000	
Inventory increase	($58,000)	
Prepaid expenses increase	($6,000)	
Depreciation expense	$61,000	
Accounts payable decrease	($16,000)	
Accrued expenses payable increase	$11,000	$57,000

Cash Flow from Investing Activities

Capital expenditures	($163,000)

Cash Flow from Financing Activities

Short-term notes payable increase	($50,000)	
Long-term notes payable increase	$125,000	$75,000

Decrease in cash during year	($31,000)
Beginning cash balance	$456,000
Ending cash balance	$425,000

The beginning and ending balances of certain accounts in a company's balance sheet are as follows:

	Beginning Balance	Ending Balance	Changes
Accounts Receivable	$500,000	$465,000	($35,000)
Inventory	$780,000	$860,000	$80,000
Prepaid Expenses	$110,000	$105,000	($5,000)
Accounts Payable	$350,000	$325,000	($25,000)
Accrued Expenses Payable	$165,000	$175,000	$10,000

The business records $145,000 depreciation expense for the year and its net income is $258,000 for the year. Determine its cash flow from operating activities for the year. Present your answer in the indirect format for cash flow from operating activities in the statement of cash flows.

Net Income	$258,000
Accounts receivable decrease	$35,000
Inventory increase	($80,000)
Prepaid expenses decrease	$5,000
Depreciation expense	$145,000
Accounts payable decrease	($25,000)
Accrued expenses payable increase	$10,000
Cash Flow from Operating Activities	$348,000

12 Referring to the scenario in Question 11, assume that the facts remain the same except that the business doesn't record depreciation expense in the year. Instead, it leases all its fixed assets and pays rent. The rent expense for the year is $145,000. (Note that the rent expense is the same amount as depreciation expense in Question 11.) Determine its cash flow from operating activities for the year. Present your answer for reporting cash flow from operating activities according to the indirect format (as illustrated in Figure 8-4).

Net Income	$258,000
Accounts receivable decrease	$35,000
Inventory increase	($80,000)
Prepaid expenses decrease	$5,000
Accounts payable decrease	($25,000)
Accrued expenses payable increase	$10,000
Cash Flow from Operating Activities	$203,000

 For added insight, compare this answer with the answer to Question 11. Cash flow from profit in this situation is $145,000 less than in the scenario for Question 11 because the business didn't record depreciation expense. Instead, it paid $145,000 rent expense during the year.

Chapter 9

Choosing Accounting Methods

. . . .

In This Chapter
▶ Selecting the best cost of goods sold expense method for the business
▶ Depreciating in the fast and slow lanes
▶ Deciding when to bite the bad-debts bullet

. . . .

You may think that two businesses that are identical in every financial respect and have identical transactions during the year would report identical financial statements. You'd be wrong. The two businesses would have identical financial statements only if they made identical accounting choices, and that's very unlikely. Different businesses make different accounting decisions.

Accounting is more than just reading the facts or interpreting the financial outcomes of business transactions. Accounting also requires accountants to choose between alternative accounting methods. Similar to the conservative states and liberal states addressed in politics, accounting has:

- **Conservative accounting methods:** These accounting methods delay the recording of revenue and accelerate the recording of expenses. Profit is reported slowly.

- **Liberal accounting methods:** These accounting methods accelerate the recording of revenue and delay the recording of expenses. Profit is reported quickly.

In rough terms, conservative accounting methods are pessimistic, and liberal methods are optimistic. The choice of accounting methods also affects the values reported for assets, liabilities, and owners' equities in the balance sheet.

Accounting methods must stay within the boundaries of *generally accepted accounting principles* (GAAP). A business can't conjure up accounting methods out of thin air. GAAP isn't a straitjacket; it leaves plenty of wiggle room, but the one fundamental constraint is that a business must stick with its accounting method when it makes a choice. *Consistency* is the rule; the same accounting methods must be used year after year. (The Internal Revenue Service (IRS) allows businesses to change their accounting methods once in a while, but the justification has to be persuasive.)

Getting Off to a Good Start

A new business with no accounting history has to make its accounting decisions for the first time. If the business sells products, it has to select which cost of goods sold expense method to use. If it owns fixed assets, it has to select which depreciation method to use. If it makes sales on credit, it has to decide which bad debts expense method to use. These are three of the many accounting decisions a business has to make.

The choices of accounting methods for these three expenses — cost of goods sold, depreciation, and bad debts — can make a sizable difference in the amount of profit or loss recorded for the year. Choosing conservative accounting methods for these three expenses can cause profit for the year to be lower by a relatively large percent compared with using liberal accounting methods for the expenses. The comprehensive problems at the end of the chapter demonstrate this point.

To explain these expense accounting methods I use a start-up business example. This new business has no accounting history. It must make these expense accounting decisions for the first time. Assume that the business put off making these accounting choices until the end of its first year. Everyone was very busy during the year getting the venture off the ground. Furthermore, waiting until the end of the year gave management and the chief accountant a year to learn more about the operating environment of the business and the kinds of problems the business faces.

One year has passed; it's now the end of the first year of business. One of the things a business does at the end of the year is to prepare a listing of all its accounts, which serves as the main source of information for preparing its financial statements. Figure 9-1 presents the accounts of the company at the end of its first year of business. Note that the total of accounts with debit balances equals the total of accounts with credit balances. (Chapter 3 explains debits and credits.) So, there are no bookkeeping errors (or, at least, none that would cause these totals to be out of balance).

| | End of First Year | |
	Debits	Credits
Cash	$559,750	
Accounts Receivable	$645,000	
Allowance for Doubtful Accounts		$0
Inventory	$3,725,000	
Prepaid Expenses	$185,000	
Property, Plant & Equipment	$1,150,000	
Accumulated Depreciation		$0
Accounts Payable		$309,500
Accrued Expenses Payable		$108,500
Short-term Notes Payable		$350,000
Long-term Notes Payable		$500,000
Owners' Equity – Capital Stock		$1,500,000
Owners' Equity – Retained Earnings		$0
Sales Revenue		$4,585,000
Cost of Goods Sold Expense	$0	
Depreciation Expense	$0	
Bad Debts Expense	$0	
Selling & General Expenses	$1,033,000	
Interest Expense	$55,250	
Totals	$7,353,000	$7,353,000

Figure 9-1: Listing of accounts of the business at end of its first year.

At this point the chief accountant sits down with top management to decide which accounting methods the business should use to record cost of goods sold expense, depreciation expense, and bad debts expense. The financial statements for the first year cannot be prepared until these accounting choices are made and the three expenses are recorded.

Q. Review the company's year-end listing of accounts' balances shown in Figure 9-1.

a. How can you tell from this listing of accounts that the business has not recorded its following three expenses for the year?

- **Bad debts expense:** Caused by uncollectible accounts receivable

- **Cost of goods sold expense:** For the cost of products sold; the revenue from these sales has been recorded in the sales revenue account

- **Depreciation expense:** For the use of fixed assets (property, plant, and equipment) during the year

b. Also, did you notice that there is no income tax expense account? What is the explanation for this omission?

A. **a.** Taking the expenses in the order listed:

- The ending balances in the bad debts expense account and in the allowance for doubtful account are both zero. Therefore, no bad debts expense has been recorded

- The balance in the cost of goods sold expense account is zero; also, the balance in the inventory account is very large compared with the balance in the sales revenue account. Therefore, no cost of goods sold expense has been recorded

- The balance in the accumulated depreciation account is zero, and the balance in the depreciation account is zero. Therefore, no depreciation expense has been recorded

b. The reason for no income tax expense is that this business is a *pass-through entity* for income tax purposes. This means that its annual taxable income or loss is passed through to its individual owners who pick up their respective shares of the taxable income or loss in their individual income tax returns. The business itself doesn't pay income tax. (The main types of businesses that are pass-through income tax entities are partnerships, small business corporations, and limited liability companies.)

1. Does the interest expense in Figure 9-1 look reasonable, or does it need an adjustment at the end of the year?

Solve It

2. In Figure 9-1 the Owners' Equity — Retained Earnings account has a zero balance. Why?

Solve It

3. In Figure 9-1, note the Prepaid Expenses asset account at the end of the year. What are three examples of such prepaid costs? Are the methods for allocating these costs to expense fairly objective and noncontroversial?

Solve It

4. In Figure 9-1, note the Accrued Expenses Payable liability account at the end of the year. What are two or three examples of such accrued costs? Are the methods for allocating these costs to expense fairly objective and noncontroversial?

Solve It

Determining Whether Products Are Unique or Fungible

In deciding on its cost of goods sold expense method of accounting, the first step a business does is to determine whether the products it sells are *fungible* or *unique*. A unique product is the only one of its kind; no other product is like it in all respects. For example, given the wide range of options, equipment, colors, and models, every car on the lot of a new auto dealer may be different. Another example of a business that sells unique products is a jeweler that sells high priced rings, necklaces, brooches, and so on. Each piece is different than the others.

Fungible means that products are interchangeable and virtually indistinguishable from one another. The products may have different serial numbers, but customers are indifferent regarding which specific products they receive. Most products you buy in a grocery store or fungible. The iPods that Apple sells are fungible. Apple sells different models of iPods, but within each model category the products are fungible.

When the products it sells are unique, the business uses the *specific identification method* to record cost of goods sold expense. The business keeps a separate record for the cost of each product. The cost of each product is charged to cost of goods sold expense when that particular product is sold.

Generally speaking, unique (non-fungible) products are higher priced than fungible products. Also, unique products are bought one at a time, whereas fungible products are bought in batches. The cost per unit of each successive batch typically fluctuates over time. This poses a dilemma; the business must choose which accounting method to use for recording cost of goods sold expense, which the next section explains.

Contrasting Cost of Goods Sold Expense Methods (for Fungible Products)

Over the years, the accounting profession hasn't managed to settle on just one method for recording cost of goods sold expense and inventory cost (for fungible products). Different methods have been allowed for many years. A business is entirely at liberty to choose whichever method it wishes from among the generally approved methods, which are as follows

- ✔ **Average cost method:** The costs of different batches of products are averaged to determine cost of goods sold expense and ending inventory cost.

- ✔ **First-in, first-out (FIFO) method:** The costs of batches are charged to cost of goods sold in the order the batches are acquired, and the cost of ending inventory is from the most recent batch(es) acquired.

- ✔ **Last-in, first-out (LIFO) method:** The costs of batches are charged to cost of goods sold in the reverse order that the batches were acquired, and the cost of ending inventory is from the oldest batch(es) acquired.

The one universal rule is that a business can't mark up its ending inventory (that is, its stockpile of unsold products on hand at the end of the year) to the current replacement cost values of the products. In short, GAAP doesn't allow market value appreciation of inventory to be recorded.

From the listing of accounts in Figure 9-1, you can see that the company's inventory account has a relatively large balance. Product purchases during the year were debited in this account, but no credits have been made for the cost of goods sold during the year. Clearly, the appropriate amount should be removed from the inventory asset account and charged to cost of goods sold expense account.

Q. Suppose the business made five purchases during the year. It bought 100,000 units of the one product it sells. Suppose, further, that the cost per unit in all five purchases was the same. In other words, there was no change in the purchase cost per unit during the year. This is not too likely, but this scenario provides is a good jumping off point for explaining cost of goods sold expense. During the year, the business sold 80,000 units of product. The revenue from these sales was $4,585,000 (see the sales revenue account in Figure 9-1). What amount of gross profit (margin) did the business earn from sales of products during the year?

A. To determine gross profit, you must first determine the cost of the 80,000 units sold during the year. In this scenario the purchase cost per unit of the products sold by the business remained constant during the year. So, there is only one method to determine cost of goods sold: (80,000 units sold/100,000 units purchased x $3,725,000 cost of purchases = $2,980,000 cost of goods sold). In other words, 80 percent of the goods purchased and available for sale were sold during the year and, therefore, 80 percent of the total cost of purchases should be charged to cost of goods sold. The following journal entry is made:

Cost of goods sold expense	$2,980,000
Inventory	$2,980,000

Therefore, the gross margin for the year is:

Sales revenue	$4,585,000
Cost of goods sold expense	$2,980,000
Gross margin	$1,605,000

The cost per unit of products purchased (or manufactured) usually does not stay the same from batch to batch. Usually the cost per unit fluctuates from batch to batch. This fluctuation creates an accounting problem. Three different methods are used to deal with the fluctuation of cost per unit from batch to batch, which I explain in the following sections.

Figure 9-2 presents the history of products purchased by the business during its first year. The business made five purchases, and the costs per unit (purchase prices) drifted up from purchase to purchase. The business sells only one product, which minimizes the number crunching. (Of course, most businesses sell a variety of products.) I use the information in Figure 9-2 to illustrate the three methods of accounting for cost of goods sold and the cost of inventory.

	Quantity	Per Unit	Cost
First purchase	24,000 units	$35.40	$849,600
Second purchase	22,500 units	$35.44	$797,400
Third purchase	20,000 units	$37.65	$753,000
Fourth purchase	10,000 units	$38.50	$385,000
Fifth purchase	23,500 units	$40.00	$940,000
Totals	100,000 units		$3,725,000

Figure 9-2: History of inventory acquisitions during the first year.

Averaging things out

Many accountants argue that when the acquisition cost per unit fluctuates the thing to do is to use the *average cost* of products to determine cost of goods sold expense. The logic of the *average cost method* goes like this: Five batches of products were purchased at different prices, so it's best to lump together all five purchases and determine the *average cost per unit.* From the data in Figure 9-2, the average cost per unit purchased during the year is calculated as follows:

$3,725,000 total cost of purchases ÷ 100,000 units = $37.25 average cost per unit

The cost of goods sold expense for the products sold during the year is calculated as follows:

80,000 units sold during year × $37.25 average cost per unit = $2,980,000 cost of goods sold expense

Alternatively, if you know that the business sold 80,000 of the 100,000 units available during the year, you can calculate cost of goods sold expense the following way:

(80,000 ÷ 100,000) × $3,725,000 total cost of purchases = $2,980,000 cost of goods sold expense

Unless you've been asleep at the wheel, you should have noticed that the average cost method gives the same answer for cost of goods sold expense as in the example scenario just above in which it is assumed that the purchase cost per unit remained the same during the year. That's the effect of calculating an average. The five different costs per unit figures (see Figure 9-2) are condensed to one average number, as if this had been the cost per unit during the year.

Using the average cost method, the $37.25 average cost per unit is used for the company's 20,000 units of ending inventory (100,000 units acquired less 80,000 units sold):

20,000 units of inventory × $37.25 average cost per unit = $745,000 cost of ending inventory

Summing up, the $3,725,000 total cost of products purchased during the first year of business is divided between $2,980,000 cost of goods sold expense and $745,000 cost of ending inventory.

The *average cost method* is not as easy to use in actual practice as this example may suggest. With this method, you face questions such as how often should you determine the average cost per unit? Should you calculate the average just once a year, once each quarter, or once each month? Before computers came along, calculating an average cost per unit was a pain in the posterior.

5. During its first year, a business made seven acquisitions of a product that it sells. Figure 9-3 presents the history of these purchases. Compare the purchases history in Figure 9-3 with the one in Figure 9-2. Does the average cost method make more sense or seem more persuasive in one case over the other?

Solve It

---

6. Refer to the purchase history in Figure 9-3. The bookkeeper said he was using the average cost method. He calculated the average of the seven purchase costs per unit and multiplied this average unit cost by the 158,100 units sold during the year. His average cost per unit is $24.76 (rounded). Is this the correct way to apply the average cost method? If not, what is the correct answer for cost of goods sold expense for the year?

Solve It

	Quantity	Per Unit	Cost
First purchase	14,200 Units	$25.75	$365,650
Second purchase	42,500 Units	$23.85	$1,013,625
Third purchase	16,500 Units	$24.85	$410,025
Fourth purchase	36,500 Units	$23.05	$841,325
Fifth purchase	6,100 Units	$26.15	$159,515
Sixth purchase	52,000 Units	$23.65	$1,229,800
Seventh purchase	18,200 Units	$26.00	$473,200
Totals	186,000 Units		$4,493,140

Figure 9-3: Acquisition history of products.

Going with the flow: The FIFO method

My Uncle Fred worked many years on the receiving and shipping docks of several businesses. If you asked Fred how to calculate the cost of goods sold, he would point out that the first goods into inventory are the first to be delivered to customers when products are sold. In other words, the sequence follows a *first-in, first-out* order. Businesses don't buy an initial stock of products, put them away in a dark corner, and then take a long time to deliver these products to customers. (Well, wineries may be an exception to this general rule.) The first-in, first-out flow of products delivered to customers means that the business's inventory of products at the end of the year comes from its most recent purchase(s).

The *first-in, first-out* (FIFO) method of determining cost of goods sold expense follows the flow of products taken out of inventory for delivery to customers. In the example, 80,000 units of product were sold to customers. The calculation of the $2,925,000 total cost assigned to these products by the FIFO method is shown in Figure 9-4. The first 24,000 units sold are assigned a cost of $35.40 per unit, or $849,600; the next 22,500 units sold are assigned a cost of $35.44 per unit, or $797,400; and so on.

	Quantity	Per Unit	Cost
First purchase	24,000 units	$35.40	$849,600
Second purchase	22,500 units	$35.44	$797,400
Third purchase	20,000 units	$37.65	$753,000
Fourth purchase	10,000 units	$38.50	$385,000
Fifth purchase	3,500 units	$40.00	$140,000
Goods sold	80,000 units		$2,925,000

Figure 9-4: Cost of goods sold expense calculation by the FIFO method.

The entry to record cost of goods sold expense for the year using the FIFO method is

Cost of goods sold expense	$2,925,000	
Inventory		$2,925,000

TIP

In internal accounting reports to managers, the accountant presents the cost per unit sold and compares it with the sales price during the year to determine the *profit margin per unit*. Using the FIFO method, the cost per unit sold is:

$2,925,000 cost of goods sold ÷ 80,000 units sold = $36.5625, or $36.56 rounded cost per unit sold during year

This cost per unit sold doesn't equal any of the five acquisition costs, nor does it equal the average cost per unit purchased during the year, which is $37.25. Business managers are used to dealing with averages, so this discrepancy shouldn't be a problem — although, whenever you're dealing with an average, it's important to know and take into account how the average is determined.

REMEMBER

What about ending inventory? By the FIFO method, the cost of ending inventory equals the cost of the most recent acquisition(s) — because the cost of earlier acquisitions are charged to cost of goods sold expense for the year. In the example, $2,925,000 is charged to cost of goods sold expense, which leaves a remainder of $800,000 in the inventory account: ($3,725,000 cost of purchases during the year – $2,925,000 to cost of goods sold = $800,000 cost of inventory). The cost of ending inventory is based on the cost of the last, or fifth, purchase and consists of 20,000 units at $40.00 cost per unit for the total cost of $800,000 (data from Figure 9-2). The total quantity of the last (fifth) purchase was 23,500 units (3,500 units were charged to cost of goods sold expense, and the other 20,000 units remain in ending inventory).

7. Figure 9-3 presents the inventory acquisition history of a business for its first year. The business sold 158,100 units during the year. By the FIFO method, determine its cost of goods sold expense for the year and its cost of ending inventory.

Solve It

8. In the example shown in Figure 9-3, the purchase cost per unit bounces up and down over successive acquisitions, and the quantities purchased each time vary quite a bit. Do these two factors play a role in the choice of a cost of goods sold method?

Solve It

Going against the flow: The LIFO method

The FIFO method (see the preceding section) has a lot going for it: It follows the actual sequence of products delivered out of inventory to customers, and it's relatively straightforward to apply. But (and this is a very big but), federal income tax law allows businesses to use an opposite method to determine annual taxable income. This feature of the tax law has led to the widespread adoption of the method, called *last-in, first-out,* or LIFO. The method reverses the sequence in which products sold are removed from inventory and charged to cost of goods sold expense.

Figure 9-5 shows how the cost of 80,000 units sold is calculated by the LIFO method. In accordance with the reverse sequence basis of LIFO, the purchases batches are listed in reverse chronological order. The logic behind the LIFO method is that products sold must be replaced in order to stay in business. The closest approximations to replacement costs are the costs of the most recent purchases.

The entry to record cost of goods sold expense for the year using the LIFO method is

| Cost of goods sold expense | $3,017,000 |
| Inventory | $3,017,000 |

	Source	Quantity	Per Unit	Cost
Figure 9-5:	Fifth purchase	23,500 units	$40.00	$940,000
Cost of	Fourth purchase	10,000 units	$38.50	$385,000
goods sold expense	Third purchase	20,000 units	$37.65	$753,000
calculation	Second purchase	22,500 units	$35.44	$797,400
by the LIFO method.	First purchase	4,000 units	$35.40	$141,600
	Goods sold	80,000 units		$3,017,000

Using the LIFO method in internal reports to managers, the cost per unit sold for the year is

$3,017,000 cost of goods sold ÷ 80,000 units sold = $37.7125, or $37.71 rounded cost per unit sold during year

As with the FIFO method, the LIFO average cost per unit sold doesn't equal any of the five acquisition costs, nor does it equal the average cost per unit purchased during the year, which is $37.25. Business managers are used to dealing with averages, though, so this discrepancy shouldn't be a problem. However, whenever dealing with an average, it is important to know how the average is determined and take that information into account.

What about ending inventory? The cost of ending inventory by the LIFO method depends on whether the business during the year increased the number of products held in inventory. Assume that the business did in fact increase its quantity of inventory (it acquired more units than it sold during the year). In this case, the cost of ending inventory equals the cost of its beginning inventory and the cost of the additional units, which is based on the per unit costs from the earliest acquisitions during the year. On the other hand, when a business decreases its inventory during the year its ending inventory cost is based on the cost(s) per unit in its beginning inventory.

In the example, the cost of ending inventory is $708,000: ($3,725,000 cost of purchases during the year – $3,017,000 to cost of goods sold = $708,000 cost of inventory). In other words, the cost of its ending inventory comes from the oldest purchase and consists of 20,000 units at $35.40 cost per unit for a total cost of $708,000.

In the example, the ending balance sheet reports inventory at $708,000 cost value by the LIFO method versus $800,000 cost value by the FIFO method, which is a fairly sizable difference. FIFO gives a more up-to-date inventory cost in the balance sheet. But, nevertheless, many businesses use LIFO because it minimizes taxable income in their federal income tax returns (assuming an inflationary trend of acquisition costs over time). Reporting ending inventory based on the earliest acquisition cost is the Achilles' heel of the LIFO method.

Assume a business has been using LIFO for, say, 40 years. This means that some part of its inventory cost goes back to costs it paid 40 years ago. (As a matter of fact, Caterpillar Inc. has been using LIFO for more than 50 years.) If the difference between the current cost value of inventory (as measured by FIFO) and the LIFO cost is significant the business discloses this discrepancy in a footnote to its financial statements.

9. Figure 9-3 presents the inventory acquisition history of a business for its first year. The business sold 158,100 units during the year. By the LIFO method, determine its cost of goods sold expense for the year and its cost of ending inventory.

Solve It

10. Suppose the business whose inventory acquisition history appears in Figure 9-3 sold all 186,000 units that it had available for sale during the year. In this situation, does the business's choice of cost of goods sold expense method make any difference?

Solve It

Appreciating Depreciation Methods

The basic theory of depreciation accounting is unarguable: The amount of capital a business invests in a fixed asset, less its estimated future residual (salvage) value when it will be disposed of, should be allocated in a rational and systematic manner over its estimated useful life to the business.

A fixed asset's cost shouldn't be charged entirely to expense in the year the asset's acquired. Doing so would heavily penalize the year of acquisition and relieve future years from any share of the cost. But the opposite approach is equally bad: The business shouldn't wait until a fixed asset is eventually disposed of to record the expense of using the asset. Doing so would heavily penalize the final year and relieve earlier years from any share of the fixed asset's cost.

Essentially, cost less residual value should be apportioned to every year of the fixed asset's use. (Land has perpetual life, and therefore, its cost isn't depreciated.) The theory of depreciation is relatively simple, but the devil is in the details. And, I mean *details!*

Frankly, there's not much point in discussing the finer points of depreciation accounting. I could refer you to many books written by accounting scholars on depreciation. But as a practical matter the federal income tax law dictates the depreciation methods and practices used by most businesses. The IRS publication "How To Depreciate Property" (2005 edition) runs 112 pages. You ought to read this pamphlet — if you have the time, and the stamina.

Let me step on the soapbox for a moment. The depreciation provisions in the income tax law are driven mainly by political and economic incentives, to encourage businesses to upgrade and modernize their investments in long-term operating assets. By and large, businesses follow income tax regulations on depreciation. As the result, useful lives for depreciating fixed assets are too short, salvage value is generally ignored, and depreciation is stacked higher in the early years. In other words: fixed assets generally last longer than their income tax depreciation lives; when disposed of fixed assets often have some salvage value; and, a strong case can be made for allocating an equal amount of depreciation to each year over the useful life of many fixed assets. In short, actual depreciation practices deviate from depreciation theory. Okay, I'm off my soapbox now.

Figure 9-1 shows the accounts of a business at the end of its first year of operations. No depreciation expense for the year has been recorded yet, but obviously, some amount of depreciation must be recorded. The business purchased all its fixed assets during the first week of the year, and the assets were placed in service immediately, so the business is entitled to record a full year's depreciation on its fixed assets. (Special partial-year rules apply when assets are placed in service at other times during the year.)

The company's plant, property, and equipment account consists of the following components:

Land	$150,000
Building	$468,000
Machines	$532,000
Total	$1,150,000

The cost of land is *not* depreciated. Land stays on the books at original cost as long as the business owns the land. Ownership of land is a right in perpetuity, which does not come to an end. Land does not wear out in the physical sense, and generally holds its economic value over time. Buildings, machines and other fixed assets, on the other hand, wear out with use over time and generally reach a point where they have no economic value.

Assume the business decides to maximize the amount of depreciation recorded in the year, according to the provisions of the income tax law.

Q. What depreciation amounts for the year should be recorded on the business's building and machines?

A. Under the federal income tax law, the cost of a building used by a business in its operations is depreciated over 39 years by the *straight-line depreciation method* of allocation. Therefore, the depreciation on the building for the year equals $12,000 ($468,000 cost ÷ 39 years = $12,000 depreciation per year).

Under the federal income tax law, the machines used by the business fall into the seven-year useful life class, and they can be (but don't have to be) depreciated by the *double-declining balance method* of allocation. This is an *accelerated depreciation method* of allocation that front-loads depreciation, which means that more depreciation is allocated to the early years and less to the later years of the asset's useful life. The applicable percent for the first year is double the straight-line rate. Therefore, ²⁄₇ of the cost of the machines is charged to depreciation in the first year: $532,000 × ²⁄₇ = $152,000 depreciation in the first year.

In years two, three, and four, the percent is the same but is applied on the *declining balance*, which equals cost less accumulated depreciation at the start of the year. So, for example, in the second year, ²⁄₇ is multiplied by the original cost of the machines minus the first year's depreciation. The business converts to the straight-line depreciation method for the last three years. In these three years, the straight-line depreciation amount is higher on the declining balance than the amount determined by the accelerated rate. By switching to the straight-line depreciation method for the last three years, the original cost of the machines is fully depreciated over the seven-year life of the assets. (Cost wouldn't be fully depreciated if the accelerated rate were used in the last three years.)

11. Determine the annual depreciation amounts on the machines for years two through seven according to the double declining accelerated depreciation method. Also, determine the declining balance of the machines at the end of each year (cost less accumulated depreciation), which is also called the *book value* of the fixed assets.

Solve It

12. Instead of using the double-declining depreciation method for its machines, suppose the business used the straight-line depreciation method over seven years. Determine the year-by-year difference in bottom-line profit with the straight-line depreciation method. (Remember that the business doesn't pay income tax because it's a pass-through tax entity.)

Solve It

Timing Bad Debts Expense

Most businesses extend credit to others, whether that means making sales on credit to other businesses, loaning money to their officers, or loaning money to their vendors and employees. The act of extending credit is backed by some good business reasons, but businesses that do so also take the risk of not being paid. Some debtors may not pay up or pay the full amount owed. Retailers have to live with some amount of shoplifting losses, despite their best efforts to prevent it. In like manner, businesses that extend credit to their customers and make loans have to live with some amount of bad debts expense, despite their best efforts to screen customers and to collect overdue debts. *Bad debts* is the general term for these *uncollectible receivables*.

A business has two options for how it records its bad debts expense:

- **Specific write-off method:** No entry is made for bad debts expense until specific receivables are actually written-off as uncollectible. A receivable is not written off until every conceivable collection effort has been made and the debt has been discharged through bankruptcy proceedings or until the customer (or other debtor) has vanished and can't be traced. One disadvantage of this method is that the receivables asset could be overstated because specific accounts have not as yet been identified as uncollectible that will in fact prove to be uncollectible in the future.

- **Allowance method:** Based on its collection experience with its credit customers (and other debtors) a business records bad debts expense before individual, specific receivables are identified as being uncollectible. The business estimates its bad debts expense, before all the facts are in regarding which particular receivables will have to be written-off as uncollectible. This is a more conservative method than the specific write-off method because bad debts expense is recorded sooner. One disadvantage is that the future amount of bad debts (receivables that will eventually be written-off) has to be estimated. Another disadvantage is that the income tax law does not permit this method to be used by most businesses.

From the data in Figure 9-1, you can see that the business's accounts receivable balance is $645,000 at year-end. The business hasn't loaned money to employees, officers, or vendors. (Non-customer loans are recorded in other accounts, such as loans to officers.) The business didn't write off any customers' receivables during the year; however, at year-end, the amounts owed to the business by a few customers are several months overdue. The business shut off credit to these customers and sent them dun (please pay now) letters. The customers have assured the business that they will pay but just need more time, so they say.

The business has done everything it can to get the customers to pay up, short of bringing legal action. As far as the business knows, none of these customers have declared bankruptcy, but the business has heard a rumor that one customer has contacted a lawyer about bankruptcy. The total amount overdue from these deadbeat customers is $18,500, and the business is of the opinion that the $18,500 will not be collected.

In addition, some other customers are two or three months overdue in paying their accounts. The business understands that some of these debts may end up being uncollectible, but it's still hopeful that these overdue accounts will be collected in full.

Q. Given the preceding background information, how much bad debts expense should the business record at the end of its first year according to:

a. the *specific write-off method* for bad debts expense

b. the *allowance method* for bad debts expense (see information below for this part of the question)?

A. Frankly, coming up with a bad debts expense amount for the year under either bad debts expense accounting method is somewhat arbitrary. Only time will tell exactly how much of the total $645,000 accounts receivable will not be collected.

a. The $18,500 seriously overdue amount of accounts receivable is written off by the specific write-off method for recording bad debts expense. The entry is as follows :

Bad Debts Expense	$18,500
Accounts Receivable	$18,500

The specific accounts receivable making up this $18,500 have been identified. Considering that the company has identified specific customers and made reasonable efforts to collect the amounts owed to it, the receivables should be written off and charged to bad debts expense. This amount of expense is allowed for federal income tax purposes.

After making this write-off entry, the accounts receivable balance is $626,500 ($645,000 balance before write off – $18,500 write off = $626,500 adjusted balance of accounts receivable). Some of this total amount of accounts receivable probably will turn out to be uncollectible. But the specific write-off method does not record these future write-offs at this time. The bad debts expense for the first year is $18,500 and the accounts receivable balance reported in its year-end balance sheet is $626,500.

b. Using the allowance method for recording bad debts expense an additional amount of bad debts expense is recorded for the yet-to-be identified uncollectible receivables. Of course, the accountant has to estimate the amount of future write-offs. (The argument is that some estimate is better than none.) Suppose a conservative estimate of these additional bad debts is $20,000. However, specific customers' accounts haven't been identified for this estimated bad debts amount.

During the year, $18,500 has already been recorded in the bad debts expense account. As the specific receivables were identified as uncollectible during the year the business had no choice but to write-off the receivables and record bad debts expense. Using the allowance method the accountant makes the following additional entry at the end of the year, which increases the bad debts expense account:

Bad Debts Expense	$20,000
Allowance for Doubtful Accounts	$20,000

The Allowance for Doubtful Accounts account is the contra account to the accounts receivable asset account. Its balance is deducted from the asset account's balance in the balance sheet. After giving effect to this year-end entry, the company's bad debts expense for the year is $38,500 ($18,500 actually written-off during the year + $20,000 estimated uncollectible receivables to be written-off in the future). In its year-end balance sheet the business reports accounts receivable at $626,500 and the $20,000 balance in the allowance for doubtful account is deducted from accounts receivable. So, the net amount of accounts receivables in its ending balance sheet is $606,500.

The IRS doesn't allow most businesses to use the allowance bad debts expense method to determine annual taxable income. (This is a terrible pun, isn't it?) Under the income tax rules, specific accounts receivable must actually be written off in order to deduct bad debts as an expense for determining taxable income. (For more information, you can refer to IRS Publication 535, "Business Expenses" (2005), and pay particular attention to the chapter on business bad debts.)

13. The chief accountant of the business outlined in the example question is from the double-breasted, dull grey suit, old guard school of accounting. He argues that a customer's account receivable should be written off as uncollectible when it becomes more than 30 days old. The normal credit term offered by the business to customers is 30 days. At the end of its first year, $278,400 of the company's $645,000 accounts receivable is more than 30 days old. What bad debts expense entry would the chief accountant make at the end of the year if he had his way? Do you agree with his approach?

14. The president of the business outlined in the example question attends an industry update seminar at which the speaker says that the average bad debts experience of businesses in this field is about 1 percent of sales. Assume that the business adopts this method. Determine its bad debts expense for the first year and for the balances in its accounts receivable and allowance for doubtful accounts at the end of the year.

Solve It

The following two questions are comprehensive for this chapter. They draw upon the discussion throughout the chapter and the answers to the example questions in the chapter. In answering these two comprehensive questions you should also refer to the figures in the chapter.

15. Prepare the company's income statement for its first year of business using the conservative accounting methods for cost of goods sold expense, depreciation expense, and bad debts expense.

Solve It

16. Prepare the company's income statement for its first year of business using the liberal accounting methods for cost of goods sold expense, depreciation expense, and bad debts expense.

Solve It

Answers to Problems on Choosing Accounting Methods

The following are the answers to the practice questions presented earlier in this chapter.

1 Does the interest expense in Figure 9-1 look reasonable, or does it need an adjustment at the end of the year?

Asking this kind of question at the end of the year is always a good thing for an accountant to do, to make sure than no account that needs adjustment at year-end is overlooked. In this situation, interest expense is $55,250 (see Figure 9-1). The sum of the business's two notes payable accounts in the year-end listing of accounts is $850,000. From Figure 9-1, you don't know for sure whether these two notes payable were borrowed for the entire year. Assuming that the notes were outstanding the entire year, the following applies:

$55,250 interest expense ÷ $850,000 notes payable = 6.5 percent annual interest rate

If the notes payable were outstanding for less than the full year, then the effective annual interest rate would be higher. Ultimately, the interest expense account probably doesn't need adjusting at the end of the year. The business probably has recorded all interest expense for the year, so it's unlikely that an adjusting entry needs to be recorded at year-end for interest expense.

2 In Figure 9-1 the Owners' Equity — Retained Earnings account has a zero balance. Why?

The final entry of the year is the closing entry in which the net profit or loss for the year is entered into the retained earnings account. The closing entry isn't made until all expenses for the year are recorded. Because the business has just concluded its first year, its retained earnings account had a zero balance at the start of the year. The closing entry to transfer net profit or loss for the year into the account hasn't been made, so retained earnings still has a zero balance. After the accountant records net profit or loss into retained earnings, the account will have a balance, of course.

3 In Figure 9-1, note the Prepaid Expenses asset account at the end of the year. What are three examples of such prepaid costs? Are the methods for allocating these costs to expense fairly objective and noncontroversial?

Three examples of prepaid expenses are:

- **Insurance premiums:** Paid in advance of the insurance coverage. When the premium is paid, the amount is recorded in the prepaid expenses asset account and then the cost is allocated to each month of insurance coverage.

- **Office and operating supplies:** Bought in quantities that last several months. The cost of these purchases is recorded in the prepaid expenses asset account and then allocated to expense as the supplies are used.

- **Property taxes:** Paid at the beginning of the tax year in some states, counties, and cities. The tax paid for the coming year is recorded in the prepaid expenses asset account and then allocated to property tax expense each month or quarter.

Generally speaking, the allocation of these and other prepaid expenses is objective and noncontroversial. Different accountants use the same allocation methods. However, most businesses don't bother to record relatively minor prepaid costs in the asset account and instead record the costs immediately as expenses. For example, a business may give its delivery truck drivers quarters to feed parking meters as they make deliveries to customers. Theoretically, the amount shouldn't be recorded as an expense until the quarters are actually used, but most companies record the expense as soon as they distribute the quarters.

4 In Figure 9-1, note the Accrued Expenses Payable liability account at the end of the year. What are three examples of such accrued costs? Are the methods for allocating these costs to expense fairly objective and noncontroversial?

Three examples of accrued costs are:

- **Vacation and sick pay:** Businesses should accrue the costs of vacation and sick pay that are "earned" by their employees each pay period. (I stress the word "earned" because the actual accumulation of these employee benefits may not be clear-cut and definite. If the business has a collective bargaining contract with its employees these benefits usually are well-defined.)

- **Warranties and guarantees:** Most products sold by businesses come with a warranty or guarantee. After the point of sale, the business incurs costs to service, repair, or replace a product under the terms of its warranty or guarantee. The business should forecast the future costs of fulfilling these obligations.

- **Property taxes:** The business should determine the amount of the property taxes that are paid at the end of the tax year (in arrears) and accumulate the expense during the year.

The accrual of these and other costs isn't cut and dried and tends to be somewhat controversial. The allocation of accrued costs has many shades of gray — there aren't any "bright" lines to delineate which particular costs should be accrued and which ones don't have to be.

5 During its first year, a business made seven acquisitions of a product that it sells. Figure 9-3 presents the history of these purchases. Compare the purchases history in Figure 9-3 with the one in Figure 9-2. Does the average cost method make more sense or seem more persuasive in one case over the other?

This is a hard question to answer, to be frank, because the appropriateness of the average cost method depends on how you look at it. You could argue that you have a little more reason to use the average cost method in the Figure 9-3 scenario because the purchase price bounces up and down, whereas in the Figure 9-2 scenario, the purchase prices are on an upward trend. But, by and large, accountants do not consider whether prices fluctuate up and down or are on a steady up escalator in making the decision to use the average cost method. Accountants like the "leveling out" effect of the average cost method. This is main reason why they prefer the method.

6 Refer to the purchase history in Figure 9-3. The bookkeeper said he was using the average cost method. He calculated the average of the seven purchase costs per unit and multiplied this average unit cost by the 158,100 units sold during the year. His average cost per unit is $24.76 (rounded). Is this the correct way to apply the average cost method? If not, what is the correct answer for cost of goods sold expense for the year?

The bookkeeper made a mistake because the average cost method doesn't use the simple average of purchases prices. The average cost method uses the *weighted* average of acquisition prices, which means that each purchase price is weighted by the quantity bought at that price. In the Figure 9-3 scenario, the $26.15 purchase price carries much less weight because only 6,100 units were bought at this price. The $23.05 purchase price carries more weight because 36,500 units were bought at this price.

The correct average cost per unit is calculated as follows:

($4,493,140 total cost of purchases ÷ 186,000 units purchased) = $24.1567, or $24.16 rounded

Therefore, the correct cost of goods sold expense for the period is $3,819,169. You can calculate this amount by multiplying the exact average cost per unit by the 158,100 units sold, or you can calculate it as follows:

(158,100 units sold ÷ 186,000 units available for sale) × $4,493,140 total cost of goods available for sale = $3,819,169 cost of goods sold expense

7　Figure 9-3 presents the inventory acquisition history of a business for its first year. The business sold 158,100 units during the year. By the FIFO method, determine its cost of goods sold expense for the year and its cost of ending inventory.

The cost of goods sold expense by the FIFO method is determined as follows:

Source	Quantity	Per Unit	Cost
First purchase	14,200 Units	$25.75	$365,650
Second purchase	42,500 Units	$23.85	$1,013,625
Third purchase	16,500 Units	$24.85	$410,025
Fourth purchase	36,500 Units	$23.05	$841,325
Fifth purchase	6,100 Units	$26.15	$159,515
Sixth purchase	42,300 Units	$23.65	$1,000,395
Totals	158,100 Units		$3,790,535

The cost of ending inventory includes some units from the sixth purchase and all units from the seventh purchase, which is summarized in the following schedule:

Source	Quantity	Per Unit	Cost
Sixth purchase	9,700 Units	$23.65	$229,405
Seventh purchase	18,200 Units	$26.00	$473,200
Totals	27,900 Units		$702,605

8　In the example shown in Figure 9-3, the purchase cost per unit bounces up and down over successive acquisitions, and the quantities purchased each time vary quite a bit. Do these two factors play a role in the choice of a cost of goods sold method?

Generally speaking, the volatility of acquisition costs per unit isn't a critical factor in choosing a cost of goods sold expense method, nor is the variation in acquisition quantities. The reasons for selecting one method over another don't depend on these two factors.

9　Figure 9-3 presents the inventory acquisition history of a business for its first year. The business sold 158,100 units during the year. By the LIFO method, determine its cost of goods sold expense for the year and its cost of ending inventory.

The cost of goods sold expense as determined by the LIFO is as follows:

Source	Quantity	Per Unit	Cost
Seventh purchase	18,200 Units	$26.00	$473,200
Sixth purchase	52,000 Units	$23.65	$1,229,800
Fifth purchase	6,100 Units	$26.15	$159,515
Fourth purchase	36,500 Units	$23.05	$841,325
Third purchase	16,500 Units	$24.85	$410,025
Second purchase	28,800 Units	$23.85	$686,880
Totals	158,100 Units		$3,800,745

The cost of ending inventory includes all the units from the first purchase and some from the second purchase, which is summarized as follows:

Source	Quantity	Per Unit	Cost
Second purchase	13,700 Units	$23.85	$326,745
Third purchase	14,200 Units	$25.75	$365,650
Totals	27,900 Units		$692,395

10　Suppose the business whose inventory acquisition history appears in Figure 9-3 sold all 186,000 units that it had available for sale during the year. In this situation, does the business's choice of cost of goods sold expense method make any difference?

No, all three methods (average cost, FIFO, and LIFO) give the same result. The $4,493,140 total purchase cost of the 186,000 units would be charged to cost of goods sold expense.

11 Determine the annual depreciation amounts on the machines for years two through seven according to the double declining method. Also, determine the *book value* (cost less accumulated depreciation) at the end of each year.

The complete depreciation schedule of the machines over their estimated seven years of life is presented as follows:

Year	Cost less Accumulated Depreciation at Start of Year	Annual Depreciation	Fraction Applied on Declining Balance
1	$532,000	$152,000	2/7
2	$380,000	$108,571	2/7
3	$271,429	$77,551	2/7
4	$193,878	$55,394	2/7
5	$138,484	$46,161	See Note
6	$92,323	$46,161	See Note
7	$46,161	$46,161	See Note
Total		$532,000	

Note: The $138,484 balance at the start of Year 5 is allocated to years 5, 6, and 7 by straight-line method.

Note the "Cost less Accumulated Depreciation at Start of Year" column in the schedule. These are the book values of the asset at the start of each year, which are the same as the book value at the end of the previous year. For instance, the $380,000 book value at the start of year 2 is the same as the book value at the end of year 1. And so on. At the end of year 7 the book value is down to zero, because the $532,000 accumulated depreciation equals the original cost of the asset.

12 Instead of using the double-declining depreciation method for its machines, suppose the business used the straight-line depreciation method over seven years. Determine the year-by-year difference in bottom-line profit with the straight-line depreciation method. (Remember that the business doesn't pay income tax because it's a pass-through tax entity.)

Year	Double Declining Depreciation	Straight-line Depreciation	Net Income Difference Using Straight-line Depreciation
1	$152,000	$76,000	$76,000
2	$108,571	$76,000	$32,571
3	$77,551	$76,000	$1,551
4	$55,394	$76,000	($20,606)
5	$46,161	$76,000	($29,839)
6	$46,161	$76,000	($29,839)
7	$46,161	$76,000	($29,839)
Totals	$532,000	$532,000	$0

13 The chief accountant of the business outlined in the example question is from the double-breasted, dull grey suit, old guard school of accounting. He argues that a customer's account receivable should be written off as uncollectible when it becomes more than 30 days old. The normal credit term offered by the business to customers is 30 days. At the end of its first year, $278,400 of the company's $645,000 accounts receivable is more than 30 days old. What bad debts expense entry would the chief accountant make if he had his way at the end of the year? Do you agree with his approach?

If the chief accountant had his way, he would make the following entry:

Bad Debts Expense	$278,400
Accounts Receivable	$278,400

I certainly don't agree with writing off such a large amount of accounts receivable. In the real world of business, many customers don't pay on time; indeed, late payment by some customers is expected any time credit's extended. The business would like to receive all payments for its credit sales on time, of course, but it knows that many of its customers probably won't make their payments within 30 days. The chief accountant needs to get real and understand that many customers slip beyond the 30-day credit period but eventually pay for their purchases.

14 The president of the business outlined in the example question attends an industry update seminar at which the speaker says that the average bad debts experience of businesses in this field is about 1 percent of sales. Assume the business adopts this method. Determine its bad debts expense for the first year and for the balances in its accounts receivable and allowance for doubtful accounts at the end of the year.

The year-end adjusting entry is as follows:

Bad Debts Expense	$45,850
Allowance for Doubtful Accounts	$45,850

To record bad debts expense equal to 1.0% of total sales for year.

The business also records the write off specific customers' accounts that have been identified as uncollectible. The write-off entry is as follows:

Allowance for Doubtful Accounts	$18,500
Accounts Receivable	$18,500

To record write off of uncollectible accounts.

Based on the information provided in the example, using 1 percent of sales to estimate bad debts expense seems too high for this particular business. And, as I mention in the chapter, the IRS doesn't allow the allowance method for income tax purposes.

15 Prepare the company's income statement for its first year of business using the conservative accounting methods for cost of goods sold expense, depreciation expense, and bad debts expense.

Using LIFO for cost of goods sold expense, accelerated depreciation for machines, and the allowance method for bad debts expense, the income statement of the business for its first year is as follows:

Income Statement for First Year

Sales Revenue		$4,585,000
Cost of Goods Sold Expense:		
Beginning inventory	$0	
Purchases	$3,725,000	
Available for sale	$3,725,000	
Ending inventory	$708,000	$3,017,000
Gross Profit		$1,568,000
Depreciation expense	$164,000	
Bad debts expense	$38,500	
Selling and General Expenses	$1,033,000	$1,235,500
Operating Profit before Interest		$332,500
Interest Expense		$55,250
Net Income		$277,250

16 Prepare the company's income statement for its first year of business using the liberal accounting methods for cost of goods sold expense, depreciation expense, and bad debts expense.

Using FIFO for cost of goods sold expense, straight-line depreciation for machines, and the specific charge off method for bad debts expense, the income statement of the business for its first year is as follows:

Income Statement for First Year

Sales Revenue		$4,585,000
Cost of Goods Sold Expense:		
Beginning inventory	$0	
Purchases	$3,725,000	
Available for sale	$3,725,000	
Ending inventory	$800,000	$2,925,000
Gross Profit		$1,660,000
Depreciation expense	$88,000	
Bad debts expense	$18,500	
Selling and General Expenses	$1,033,000	$1,139,500
Operating Profit before Interest		$520,500
Interest Expense		$55,250
Net Income		$465,250

For additional insight, compare the net income in your answer using liberal accounting methods to your answer to Question 15, which asks you to use conservative accounting methods. You'll find that net income is $188,000 higher using liberal accounting methods, or 68 percent higher than the profit determined by using conservative accounting methods in Question 15.

Part III
Managerial, Manufacturing, and Capital Accounting

The 5th Wave   By Rich Tennant

"I ran an evaluation of our last pie chart.
Apparently it's boysenberry."

In this part . . .

The first chapter in this part explains the accountant's essential role in helping business managers do their jobs well. In broad terms, managers need financial information for planning, control, and decision-making. Accountants should develop profit analysis models that managers can use efficiently — so they make optimal decisions based on the key factors that drive profit.

For manufacturing businesses, accountants have the additional function of determining the product cost of the goods produced by the business. In Chapter 11, I explain plain words manufacturing cost accounting fundamentals. The chapter explains the importance of calculating the burden rate for indirect fixed manufacturing overhead costs that is included in product cost, and how production output (not just sales) affects profit for the period.

Chapter 12 explains nominal and effective interest rates, how compounding works both for and against you, and return on investment (ROI) measures. At their core, interest and investment ratios are based on accounting methods.

Chapter 10

Analyzing Profit Behavior

Business managers need a sure analytical grip on the fundamental factors that drive profit. And because profit is an *accounting* measure, chief accountants should help the business's managers understand and analyze profit performance. The trick is not to overload managers with so much detail that they can't see the forest for the trees.

Now, don't get me wrong. Detail is necessary for *management control;* managers need to keep their eyes on a thousand and one details, any one of which can spin out of control and cause serious damage to profit performance. But too much detail is the enemy of profit analysis for planning and decision-making. Management control requires gobs of detailed information. Management decision-making, in contrast, needs condensed and global information presented in a compact package that the manager can get his or her head around without getting sidetracked by too many details.

The profit analysis methods that I discuss in this chapter can be done on the back of an envelope. All you need for the number crunching is a basic hand-held calculator. More elaborate and detail-rich profit analysis methods need to be done on computers. These sophisticated profit analysis methods have their place, but before they delve into technical profit analysis, managers should be absolutely clear on the fundamental factors that determine profit. The idea is to make sure one knows how to read the dashboard before going under the hood and taking apart the engine.

This chapter tackles three main questions:

✔ How did the business make its profit?

✔ How can the business improve its profit performance?

✔ How would unfavorable changes affect the business's profit performance?

Mapping Profit for Managers

Figure 10-1 lays out an internal profit (P&L) report for the business's managers. The revenue and expense information is for the most recent year of a business that I call Company A. (I introduce two other business examples later in this chapter and call them Company B and Company C.) An internal profit report should serve as a profit map that shows managers how to get to their profit destination. The profit report in Figure 10-1 is very condensed; it's stripped down to bare essentials. It includes the five fundamental factors that drive profit performance. These key profit drivers are the following:

   ✔ **Sales volume**, or the total number of units sold during the period

   ✔ **Sales revenue per unit** (sales price)

   ✔ **Cost of goods sold expense per unit** (product cost)

   ✔ **Variable operating expenses per unit**

   ✔ **Fixed operating expenses** for the period

The other dollar amounts in the profit report (Figure 10-1) depend on these five profit drivers. For instance, the $24,000,000 sales revenue amount equals the 120,000 units sales volume times the $200 sales revenue per unit (or sales price). And, the $25 fixed operating expenses per unit amount equals the $3,000,000 total fixed operating expenses for the period divided by the 120,000 units sales volume.

	Company A	
	Totals	Per Unit
Sales volume, in units	120,000	
Sales revenue	$24,000,000	$200.00
Cost of goods sold expense	$15,600,000	$130.00
Gross margin	$8,400,000	$70.00
Variable operating expenses	$3,600,000	$30.00
Contribution margin	$4,800,000	$40.00
Fixed operating expenses	$3,000,000	$25.00
Operating profit	$1,800,000	$15.00

Figure 10-1: Internal profit (P&L) report (highlighting profit drivers).

Don't confuse the internal profit report presented in Figure 10-1 with the income statement in the external financial reports a business distributes to its owners and creditors. (I discuss externally reported financial statements in Chapters 5, 6, and 8.) The internal profit report (Figure 10-1) includes sales volume and per unit values, which aren't disclosed in externally reported income statements. Also, the internal profit report separates operating expenses into *variable* and *fixed* categories, which isn't done in externally reported income statements.

The last line in Figure 10-1 is *operating* profit, which is profit before interest and income tax. Interest and income tax are deducted to reach a business's final, bottom-line net income. Income tax is a very technical topic, which makes it difficult to generalize. Some businesses are pass-through entities and don't pay income tax directly. Some businesses receive special tax breaks, and some businesses operate overseas where income taxes are quite different than in the United States.

Standard terminology doesn't exist in the area of management profit reporting and analysis. Instead of *gross margin,* you may see *gross profit.* Instead of *operating profit,* you may see *operating earnings* or *earnings before interest and income tax* (EBIT). You may even see other terms than these. Despite the diversity of terminology, in the context of a profit report, the meanings of terms used are usually clear enough.

Before using the five profit factors for analyzing profit performance, a good thing to do is to "walk down the profit ladder" in the internal profit report (Figure 10-1). The top rung of the ladder is *sales revenue,* which equals sales price times sales volume. You can think of sales revenue as profit before any expenses are deducted. If the business sells products, the first expense deducted against sales revenue is *cost of goods sold,* which equals product cost (cost of goods sold expense per unit) times sales volume. (Chapter 9 explains the different accounting methods for recording this expense.) Deducting cost of goods sold from sales revenue gives you *gross margin.* Managers keep a close watch on the *gross margin ratio,* which for Company A equals 35 percent ($70 gross margin per unit ÷ $200 sales price = 35% gross margin ratio). Even a relatively small shift in this ratio can have huge impacts on profit.

Virtually all businesses have *variable operating expenses,* which are costs that move in tandem with changes in sales revenue. One example of a variable expense is the commissions paid to salespersons, which typically are a certain percent of sales revenue. Other examples of variable expenses that fluctuate with sales are delivery expenses and bad debts from credit sales. Total variable operating expenses equal variable operating expenses per unit times sales volume. Deducting variable operating expenses from gross margin produces *contribution margin,* or profit before fixed operating expenses are considered.

Businesses commit to a certain level of *fixed operating expenses* for the year. Examples of fixed expenses are property taxes, employees on fixed salaries, insurance, depreciation, legal and accounting, and so on. In the short run, fixed costs behave like the term implies — they're relatively fixed and constant in amount regardless of whether sales are high or low. Fixed costs aren't sensitive to fluctuations in sales over the short term. Company A's $3,000,000 fixed operating expenses for the period are divided by its 120,000 units sales volume to determine the $25 fixed operating expenses per unit in Figure 10-1.

The final step in the walk down the profit ladder is deducting fixed operating expenses from contribution margin. The remainder is the business's *operating profit* for the year. The business earned $1,800,000 operating profit for the year, which is 7.5 percent of its sales revenue for the year. Internal operating profit (P&L) reports often include ratios (percents) for each line item based on sales revenue, so managers can track changes in these important ratios period to period.

Q. Refer to the Company A example presented in Figure 10-1. Purely hypothetically, suppose the business could have sold either 5 percent more sales volume or it could have sold the same sales volume at a 5 percent higher sales price. Assume other profit factors remain the same. Which change — the 5 percent higher sales volume, or the 5 percent higher sales price — would have been better for operating profit?

A. Well, 5 percent additional sales volume means the business would have sold 6,000 more units than in the Figure 10-1 scenario: (120,000 units sales volume in Figure 10-1 × 5% = 6,000 additional units). Each additional unit sold would earn $40 contribution margin per unit (see Figure 10-1). So, total contribution margin would have been $240,000 higher. The business's fixed operating expenses would not have increased with such a relatively small increase in sales volume. Therefore, its operating

profit would have been $240,000 higher. Would the sales price increase have been any better? You bet it would!

A 5 percent jump means sales price would have been $10 per unit higher: ($200 sales price in Figure 10-1 × 5% = $10 increase in sales price). This would have increased the contribution margin per unit from $40 (see Figure 10-1) to $50. Therefore, the business's total contribution margin would have been $6,000,000: ($50 contribution per unit × 120,000 units sales volume = $6,000,000 contribution margin). This would be an increase of $1,200,000 over the contribution margin in the Figure 10-1 scenario. There's no reason to think that fixed operating expenses would be any different at the higher sales price, so operating profit would have increased $1,200,000.

In short, the 5 percent gain in sales price would have been much better for operating profit, compared with the 5 percent step up in sales volume.

Analyzing Operating Profit

When handed an internal operating profit report like the one presented in Figure 10-1, a business manager may say "thanks for the information" and leave it at that. An internal profit report like the one in Figure 10-1 is prepared according to the standard accounting approach, which reports *totals* for sales revenue and expenses for the period and which starts with sales revenue and works its way down to bottom line profit (operating profit in the Figure 10-1 example). There's nothing wrong with this sort of report. Indeed, managers would be surprised not to get such profit reports on a regular basis.

However, the layout of the typical accounting internal profit report is cumbersome for analyzing profit behavior. As you know, business managers are busy people. They don't have a lot of time to wade through an accounting profit report to analyze the impact of a change in sales volume, or a change in sales price, or a change in any of the key factors that drive profit. An accounting profit report is not the best format for the efficient analysis of profit behavior.

Busy business managers can analyze the profit performance of their business more efficiently using compact profit models based on the five fundamental profit drivers. There are different analysis methods, each having certain advantages. Managers are best advised to be familiar with three profit analysis methods:

- Contribution margin minus fixed costs method
- Excess over breakeven method
- Minimizing fixed costs per unit method

Analysis method #1: Contribution margin minus fixed costs

The basis of this method is that fixed costs have a first claim on contribution margin, and what's left over is operating profit. This method starts with *contribution margin per unit*, which is the catalyst of profit. To make profit, the business has to have an adequate margin per unit. The second step of this method is to multiply contribution margin per unit by sales volume. Earning a margin on each unit sold doesn't help much if a business doesn't sell many units. (Which reminds me of the old joke, "A business loses a little on each sale, but makes it up on volume.")

Using this method Company A's profit for the year is analyzed as follows:

Analysis method #1: Contribution margin minus fixed costs (see Figure 10-1 for data)

Contribution margin per unit	$40
Times annual sales volume, in units	120,000
Equals total contribution margin	$4,800,000
Less fixed operating expenses	$3,000,000
Equals operating profit	$1,8000,000

Analysis method #2: Excess over breakeven

The thinking behind this method is that a business has to first recover its fixed costs by selling enough units before it starts making profit.

This profit analysis technique pivots on the *breakeven volume* of the business, which you calculate as follows for Company A (see Figure 10-1 for data):

> $3,000,000 annual fixed operating expenses ÷ $40 contribution margin per unit = 75,000 units breakeven point (volume)

Every additional unit sold over the breakeven volume brings in *marginal profit* (also referred to as *incremental profit*.) The underlying theme of this method is that after you sell enough units to recoup your fixed operating expenses for the year, you're "home free" as it were. (Of course, you can't forget about interest expense and income tax.)

Using this method Company A's profit for the year is analyzed as follows:

Analysis method #2: Excess over breakeven (see Figure 10-1 for data)

Annual sales volume for year, in units	120,000
Less annual breakeven volume, in units	75,000
Equals excess over breakeven, in units	45,000
Times contribution margin per unit	$40
Equals operating profit	$1,800,000

Analysis method #3: Minimizing fixed costs per unit

The thinking behind this method of analyzing profit is that a business has to spread its fixed costs over enough sales volume to drive the average fixed cost per unit below its contribution per unit. In this way, the business makes operating profit.

In this method of profit analysis, you compare the contribution margin per unit with *fixed operating expenses per unit*, which you calculate by dividing annual fixed operating expenses by the number of units sold. For Company A, its average fixed operating expenses per unit are

> $3,000,000 annual fixed operating expenses ÷ 120,000 units sold = $25 fixed operating expenses per unit sold

The spread between the contribution margin per unit and the average fixed costs per unit gives the profit per unit, which is scaled up by sales volume as follows:

Analysis method #3: Minimizing fixed costs per unit (see Figure 10-1 for data)

Contribution margin per unit	$40
Less average fixed operating expenses per unit	$25
Equals average profit per unit	$15
Times annual sales volume, in units	120,000
Equals operating profit	$1,800,000

0. Suppose Company A had sold 125,000 units during the year, instead of the 120,000 units in the Figure 10-1 scenario. Using each of the three analysis methods just explained, determine Company A's operating profit at the 125,000 units sales volume level. Assume other profit factors remain the same.

A. The operating profit of Company A is analyzed for this scenario according to the three methods of profit analysis.

Analysis method #1: Contribution margin minus fixed costs (see Figure 10-1 for data)

Contribution margin per unit	$40
Times annual sales volume, in units	125,000
Equals total contribution margin	$5,000,000
Less fixed operating expenses	$3,000,000
Equals operating profit	$2,000,000

Analysis method #2: Excess over breakeven (see Figure 10-1 for data)

Annual sales volume for year, in units	125,000
Less annual breakeven volume, in units	75,000
Equals excess over breakeven, in units	50,000
Times contribution margin per unit	$40
Equals operating profit	$2,000,000

Analysis method #3: Minimizing fixed costs per unit (see Figure 10-1 for data)

Contribution margin per unit	$40
Less average fixed operating expenses per unit	$24
Equals average profit per unit	$16
Times annual sales volume, in units	125,000
Equals operating profit	$2,000,000

---

1. One of Company A's marketing managers was overheard to comment, "If we had sold 10 percent more units than we did in the year, our profit would have been 10 percent higher." Do you agree with this comment? (Figure 10-1 presents Company A's operating profit report for the year.)

Solve It

2. Instead of the scenario shown in Figure 10-1 assume that Company A had a bad year. Its internal operating profit report for this alternative scenario is presented below. Using the three methods explained in this section, analyze why the business suffered a loss for the year.

	Totals	Per Unit
Sales volume, in units	120,000	
Sales revenue	$21,000,000	$175.00
Cost of goods sold expense	$15,600,000	$130.00
Gross margin	$5,400,000	$45.00
Variable operating expenses	$3,150,000	$26.25
Contribution margin	$2,250,000	$18.75
Fixed operating expenses	$3,000,000	$25.00
Operating profit (loss)	($750,000)	($6.25)

Solve It

3. Figure 10-2 presents profit performance information for two businesses for their most recent years. Using the three profit analysis methods explained in this section, analyze the profit performance of Company B. (You may note that both businesses in Figure 10-2 earned exactly the same amount of operating profit as the Company A business example for which I explain three profit analysis methods in this section. This similarity allows you to compare the key differences between businesses that earn the same profit.)

	Company B		Company C	
	Totals	Per Unit	Totals	Per Unit
Sales volume, in units	50,000		1,500,000	
Sales revenue	$15,000,000	$300.00	$36,000,000	$24.00
Cost of goods sold expense	$7,500,000	$150.00	$27,000,000	$18.00
Gross margin	$7,500,000	$150.00	$9,000,000	$6.00
Variable operating expenses	$3,750,000	$75.00	$4,200,000	$2.80
Contribution margin	$3,750,000	$75.00	$4,800,000	$3.20
Fixed operating expenses	$1,950,000	$39.00	$3,000,000	$2.00
Operating profit	$1,800,000	$36.00	$1,800,000	$1.20

Figure 10-2: Internal profit (P&L) reports for two business examples.

Solve It

4. Please refer to Figure 10-2. Using the three profit analysis methods explained in this section, analyze the profit performance of Company C. (You may note that both businesses in Figure 10-2 earned exactly the same amount of operating profit as the Company A business example for which I explain three profit analysis methods in this section. This similarity allows you to compare the key differences between businesses that earn the same profit.)

Solve It

Analyzing Return on Capital

Evaluating the financial performance of a business includes looking at how its profit stacks up against the capital used by the business. Figure 10-1 presents Company A's profit performance for the year down to the operating profit before interest and income tax. Did the business earn enough operating profit relative to the *capital* it used to make this profit?

Suppose, purely hypothetically, that Company A used $100,000,000 capital to earn its $1,800,000 operating profit. In this situation, the business would have earned a measly 1.8 percent *rate of return* on the capital used to generate the profit:

$1,800,000 operating profit ÷ $100,000,000 capital = 1.8 percent rate of return

By almost any standard, 1.8 percent is a dismal return on capital performance.

In general terms, the amount of capital a business uses equals its total assets minus its operating liabilities that don't charge interest. The main examples of non–interest bearing operating liabilities are accounts payable from purchases on credit and accrued expenses payable. (I discuss these two liabilities in Chapters 6 and 7.) Operating liabilities typically account for 20 percent or more or a business's total assets. The remainder of its assets (total assets less total operating liabilities) is the amount of capital the business has to raise from two basic sources: borrowing money on the basis of *interest-bearing debt* instruments, and raising *equity (ownership) capital* from private or public sources.

Assume the following:

Company A's Sources of Capital:

Debt	$4,000,000
Owners' equity	$8,000,000
Total capital	$12,000,000

Company A's *return on capital* for the year is:

$1,800,000 operating margin ÷ $12,000,000 capital = 15.0 percent return on capital

Company A's interest expense for the year on its debt is $240,000. Deducting interest from the $1,800,000 operating profit earned by the business gives $1,560,000 profit before income tax. The *rate of return on equity* (before income tax) for the business is calculated as follows:

$1,560,000 profit before income tax ÷ $8,000,000 owners' equity = 19.5 percent return on equity

Q. Company A earned 15.0 percent return on capital (see the preceding calculation), but its return on equity is 19.5 percent, which is quite a bit higher. How do you explain the difference?

A. The higher rate of return on equity is due to a *financial leverage gain* for the year.

Debt supplies ⅓ of the company's capital ($4,000,000 ÷ $12,000,000 total capital = ⅓). The business earned 15 percent return on its debt capital ($4,000,000 debt × 15 percent rate of return = $600,000 return on debt capital). Because interest is a contractually fixed amount per period, the business had to pay only $240,000 interest for the use of its debt capital.

The excess of operating profit earned on debt capital over the amount of interest is called *financial leverage gain*. Company A made $360,000 financial leverage gain for the year ($600,000 operating profit earned on debt capital − $240,000 interest paid on debt = $360,000 financial leverage gain).

The owners supply ⅔ of the total capital of the business, so their share of the $1,800,000 operating profit earned by the business equals $1,200,000 ($1,800,000 operating profit × ⅔ = $1,200,000 share of operating profit). In addition, the owners pick up the $360,000 financial leverage gain. Therefore, the profit before income tax for owners equals $1,560,000 ($1,200,000 owners' share of operating profit + $360,000 financial leverage gain = $1,560,000 profit before income tax). The $1,560,000 profit before income tax yields the 19.5 percent on equity that triggered this question.

Financial leverage is a double-edged sword. Suppose, for example, that in the example scenario, Company A earned only $240,000 operating profit for the year. Interest is a contractual obligation that can't be avoided. In this situation, all Company A's operating profit would go to its debt holders, and profit after interest (before income tax) for its owners would be zero. The business would have had a *financial leverage loss* that wiped out profit for its owners. When a business suffers an operating loss, the burden of interest expense compounds the felony and makes matters just that much worse for shareowners.

5. Assume the following:

Company B's Sources of Capital:

Debt	$8,000,000
Owners' equity	$4,000,000
Total capital	$12,000,000

See Figure 10-2 for Company B's operating profit performance for the year. The business paid $480,000 interest for the year. Calculate its financial leverage gain (or loss) for the year.

Solve It

6. Assume the following:

Company C's Sources of Capital:

Debt	$6,000,000
Owners' equity	$6,000,000
Total capital	$12,000,000

See Figure 10-2 for Company C's profit data for the year. The business paid $360,000 interest for the year. Calculate its financial leverage gain (or loss) for the year.

Solve It

7. Suppose that Company B's fixed operating expenses were $3,030,000 for the year. Otherwise, other profit factors are the same as in Figure 10-2. Using the sources of capital and interest expense presented in Question 5, calculate Company B's financial leverage gain (or loss) for the year.

Solve It

8. Suppose that Company C's fixed operating expenses were $4,440,000 for the year. Otherwise, other profit factors are the same as in Figure 10-2. Using the sources of capital and interest expense presented in Question 6, calculate Company C's financial leverage gain (or loss) for the year.

Solve It

Improving Profit Performance

Business managers are always looking for ways to improve profit performance (or they should be). One obvious way to improve profit is to sell more units — to move more units out the door without reducing sales prices. A business may have to increase its market share to sell more volume, which is no easy task as I'm sure you know. Or perhaps the business is in a growing market and doesn't have to increase its market share. In any case, the logical place to begin profit improvement analysis is an increase in sales volume.

Selling more units

Every business would like to have sold more units than they did during the most recent period. Take the publisher of this book for example, Wiley Publishing, Inc. I'm certain that the company would like to have sold more copies of Dummies books than the actual number sold during the past year. All businesses are on the lookout for how to increase sales volume. A fundamental growth strategy is to increase sales volume.

Q. According to Figure 10-1, Company A sold 120,000 units during the year. If the business had sold 5 percent more units, would its profit have been 5 percent higher? You might quickly review the answer to the example question in the section "Mapping Profit For Managers," which I extend in the following answer.

A. Before I can answer this question, I need to address an important point: When you start simulating increases in sales volume, you have to make assumptions every step of the way. In this case, the question asks you to simulate a 5 percent (6,000 additional units) increase in sales volume to

see what happens in the profit example (shown in Figure 10-1). In order to answer the question, you have to assume

- That the sale price (average sales revenue per unit) stays the same at $200 per unit

- That the product cost per unit remains the same at $130 per unit

- That variable operating expenses hold the same at 15 percent of sales revenue

- That Company A's fixed operating expenses stay the same at $3,000,000 for the year

The last assumption is an important one to understand because it means that the business has enough unused, or untapped, capacity to sell an additional 6,000 units of product. In other words, you're assuming that there was some slack in the organization such that it could have sold 6,000 more units without stepping up its fixed costs to support the higher sales volume. For relatively small changes in sales volume, that circumstance is probably true in most situations. But on the other hand, what if the question had asked you to simulate an increase in sales volume of 30, 40, or 50 percent? With a change of this extent, a business probably would have to hire more people, buy more delivery trucks, buy or rent more warehouse space, and so on — with the result that its fixed operating expenses would be higher at the higher sales volume level.

Capacity is a broad concept that refers to the capability of a business to handle sales activity. It encompasses all the resources needed to make sales, including employees, machines, manufacturing and warehouse space, retail space, and so on. Many of the costs of capacity are fixed in nature.

Keeping in mind the assumptions listed, operating profit would have increased much more than 5 percent if Company A had sold 5 percent more units during the year. The key point is this: Contribution margin would stay the same at $40 per unit because sales price, product cost, and variable operating expenses per unit all remain the same (see Figure 10-1). So the additional 6,000 units would have generated $240,000 additional contribution margin:

$40 contribution margin per unit × 6,000 units sales volume increase = $240,000 contribution margin increase

Assuming that fixed operating expenses remain the same at the higher sales volume, operating profit increases $240,000 from a 5 percent increase in sales volume. This is an increase of over 13 percent:

$240,000 operating profit increase × $1,800,000 operating profit = 13.3 percent increase in contribution margin

In the end, a sales volume increase of only 5 percent would increase operating profit over 13 percent! How do you like that?

In the example scenario, the bigger 13.3 percent swing in profit compared with the 5 percent change in sales volume is referred to as *operating leverage*. At the higher sales volume, the business gets more leverage, or better utilization, from its fixed operating expenses. At a lower sales volume, the percent drop in profit would be more severe than the percent drop in sales volume. In other words, the magnifying effect of operating leverage works both ways.

---

9. Suppose Company B sold 10 percent more units during the year than it did according to Figure 10-2. Determine Company B's operating profit for this scenario. (Assume fixed operating expenses remain the same at the higher sales volume.)

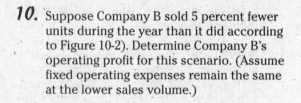

Solve It

10. Suppose Company B sold 5 percent fewer units during the year than it did according to Figure 10-2). Determine Company B's operating profit for this scenario. (Assume fixed operating expenses remain the same at the lower sales volume.)

Solve It

11. Suppose Company C sold 5 percent more units during the year than it did according to Figure 10-2. Determine Company C's operating profit for this scenario. (Assume fixed operating expenses remain the same at the higher sales volume.)

Solve It

12. Suppose Company C sold 10 percent fewer units during the year than it did according to Figure 10-2. Determine Company C's operating profit for this scenario. (Assume fixed operating expenses remain the same at the lower sales volume.)

Solve It

Improving margin per unit

Another way to improve operating profit is to increase the *contribution margin per unit,* without increasing sales volume. Actually improving contribution margin per unit is very difficult in the real world of business. To increase contribution margin per unit you have to increase sales price, decrease product cost, decrease variable operating expenses per unit, or some combination of these. None of these profit factors are easy to improve in the real world of business, that's for sure.

Q. Suppose Company A (see Figure 10-1) wants to improve its contribution margin per unit as the means to order to increase its operating profit $240,000. Assume its 120,000 units sales volume remains the same. Assume, further, that the business targeted its product cost as the most feasible way to improve contribution margin per unit. So, assume that sales price, variable operating expenses per unit, and fixed operating expenses remain the same. How

much would product cost have to improve to achieve the $240,000 increase in operating profit?

A. The needed improvement in contribution margin per unit is calculated as follows:

$240,000 desired increase in operating profit ÷ 120,000 units sales volume = $2 improvement needed in contribution margin per unit

Therefore, the business would have to reduce its product cost (cost of goods sold per unit) by $2, from $130 to $128 per unit. Now, this may not sound like such a difficult task. However, the business may have already cut its product cost to the bone. Trying to squeeze another $2 reduction out of product cost may not be realistic. If the business cannot reduce product cost $2 per unit, it has to look at sales price or variable operating expenses per unit in order to improve contribution margin. Raising sales price $2 per unit, or lowering variable operating expenses $2 per unit may be no easier than reducing product cost $2 per unit.

13. Suppose that Company B was able to improve (lower) its product cost per unit $10. Assume that all other profit factors for Company B remain the same as shown in Figure 10-2. Determine its operating profit for this scenario. Also, how does this change affect the company's breakeven sales volume?

14. Suppose that Company C's product cost increases $0.50 per unit. Assume that all other profit factors for Company C remain the same as shown in Figure 10-2. Determine its operating profit for this scenario. Also, how does this change affect the company's breakeven sales volume?

In the preceding example I focus on lowering product cost as one basic way to improve contribution margin per unit. Another basic strategy for improving contribution margin per unit is to increase sales price. Sales prices are the province of marketing managers. I'd be the first to admit that I am not a marketing expert. Setting sales prices is a complex decision involving consumer psychology and many other factors. Nevertheless, in discussing the general topic of how to improve contribution margin per unit I should say a few words about raising sales price — mainly to show the powerful impact of a higher sales price.

You don't get too far in discussing raising sales price without bumping into a problem concerning variable operating expenses per unit. Most businesses have *two* types of variable operating expenses. Some vary with *sales volume* (the number of units sold) and some vary with *sales revenue* (the number of dollars from sales). For example, sales commissions depend on the dollar amount of sales. In contrast, packing and shipping costs depend on the number of units sold and delivered.

EXAMPLE

Q. Suppose that Company B (see Figure 10-2 for its profit data) could increase its sales price $15 per unit and sell the same number of units. Assume Company B's volume-driven variable operating expenses are $15 per unit sold, and its revenue-driven variable operating expenses are 20 percent of sales revenue. How would this $15 sales price increase affect its contribution margin per unit, total contribution margin, and operating profit?

A. If the business raises sales price $15, its volume-driven expenses per unit remain the same, but its revenue-driven expenses

increase $3 per unit, which is 20 percent of the $15 sales price increase. So, the net gain in contribution margin per unit is only $12. Therefore,

$12 net increase in contribution margin per unit × 50,000 units sales volume = $600,000 contribution margin increase

Company B's fixed operating expenses should remain the same (a sales price increase should have no bearing on a business's fixed operating expenses). Therefore, the increase in contribution margin would increase the business's operating profit $600,000.

15. Suppose that Company B had to drop its sales price $10 due to competitive pressures. All other profit factors remain the same as shown in Figure 10-2. The company's volume-driven variable expenses are $15 per unit sold, and its revenue-driven variable operating expenses are 20 percent of sales revenue. Determine Company B's operating profit for this scenario. Also, how does this change affect the company's breakeven sales volume?

Solve It

16. Suppose that Company C increased its sales price $1.50. Sales volume remains the same as shown in Figure 10-2. The company's revenue-driven variable operating expenses are 10 percent of sales revenue, and its volume-driven variable operating expenses are $0.40 per unit sold. Determine Company C's operating profit for this scenario. Also, how does this change affect the company's breakeven sales volume?

Solve It

Making Trade-Offs Among Profit Factors

I used to regularly ask my students whether, as future business managers, they would drop sales prices 10 percent in order to increase sales volume 10 percent. Invariably, they would answer, "It depends." Invariably, I would respond, "No, it doesn't." The answer is clear.

Unless you're willing to do anything to increase your market share, trading a 10 percent decrease in sales prices for a 10 percent increase in sales volume is dumb . . . and I mean *really* dumb.

Q. Company B (see Figure 10-2) decides to analyze the impact that dropping its sales price 10 percent to gain a 10 percent increase in sales volume would have on its operating profit. What would Company B's operating profit be in this scenario?

A. The following comparative schedule shows just how devastating this trade-off would be on the company's operating profit.

Operating Profit Result from 10 Percent Sales Price Decrease in Exchange for 10 Percent Sales Volume Increase

	Before	After	Change
Sales price	$300.00	$270.00	($30.00)
Product cost	$150.00	$150.00	
Variable operating expenses:			
Volume driven expenses	$15.00	$15.00	
Revenue driven expenses at 20%	$60.00	$54.00	($6.00)
Contribution margin per unit	$75.00	$51.00	($24.00)
Times Sales volume, in units	50,000	55,000	5,000
Equals Total contribution margin	$3,750,000	$2,805,000	($945,000)
Less Fixed Operating expenses	$1,950,000	$1,950,000	
Operating profit	$1,800,000	$855,000	($945,000)

This comparative schedule shows that operating profit would decrease $945,000, which is a decrease of more than 50 percent of the amount before the trade-off. See why this trade-off is a bad idea? The only argument I got from my students, especially the marketing majors, was that a business may take such an action to gain market share. But that's another argument. The accountant's job is to calculate the precipitous drop-off in operating profit in this situation.

The reason for the huge drop-off in operating profit is simple enough (although perhaps not immediately obvious). The 10 percent decrease in sales price causes contribution margin per unit to drop from $75 to $51 (see the preceding comparative schedule), which is a plunge of 32 percent in Company B's contribution margin per unit ($24 decrease ÷ $75 contribution margin per unit before sales price decrease = 32 percent decrease). A paltry 10 percent increase in sales volume can't make up for such a large drop in contribution margin per unit.

17. Suppose that Company A (see Figure 10-1) were to offer all customers special rebates as a sales incentive. As a result, assume that sales price would decrease $10 per unit, but that annual sales volume would increase to 150,000 units. Assume that the company's fixed operating expenses would not increase at the higher sales volume level (which may be stretching things a bit). Also assume that its variable operating expenses are all revenue-driven and equal to 15 percent of sales revenue. In terms of the impact on operating profit, would the rebate strategy to increase sales volume be a good trade-off for the company?

18. The example question in this section shows a scenario for Company B that involves a 10 percent reduction in sales price with a 10 percent increase in sales volume. According to the comparative schedule, it's clear that a 10 percent sales volume increase isn't nearly enough. Determine the sales volume level needed at the lower sales price to keep operating profit the same at $1,800,000.

Answers to Problems on Analyzing Profit Behavior

The following are the answers to the practice questions presented earlier in this chapter.

1 One of Company A's marketing managers was overheard to comment, "If we had sold 10 percent more units than we did in the year, our profit would have been 10 percent higher." Do you agree with this comment? (Figure 10-1 presents Company A's operating profit report for the year.)

Increasing sales volume 10 percent would have increased total contribution margin 10 percent, assuming that sales price, product cost, and variable operating expenses remained the same. So far the this answer is relatively straightforward. The next step concerns what would happen to the company's total fixed operating expenses at the higher sales volume level.

Fixed operating costs don't increase with an increase in sales volume *unless* the increase in sales volume is relatively large such that the business would have to expand its capacity to accommodate the higher sales volume. Generally speaking, a business probably can take on a 10 percent sales volume increase without having to increase its capacity, at least in the short run. (Remember, an increase in capacity requires an increase in fixed operating expenses.)

Assuming the company's total fixed operating expenses would have been the same, all of the increase in total contribution margin would "fall down" to operating profit. Operating profit, therefore, would have increased more than 10 percent. The increase in total contribution margin is more than 10 percent of operating profit because operating profit is a smaller amount than the total contribution margin amount.

2 Instead of the scenario shown in Figure 10-1 assume that Company A had a bad year. The internal operating profit report for this alternative scenario is presented below. Using the three methods explained in this section, analyze why the business suffered a loss for the year.

Refer to profit data for Company A at the end of the question in order to produce this answer.

Analysis method #1: Contribution margin minus fixed costs

Contribution margin per unit	$18.75
Times annual sales volume, in units	120,000
Equals total contribution margin	$2,250,000
Less fixed operating expenses	$3,000,000
Equals operating profit (loss)	($750,000)

Analysis method #2: Shortfall below breakeven

Annual sales volume for year, in units	120,000
Less annual breakeven volume, in units	160,000
Equals shortfall below breakeven, in units	(40,000)
Times contribution margin per unit	$18.75
Equals operating profit (loss)	($750,000)

Analysis method #3: Minimizing fixed costs per unit

Contribution margin per unit	$18.75
Less average fixed operating expenses per unit	$25.00
Equals average profit (loss) per unit	($6.25)
Times annual sales volume, in units	120,000
Equals operating profit (loss)	($750,000)

3 Figure 10-2 presents profit performance information for two businesses for their most recent years. Using the three profit analysis methods explained in this section, analyze the profit performance of Company B. (You may note that both businesses in Figure 10-2 earned exactly the same amount of operating profit as the Company A business example for which I explain three profit analysis methods in this section. This similarity allows you to compare the key differences between businesses that earn the same profit.)

Refer to profit data Figure 10-2 in order to produce this answer.

Analysis method #1: Contribution margin minus fixed costs

Contribution margin per unit	$75
Times annual sales volume, in units	50,000
Equals total contribution margin	$3,750,000
Less fixed operating expenses	$1,950,000
Equals operating profit	$1,800,000

Analysis method #2: Excess over breakeven

Annual sales volume for year, in units	50,000
Less annual breakeven volume, in units	26,000
Equals excess over breakeven, in units	24,000
Times contribution margin per unit	$75
Equals operating profit	$1,800,000

Analysis Method #3: Minimizing fixed costs per unit

Contribution margin per unit	$75
Less average fixed operating expenses per unit	$39
Equals average profit per unit	$36
Times annual sales volume, in units	50,000
Equals operating profit	$1,800,000

4 Please refer to Figure 10-2. Using the three profit analysis methods explained in this section, analyze the profit performance of Company C. (You may note that both businesses in Figure 10-2 earned exactly the same amount of operating profit as the Company A business example for which I explain three profit analysis methods in this section. This similarity allows you to compare the key differences between businesses that earn the same profit.)

Refer to profit data Figure 10-2 in order to produce this answer.

Analysis method #1: Contribution margin minus fixed costs

Contribution margin per unit	$3.20
Times annual sales volume, in units	1,500,000
Equals total contribution margin	$4,800,000
Less fixed operating expenses	$3,000,000
Equals operating profit	$1,800,000

Analysis method #2: Excess over breakeven

Annual sales volume for year, in units	1,500,000
Less annual breakeven volume, in units	937,500
Equals excess over breakeven, in units	562,500
Times contribution margin per unit	$3.20
Equals operating profit	$1,800,000

Analysis Method #3: Minimizing fixed costs per unit

Contribution margin per unit	$3.20
Less average fixed operating expenses per unit	$2.00
Equals average profit per unit	$1.20
Times annual sales volume, in units	1,500000
Equals operating profit	$1,800,000

5 Assume the following:

Company B's Sources of Capital:

Debt	$8,000,000
Owners' equity	$4,000,000
Total capital	$12,000,000

See Figure 10-2 for Company B's operating profit data for the year. The business recorded $480,000 interest for the year. Calculate its financial leverage gain (or loss) for the year.

In this case, debt holders provide two-thirds of the company's total capital ($8 million of the total $12 million capital). Thus, two-thirds of its $1,800,000 operating profit can be attributed to the debt capital used by the business, which equals $1,200,000 (⅔ × $1,800,000 = $1,200,000).

The company paid only $480,000 interest on its debt capital. So:

> $1,200,000 operating profit attributable to debt capital – $480,000 interest on debt capital = $720,000 financial leverage gain

Here's another way to calculate financial leverage gain: The company earned 15 percent return on capital ($1,800,000 operating profit ÷ $12,000,000 total capital = 15.0 percent return on capital). The company paid a 6 percent interest rate on its debt capital ($480,000 interest ÷ $8,000,000 debt = 6 percent interest rate). There's a favorable 9 percent spread between the two rates. Therefore:

> 9 percent favorable spread between return on capital and interest rate × $8,000,000 debt = $720,000 financial leverage gain.

6 Assume the following:

Company C's Sources of Capital:

Debt	$6,000,000
Owners' equity	$6,000,000
Total capital	$12,000,000

See Figure 10-2 for Company C's profit data for the year. The business recorded $360,000 interest for the year. Calculate its financial leverage gain (or loss) for the year.

In this case, debt holders provide one-half of the company's total capital ($6 million of the total $12 million capital). Thus, one-half of its $1,800,000 operating profit can be attributed to the debt capital used by the business, which equals $900,000 (½ × $1,800,000 = $900,000).

The company paid only $360,000 interest on its debt capital. So:

> $900,000 operating profit attributable to debt capital – $360,000 interest on debt capital = $540,000 financial leverage gain

7 Suppose that Company B's fixed operating expenses were $3,030,000 for the year. Otherwise, other profit factors are the same as in Figure 10-2. Using the sources of capital and interest expense presented in Question 5, calculate Company B's financial leverage gain (or loss) for the year.

For the year, Company B earned $3,750,000 total contribution margin (see Figure 10-2). If its fixed operating expenses were $3,030,000, its operating profit for the year would be only $720,000. Based on this operating profit, Company B's return on capital would be only 6 percent ($720,000 ÷ $12,000,000 total capital = 6 percent return on capital).

In this case, debt supplies two-thirds of total capital. Therefore, two-thirds of its $720,000 operating profit can be attributed to its debt capital, which is $480,000 ($720,000 operating profit × ⅔ = $480,000). The company paid $480,000 interest in the year. Thus, its financial leverage gain is zero.

 Here's another way to calculate the company's financial leverage gain/loss for the year: The business earned only 6 percent return on capital, and its interest rate on debt is 6 percent ($480,000 interest ÷ $8,000,000 debt = 6 percent). So, there's no spread, or difference, between its 6 percent return on capital and its interest rate. Therefore, there's no financial leverage gain (or loss).

8 Suppose that Company C's fixed operating expenses were $4,440,000 for the year. Otherwise, other profit factors are the same as in Figure 10-2. Using the sources of capital and interest expense presented in Question 6, calculate Company C's financial leverage gain (or loss) for the year.

For the year, Company C earned $4,800,000 total contribution margin (see Figure 10-2). If its fixed operating expenses were $4,440,000, its operating profit for the year would be only $360,000. Based on this operating profit, the company's return on capital would be a very low 3 percent ($360,000 ÷ $12,000,000 total capital = 3 percent return on capital)

In this case, debt supplies one half of total capital. Therefore, one half of its $360,000 operating profit can be attributed to its debt capital, which is $180,000 ($360,000 operating profit × ½ = $180,000). The company paid $360,000 interest in the year. Thus, it has a financial leverage *loss* equal to $180,000.

Here's another way to calculate the company's financial leverage loss for the year: The business earned only 3 percent return on capital, and its interest rate on debt is 6 percent ($360,000 interest ÷ $6,000,000 debt = 6.0 percent). So, there's an unfavorable 3 percent spread between return on capital and interest rate. The company's financial leverage loss for the year is $180,000 (3 percent unfavorable spread × $6,000,000 debt = $180,000 financial leverage loss for the year).

9 Suppose Company B sold 10 percent more units during the year than it did according to Figure 10-2. Determine Company B's operating profit for this scenario. (Assume fixed operating expenses remain the same at the higher sales volume.)

For Company B, selling 10 percent additional units equals 5,000 additional units sold. Given that its contribution margin per unit is $75, the increase in its total contribution margin is:

> 5,000 additional units × $75 contribution margin per unit = $375,000 increase in total contribution margin

Because fixed operating expenses don't increase at the higher sales volume level, the gain in total contribution margin increases operating profit $375,000. The 10 percent increase in sales volume increases operating profit 20.8 percent ($375,000 gain in operating profit ÷ $1,800,000 operating profit at the original sales volume level = 20.8 percent increase).

The percent gain in operating profit is much larger than the percent increase in sales volume. This magnification effect is called *operating leverage*.

10 Suppose Company B sold 5 percent fewer units during the year than it did according to Figure 10-2. Determine Company B's operating profit for this scenario. (Assume fixed operating expenses remain the same at the lower sales volume.)

For Company B, selling 5 percent less units equals 2,500 fewer units sold. Given that its contribution margin per unit is $75, the decrease in its total contribution margin is:

> 2,500 fewer units × $75 contribution margin per unit = $187,500 decrease in total contribution margin

Because fixed operating expenses don't decrease at the lower sales volume level, the drop in total contribution margin decreases operating profit $187,500. The 5 percent decrease in sales volume decreases operating profit 10.4 percent ($187,500 fall in operating profit ÷ $1,800,000 operating profit at the original sales volume level = 10.4 percent decrease).

The percent drop in operating profit is much larger than the percent decrease in sales volume. This magnification effect is called *operating leverage*.

11 Suppose Company C sold 5 percent more units during the year than it did according to Figure 10-2. Determine Company C's operating profit for this scenario. (Assume fixed operating expenses remain the same at the higher sales volume.)

For Company C, selling 5 percent additional units equals 75,000 additional units sold. Given that its contribution margin per unit is $3.20, the increase in its total contribution margin is:

> 75,000 additional units × $3.20 contribution margin per unit = $240,000 increase in total contribution margin

Because fixed operating expenses don't increase at the higher sales volume level, the gain in total contribution margin increases operating profit $240,000. The 5 percent increase in sales volume increases operating profit 13.3 percent ($240,000 gain in operating profit ÷ $1,800,000 operating profit at the original sales volume level = 13.3 percent increase).

12 Suppose Company C sold 10 percent fewer units during the year than it did according to Figure 10-2. Determine Company C's operating profit for this scenario. (Assume fixed operating expenses remain the same at the lower sales volume.)

For Company C, selling 10 percent less units equals 150,000 fewer units sold. Given that its contribution margin per unit is $3.20, the decrease in its total contribution margin is:

> 150,000 fewer units × $3.20 contribution margin per unit = $480,000 decrease in total contribution margin

Because fixed operating expenses don't decrease at the lower sales volume level, the drop in total contribution margin decreases operating profit $480,000. The 10 percent decrease in sales volume decreases operating profit 26.7 percent ($480,000 fall in operating profit ÷ $1,800,000 operating profit at the original sales volume level = 26.7 percent decrease).

13 Suppose that Company B was able to improve (lower) its product cost per unit $10. Assume that all other profit factors for Company B remain the same as shown in Figure 10-2. Determine its operating profit for this scenario. Also, how does this change affect the company's breakeven sales volume?

The complete schedule of changes in this scenario is as follows:

	Before	After	Change
Sales price	$300.00	$300.00	
Product cost	*$150.00*	*$140.00*	($10.00)
Variable operating expenses:			
Volume driven expenses	*$15.00*	*$15.00*	
Revenue driven expenses at 20%	*$60.00*	*$60.00*	
Contribution margin per unit	$75.00	$85.00	+ $10.00
Times Sales volume, in units	50,000	50,000	
Equals Total contribution margin	$3,750,000	$4,250,000	+ $500,000
Less Fixed Operating expenses	*$1,950,000*	*$1,950,000*	
Operating profit	$1,800,000	$2,300,000	+ $500,000

As the schedule shows, operating profit increases $500,000, which is a 27.8 percent increase from a 6.7 percent change in product cost ($10 decrease ÷ $150 = 6.7 percent decrease).

The company's breakeven decreases because contribution margin per unit is higher than it was before the product cost change:

  $1,950,000 fixed operating expenses ÷ $85 contribution margin per unit = 22,941 units breakeven volume

At the $75 contribution margin per unit, Company B's breakeven volume is 26,000 units sales volume.

14 Suppose that Company C's product cost increases $0.50 per unit. Assume that all other profit factors for Company C remain the same as shown in Figure 10-2. Determine its operating profit for this scenario. Also, how does this change affect the company's breakeven sales volume?

The impact on contribution margin and operating profit from the seemingly small increase in product cost is shown in the following comparative schedule:

	Before	After	Change
Sales price	$24.00	$24.00	
Less Product cost	$18.00	$18.50	$0.50
Less Variable operating expenses:	$2.80	$2.80	
Equals Contribution margin per unit	$3.20	$2.70	($0.50)
Times Sales volume, in units	1,500,000	1,500,000	
Equals Total contribution margin	$4,800,000.00	$4,050,000.00	($750,000.00)
Less Fixed Operating expenses	$3,000,000.00	$3,000,000.00	
Equals Operating profit	$1,800,000.00	$1,050,000.00	($750,000.00)

So, operating profit drops $750,000, from $1,800,000 to only $1,050,000, which is a 41.7 percent decrease! The reason is the relatively large drop in contribution margin per unit, from $3.20 to only $2.70, which is a 15.6 percent decline. The importance of maintaining the contribution margin per unit cannot be overstated.

If Company C's product cost increases $0.50 per unit, the company's breakeven also increases because contribution margin per unit is lower than it was before the product cost change:

  $3,000,000 fixed operating expenses ÷ $2.70 contribution margin per unit = 1,111,111 units breakeven volume

At the $3.20 contribution margin per unit, the breakeven volume is 937,500 units sales volume.

15 Suppose that Company B had to drop its sales price $10 due to competitive pressures. All other profit factors remain the same as shown in Figure 10-2. The company's volume-driven variable expenses are $15 per unit sold, and its revenue-driven variable operating expenses are 20 percent of sales revenue. Determine Company B's operating profit for this scenario. Also, how does this change affect the company's breakeven sales volume?

The circumstances cause the company's operating profit to decrease $400,000, as shown in the following schedule:

	Before	After	Change
Sales price	$300	$290	($10)
Less Product cost	$150	$150	
Less Variable operating expenses:			
Volume driven expenses	$15	$15	
Revenue driven expenses at 20%	$60	$58	($2)
Equals Contribution margin per unit	$75	$67	($8)
Times Sales volume, in units	50,000	50,000	
Equals Total contribution margin	$3,750,000	$3,350,000	($400,000)
Less Fixed Operating expenses	$1,950,000	$1,950,000	
Equals Operating profit	$1,800,000	$1,400,000	($400,000)

If Company B's sales price drops $10, the company's breakeven increases because contribution margin per unit is lower than it was before the sales price change:

$1,950,000 fixed operating expenses ÷ $67 contribution margin per unit = 29,104 units breakeven volume

At the $75 contribution margin per unit, the breakeven volume is 26,000 units sales volume.

16 Suppose that Company C increased its sales price $1.50. Sales volume remains the same as shown in Figure 10-2. The company's revenue-driven variable operating expenses are 10 percent of sales revenue, and its volume-driven variable operating expenses are $0.40 per unit sold. Determine Company C's operating profit for this scenario. Also, how does this change affect the company's breakeven sales volume?

The circumstances cause the company's operating profit to increase $2,025,000, as shown in the following schedule:

	Before	After	Change
Sales price	$24.00	$25.50	+ $1.50
Product cost	$18.00	$18.00	
Variable operating expenses:			
Volume driven expenses	$0.40	$0.40	
Revenue driven expenses at 10%	$2.40	$2.55	+ $0.15
Contribution margin per unit	$3.20	$4.55	+ $1.35
Times Sales volume, in units	1,500,000	1,500,000	
Equals Total contribution margin	$4,800,000	$6,825,000	+ $2,025,000
Less Fixed Operating expenses	$3,000,000	$3,000,000	
Operating profit	$1,800,000	$3,825,000	+ $2,025,000

If Company C's sales price increases $1.50, the company's breakeven decreases because contribution margin per unit is higher than it was before the sales price change:

$3,000,000 fixed operating expenses ÷ $4.55 contribution margin per unit = 659,341 units breakeven volume

At the $3.20 contribution margin per unit, the breakeven volume is 937,500 units sales volume.

17 Suppose that Company A (see Figure 10-1) were to offer all customers special rebates as a **sales** incentive. As a result, assume that sales price would decrease $10 per unit, but that annual sales volume would increase to 150,000 units. Assume that the company's fixed operating expenses would not increase at the higher sales volume level (which may be stretching things a bit). Also assume that its variable operating expenses are all revenue-driven and equal to 15 percent of sales revenue. In terms of the impact on operating profit, would the rebate strategy to increase sales volume a good trade-off for the company?

On the surface, this trade-off appears to be a good one that improves operating profit. After all, the company decreases sales price only 5 percent for a 25 percent jump in sales volume. Surely this must be a good deal. But look closely at the following comparative schedule:

	Before	After	Change
Sales price	$200.00	$190.00	($10.00)
Product cost	*$130.00*	*$130.00*	
Variable operating expenses:			
Volume driven expenses	*$0.00*	*$0.00*	
Revenue driven expenses at 15%	*$30.00*	*$28.50*	($1.50)
Contribution margin per unit	$40.00	$31.50	($8.50)
Times Sales volume, in units	120,000	150,000	+30,000
Equals Total contribution margin	$4,800,000	$4,725,000	($75,000)
Less Fixed Operating expenses	*$3,000,000*	*$3,000,000*	
Operating profit	$1,800,000	$1,725,000	($75,000)

As the schedule shows, operating profit actually *decreases* $75,000 in this scenario. One key to understanding this change is that the contribution margin per unit decreases 21.25 percent ($8.50 decrease ÷ $40.00 contribution margin per unit before sales price decrease = 21.25 percent). The 25 percent increase in sales volume (from 120,000 units to 150,000 units) isn't enough to make up for the drop in the all important contribution margin per unit.

18 The example question in this section shows a scenario for Company B that involves a 10 percent reduction in sales price with a 10 percent increase in sales volume. According to the comparative schedule, it's clear that a 10 percent sales volume increase isn't nearly enough. Determine the sales volume level needed at the lower sales price to keep operating profit the same at $1,800,000.

Obviously, sales volume has to increase more than 10 percent to keep operating profit at $1,800,000. The following calculation determines the exact sales volume needed to keep operating profit the same:

$3,750,000 contribution margin target ÷ $51 contribution margin after sales price decrease = 73,529 units sales volume needed to keep operating profit the same

This answer is proven in the following comparative schedule using the 73,529 units sales volume:

	Before	After	Change
Sales price	$300.00	$270.00	($30.00)
Product cost	*$150.00*	*$150.00*	
Variable operating expenses:			
Volume driven expenses	*$15.00*	*$15.00*	
Revenue driven expenses at 20%	*$60.00*	*$54.00*	($6.00)
Contribution margin per unit	$75.00	$51.00	($24.00)
Times Sales volume, in units	50,000	73,529	+23,529
Equals Total contribution margin	$3,750,000	$3,750,000	
Less Fixed Operating expenses	*$1,950,000*	*$1,950,000*	
Operating profit	$1,800,000	$1,800,000	

Chapter 11

Manufacturing Cost Accounting

· ·

In This Chapter

▶ Recognizing the different types of manufacturing costs

▶ Getting to know manufacturing journal entries

▶ Calculating product cost

· ·

*I*n addition to normal accounting matters, businesses that manufacture products face additional accounting problems that retailers and distributors do not. Throughout this chapter, I use the term *manufacture* in the broadest sense: Automobile makers assemble cars, beer companies brew beer, automobile gasoline companies refine oil, DuPont makes products through chemical synthesis, and so on. Retailers (also called *merchandisers*) and distributors, on the other hand, buy products in a condition ready for resale to the end consumer. For example, Wal-Mart and Target don't manufacture the products they sell. Other companies manufacture the products that retailers sell — although the manufacturers may put private labels on the goods (which is common practice for grocery stores and other retailers).

The chapter focuses mainly on the accounting procedures used to accumulate the basic types of manufacturing costs and how these pools of costs are used to determine product cost. A manufacturer must know product cost in order to determine its cost of goods sold expense for the period and the cost of its inventory. The chapter explores certain unavoidable problems accountants face in determining product cost. To complete the picture, the chapter also explains how unscrupulous managers can set production output to manipulate profit for the period.

Minding Manufacturing Costs

A manufacturing business, first of all, must separate between its manufacturing costs and non-manufacturing costs. Manufacturing costs are the costs of production that are included in the determination of *product cost*. Non-manufacturing costs include marketing expenses and the general and administration expenses of the business, which are referred to as *period costs*. I explain the importance of the distinction between product and period costs later in the section. First, I explain the basic types of manufacturing costs that go into the calculation of product cost.

Manufacturing costs consist of four basic types:

▶ **Raw materials:** What a manufacturer buys from other companies to use in the production of its own products. For example, General Motors buys tires from Goodyear (or other tire manufacturers) that become part of GM's cars.

▶ **Direct labor:** Compensation of employees who work on the production line.

▶ **Variable overhead:** Indirect production costs that increase or decrease as the quantity produced increases or decreases. An example is the cost of electricity that runs a company's production machines: If the business increases or decreases the use of those machines, the electricity cost increases or decreases accordingly.

230 Part III: Managerial, Manufacturing, and Capital Accounting

✔ **Fixed overhead:** Indirect production costs that do *not* increase or decrease as the quantity produced increases or decreases. These fixed costs remain the same over a fairly broad range of production output levels. Fixed manufacturing costs include:

- Salaries for certain production employees who don't work directly on the production line, such as a vice president, safety inspectors, security guards, accountants, and shipping and receiving workers

- Depreciation of production buildings, equipment, and other manufacturing fixed assets

- Occupancy costs, such as building insurance, property taxes, and heating and lighting charges

Figure 11-1 presents an internal operating profit report of a manufacturer I call Company X; the report includes information about the company's manufacturing activity and costs for the year. A business may manufacture hundreds or thousands of products, but in the example, Company X manufactures and sells only one product. The example is realistic yet avoids the clutter of too much detail. Figure 11-1 is a good platform to illustrate the fundamental accounting problems and methods of all manufacturers.

The information in the operating profit report and manufacturing activity summary in Figure 11-1 is confidential and for management eyes only. The company's competitors would love to know this information. For instance, if Company X enjoys a significant product cost advantage over its competitors, it definitely wouldn't want its cost data to get into their hands.

	Company X	
Operating Profit Report for Year	**Per Unit**	**Totals**
Sales volume, in Units		110,000
Sales Revenue	$1,400.00	$154,000,000
Cost of Goods Sold Expense (see below)	(760.00)	(83,600,000)
Gross Margin	$640.00	$70,400,000
Variable Operating Expenses	(300.00)	(33,000,000)
Contribution Margin	$340.00	$37,400,000
Fixed Operating Expenses		(21,450,000)
Operating Profit		$15,950,000

Manufacturing Activity Summary for Year	**Per Unit**	**Totals**
Annual Production Capacity, in Units		150,000
Actual Output, in Units		120,000
Raw Materials	$215.00	$25,800,000
Direct Labor	125.00	15,000,000
Variable Manufacturing Overhead Costs	70.00	8,400,000
Total Variable Manufacturing Costs	$410.00	$49,200,000
Fixed Manufacturing Overhead Costs	350.00	42,000,000
Product Cost and Total Manufacturing Costs	$760.00	$91,200,000

Figure 11-1: Internal operating profit report for Company X (a manufacturer).

Product costs

Unlike a retailer that purchases products in a condition ready for resale, a manufacturer begins by purchasing the raw materials needed in the production process. Then the manufacturer pays workers to operate the production machines and equipment and to move the products into warehouses after they're produced. All this work is done in a sprawling plant that has many indirect overhead costs. All these different production costs are funneled into *product cost*.

When manufacturing costs are incurred, they're recorded in an *inventory* account — in particular, the *work-in-process inventory account*. I explain the use of this account in the section "Taking a Short Tour of Manufacturing Entries" later in this chapter. Product costs are later recorded in the cost of goods sold expense when the products are sold.

Pay special attention to the $760.00 product cost and its components in Figure 11-1. In particular, note that the $760.00 is the sum of four separate cost components — raw materials, direct labor, variable manufacturing overhead, and fixed manufacturing overhead. All four of the component costs must be correct to end up with the correct product cost.

Product costs are said to be *capitalized* because they're viewed as a *capital investment,* which is an investment in an asset. Product costs aren't recorded to expense until the products are eventually sold, at which time the appropriate amount of cost is removed from the asset account and recorded in the cost of goods sold expense account.

Period costs

Costs that are charged to expense when they're recorded are known as *period costs*. Marketing costs (such as advertising, sales personnel, or delivery of products to customers) are period costs. These selling costs are recorded as expenses in the period the costs are incurred. General and administrative costs (such as legal and accounting, compensation of officers, or information and data processing) are also period costs. Period costs do not pass through an inventory account.

Separating period and product costs

The distinction between period and product costs is very important. What if a business deliberately recorded some of its manufacturing costs as period costs instead of as product costs? Suppose that for the year just ended, a business recorded $2,400,000 of its manufacturing costs as marketing expenses. The $2,400,000 should have gone into inventory and stayed there until the products were sold. To the extent the products haven't yet been sold at the end of the year, the business has understated the cost of its ending inventory and overstated its marketing expense for the year. Why would a business do this? To minimize its current year's taxable income, that's why.

Evidently many businesses were in the habit of misclassifying some costs as period costs (immediate expense deduction) instead of product costs. In response the IRS has laid down rules regarding what has to be treated as a manufacturing cost. Nevertheless, there are still many gray areas in which drawing a line between manufacturing and non-manufacturing costs is not entirely clear-cut. In any case, a business should be consistent from period to period regarding how it classifies its manufacturing and non-manufacturing costs.

Wages paid to production line workers are a clear example of a manufacturing cost. Salaries paid to salespeople are a marketing cost and are not part of product cost. Depreciation on production equipment is a manufacturing cost, but depreciation on the warehouse in which products are stored after being manufactured is a period cost. Similarly, moving raw materials and partially completed goods through production process is a manufacturing cost, but transporting the finished products from the warehouse to customers is a period cost. Essentially, product cost stops at the end of the production line — but every cost up to that point is a manufacturing cost.

A manufacturer must design and implement a *cost accounting system* to determine the cost of every product it manufactures and sells. The business must track the costs of all raw materials that go into the production process and the costs of all production line labor (which may involve hundreds or thousands of operations). Furthermore, the business has to determine and allocate many indirect manufacturing costs to the various products it manufactures (although in the example shown in Figure 11-1, the business produces only one product). Tracking and allocating these costs is a very challenging task, to say the least.

Q. How is the $83,600,000 cost of goods sold expense of Company X determined (see Figure 11-1)?

A. In the example (see Figure 11-1), the business recorded $91,200,000 total manufacturing costs to produce 120,000 units during the year. Therefore, the product cost per unit is $760.00: ($91,200,000 total

manufacturing costs ÷ 120,000 units production output = $760.00 product cost per unit). Based on this product cost per unit its cost of goods sold expense for the year is determined as follows:

$760.00 product cost × 110,000 units sales volume = $83,600,000 cost of goods sold expense

The business uses the LIFO (last in, first out) method: All 110,000 units sold are charged out at the $760.00 product cost per unit, which is for the latest batch of units produced. (The example treats the entire year as one production period for determining product cost, whereas in actual practice, product cost is determined monthly or quarterly.) In other words, none of the cost from its beginning inventory is charged to cost of goods sold expense. The cost of beginning inventory most likely is carried on the books at a lower product cost. If the company were to use the FIFO (first in, first out) method, some of the units sold during the year would have been charged out based on the product cost in beginning inventory. (I discuss the LIFO and FIFO methods in Chapter 9.)

---

1. The company's total manufacturing costs for the year are $91,200,000 (see Figure 11-1), but only $83,600,000 is charged to cost of goods expense. What happened to the other $7,600,000 ($91,200,000 manufacturing costs for year − $83,600,000 cost of goods sold expense for year = $7,600,000)?

Solve It

2. As you can see in Figure 11-1, Company X recorded $42,000,000 fixed manufacturing overhead costs in the year. Suppose, instead, that its fixed manufacturing overhead costs were $45,600,000 for the year, which is an increase of $3,600,000. Would the company's operating profit have been $3,600,000 lower? (Assume that variable manufacturing costs per unit and operating expenses remain the same.)

Solve It

3. Suppose that Company X uses the FIFO method instead of the LIFO method shown in Figure 11-1. The company starts the year with 25,000 units in beginning inventory at a cost of $735 per unit according to the FIFO method. During the year, it manufactures 120,000 units and sells 110,000 units (see Figure 11-1). Determine Company X's cost of goods sold expense for the year and its cost of ending inventory using the FIFO method.

Solve It

4. Company X produced 120,000 units and sold 110,000 units during the year (see Figure 11-1). Therefore, the company increased its inventory 10,000 units. Does this increase seem reasonable? Or is the company's production output compared with its sales volume out of kilter?

Solve It

Taking a Short Tour of Manufacturing Entries

When a retailer or wholesaler purchases products, it debits (increases) an inventory account. The cost of the products is held in an inventory account until the products are sold. At that time, the appropriate amount of cost is removed from the inventory account and charged to cost of goods sold expense. The amount of the cost removed from inventory is determined by which cost of goods sold expense method is used, such as FIFO or LIFO. (I discuss cost of goods sold expense methods in Chapter 9.)

In contrast to retailers and wholesalers, a manufacturer has to make more entries to get to its cost of goods sold expense. The following illustrative entries are based on the Company X manufacturing example, whose operating profit report and manufacturing activity summary appear in Figure 11-1.

Company X purchased $27,325,000 of raw materials during the year, which is slightly more than the cost of materials released into the manufacturing process. Therefore, its inventory of raw materials increased during the year. The business has a good credit rating, and purchased all its raw materials on credit. Its raw materials purchases during the year are shown in the following entry:

Raw Materials Inventory	$27,325,000
Accounts Payable	$27,325,000

When raw materials are released from inventory storage into the manufacturing process, the cost is charged to a particular job order or to a particular department. The transfers of raw materials to production during the year are shown in the following entry:

Work-in-Process Inventory	$25,800,000	
Raw Materials Inventory		$25,800,000

The *work-in-process inventory account* is a special account used by manufacturers to accumulate the costs of products working their way through the production process. These products aren't ready for sale until the production process is completed. At that time, an entry is made to move the product cost out of this temporary holding account into the finished goods inventory account — see the entry below (the second to last entry).

The company's direct labor costs consist of all elements of compensation earned by its production line workers. The largest part of the compensation of production line workers is paid in cash, but payroll taxes are withheld and fringe benefit costs are also recorded in various liability accounts. In the following entries I use *Accrued payables* as the generic title for various liability accounts used to record costs incurred by the business that are paid at a later time. The direct labor costs of the business during the period are shown in the following entry:

Work-in-Process Inventory	$15,000,000	
Cash		$xx,xxx,xxx
Payroll Taxes Payable		$x,xxx,xxx
Accrued Payables		$x,xxx,xxx

The bulk of the company's variable manufacturing overhead costs are paid in cash over the course of the year, but two liability accounts — accounts payable and accrued payables — are involved in recording many of these costs. The business's variable manufacturing overhead costs for the year are shown in the following entry:

Work-in-Process Inventory	$8,400,000	
Cash		$x,xxx,xxx
Accounts Payable		$xxx,xxx
Accrued Payables		$xxx,xxx

Most of the company's indirect fixed manufacturing overhead costs for period are paid in cash during the year, but many involve liability accounts for unpaid manufacturing costs — such as the two shown in the following entry. Also, depreciation is a major fixed overhead cost, so the accumulated depreciation account is credited in recording the depreciation cost component of fixed manufacturing overhead costs. The business's fixed manufacturing overhead costs for the year are shown in the following entry:

Work-in-Process Inventory	$42,000,000	
Cash		$xx,xxx,xxx
Accumulated Depreciation		$x,xxx,xxx
Accounts Payable		$x,xxx,xxx
Accrued Payables		$x,xxx,xxx

When the manufacturing process is completed products are moved off the production line to the warehouse. The appropriate amount of product cost is removed from the work-in-process inventory account and entered in the finished goods inventory account. The transfers of products from the production line to the finished goods warehouse during the year are shown in the following entry:

| Finished Goods Inventory | $91,200,000 | |
| Work-in-Process Inventory | | $91,200,000 |

Note: In these entries, I assume that there was no work-in-process at the beginning or end of the year. This assumption would be accurate, for instance, if the business shut down its manufacturing activity for a week or two at the end of the year to permit a fumigation of the plant or to give workers a holiday vacation. The entries would be more involved if there was work-in-process inventory at the start and end of the year.

Recording the cost of products sold during the year is shown in the following entry:

| Cost of Goods Sold Expense | $83,600,000 | |
| Finished Goods Inventory | | $83,600,000 |

Figure 11-2 presents the internal operating profit reports of two sample manufacturing companies, Company Y and Company Z. Their operating profit reports include information about their manufacturing activity for the year.

Operating Profit Report for Year	Company Y Per Unit	Company Y Totals	Company Z Per Unit	Company Z Totals
Sales volume, in Units		500,000		2,000,000
Sales Revenue	$85.00	$42,500,000	$25.00	$50,000,000
Cost of Goods Sold Expense (see below)	(56.00)	(28,000,000)	(18.45)	(36,900,000)
Gross Margin	$29.00	$14,500,000	$6.55	$13,100,000
Variable Operating Expenses	(12.50)	(6,250,000)	(2.50)	(5,000,000)
Contribution Margin	$16.50	$8,250,000	$4.05	$8,100,000
Fixed Operating Expenses		(5,000,000)		(7,500,000)
Operating Profit		$3,250,000		$600,000

Manufacturing Activity Summary for Year	Per Unit	Totals	Per Unit	Totals
Annual Production Capacity, in Units		800,000		2,500,000
Actual Output, in Units		500,000		2,500,000
Raw Materials	$15.00	$7,500,000	$7.50	$18,750,000
Direct Labor	20.00	10,000,000	2.75	6,875,000
Variable Manufacturing Overhead Costs	5.00	2,500,000	5.00	12,500,000
Total Variable Manufacturing Costs	$40.00	$20,000,000	$15.25	$38,125,000
Fixed Manufacturing Overhead Costs	16.00	8,000,000	3.20	8,000,000
Product Cost and Total Manufacturing Costs	$56.00	$28,000,000	$18.45	$46,125,000

Figure 11-2: Internal operating profit reports of Company Y and Company Z (two manufacturers).

5. Refer to Figure 11-2 for the operating profit report and manufacturing activity summary of Company Y for the year. Assume that the business had no work-in-process inventory at the start or end of the year. The business purchased $7,800,000 raw materials on credit during the year. Make the basic manufacturing entries for the business by following the series of entries explained in this section.

Solve It

6. Refer to Figure 11-2 for the operating profit report and manufacturing activity summary of Company Z for the year. Assume that the business had no work-in-process inventory at the start or end of the year. The business purchased $19,500,000 raw materials on credit during the year. Make the basic manufacturing entries for the business by following the series of entries explained in this section.

Solve It

7. Assume that Company Y uses the LIFO method to charge out raw materials to production. In this question, assume that supply shortages of raw materials meant that Company Y couldn't purchase all the raw materials it needed for production during the year, and it had to draw down its raw materials inventory. Fortunately, it had an adequate beginning inventory of raw materials to cover the gap in purchases during the year. In this situation, would the cost of raw materials issued to production be different than the $7,500,000 shown in Figure 11-2?

Solve It

8. Determine what Company Z's operating profit would have been if it had sold 2,100,000 units during the year, which is 100,000 more units than in the example shown in Figure 11-2. Assume that production output had remained the same at 2,500,000 units (the company's production output capacity).

Solve It

Calculating Product Cost: Basic Methods and Problems

Product cost, $760.00 in the example shown in Figure 11-1, consists of two quite different types of manufacturing costs: *variable costs* (including raw materials, direct labor, and variable overhead) and *fixed overhead costs*. Variable manufacturing costs remain the same *per unit* (except at very low or very high levels of production). Thus, the total of variable manufacturing costs moves up and down with increases and decreases in production output (the number of units produced). In contrast, fixed costs are rigid; these costs remain the same and unchanged over a broad range of production output levels. Many of these fixed costs would have to be paid even if the business had to shut down its manufacturing for several months.

Refer to Figure 11-1 for Company X's manufacturing cost information. Its $760.00 product cost consists of $410.00 total variable costs per unit manufactured and $350.00 fixed manufacturing overhead cost per unit.

If Company X had manufactured ten more units than it did during the year, its total variable manufacturing costs would have been $4,100 higher (10 additional units × $410 per unit = $4,100). The actual number of units produced drives total variable manufacturing costs, so even one more unit would have caused the variable costs to increase $410. But the company's total fixed manufacturing overhead costs would have been the same if it had produced ten more units, or 10,000 more units for that matter. Variable manufacturing costs are bought on a per unit basis, as it were, whereas fixed manufacturing costs are bought in bulk at fixed prices for the whole period.

Total manufacturing costs for the year are calculated as follows:

(Variable manufacturing costs per unit × Number of units produced) +
Fixed manufacturing overhead costs = Total manufacturing costs

Connecting fixed manufacturing overhead costs and production capacity

Fixed manufacturing overhead costs present certain problems in determining product cost and operating profit (that is, profit before interest and income tax expenses).

Why in the world would a manufacturer in its right mind commit to fixed manufacturing overhead costs? For example, according to Figure 11-1, Company X has $42,000,000 of these cost commitments hanging over its head for the year whether it produces 15,000 or 150,000 units or any number in between. The answer is that fixed manufacturing costs are needed to provide *production capacity* — the people and physical resources needed to manufacture products — for the year. When the business has the production plant and people in place for the year, its fixed manufacturing costs aren't easily scaled down. The business is stuck with these costs over the short run.

The fixed manufacturing overhead cost component of product cost is called the *burden rate*. The burden rate of Company X for the year is computed as follows (see Figure 11-1 for data):

$42,000,000 total fixed manufacturing overhead costs for year ÷ 120,000 units production output for period = $350 burden rate

EXAMPLE

Now, here's a very important twist on the example: Suppose Company X manufactured only 110,000 units during the period — equal to the quantity sold during the year. Its variable manufacturing costs equal $410.00 per unit. This *per unit* cost remains the same at the lower production output level. In contrast, the burden rate would be $381.82 per unit at the lower production output level ($42,000,000 total fixed manufacturing overhead costs ÷ 110,000 units production output = $381.82 burden rate). The higher burden rate causes product cost to be $31.82 higher.

Q. What would be the operating profit of Company X if its production output for the year had been 110,000 units (equal to the number of units sold) instead of the 120,000 units production output level assumed in Figure 11-1?

A. Its operating profit at the 110,000 units production output level is $12,450,000, as shown in the following schedule:

	Company X	
Operating Profit Report For Year	**Per Unit**	**Totals**
Sales volume, in Units		110,000
Sales Revenue	$1,400.00	$154,000,000
Cost of Goods Sold Expense (see below)	(791.82)	(87,100,000)
Gross Margin	$608.18	$66,900,000
Variable Operating Expenses	(300.00)	(33,000,000)
Contribution Margin	$308.18	$33,900,000
Fixed Operating Expenses		(21,450,000)
Operating Profit		$12,450,000

Manufacturing Activity Summary For Year	**Per Unit**	**Totals**
Annual Production Capacity, in Units		150,000
Actual Output, in Units		110,000
Raw Materials	$215.00	$23,650,000
Direct Labor	125.00	13,750,000
Variable Manufacturing Overhead Costs	70.00	7,700,000
Total Variable Manufacturing Costs	$410.00	$45,100,000
Fixed Manufacturing Overhead Costs	381.82	42,000,000
Product Cost and Total Manufacturing Costs	$791.82	$87,100,000

TIP

A key point of this example is that Company X's product cost is $31.82 higher simply because it produces fewer units. The same total amount of fixed manufacturing overhead costs is spread over fewer units of production output. The higher product cost means that cost of goods sold expense is higher, and therefore, operating profit is lower. At the 120,000 units production output level, operating profit is $15,950,000 (see Figure 11-1). But at the 110,000 units production output level, operating profit dips to $12,450,000, which is a decrease of $3,500,000. This decrease gets the attention of business managers, that's for sure!

9. Company Y was on track to sell 550,000 units in the year, but late in the year, a major customer canceled a large order for 50,000 units. The business reduced its production output to 500,000 units, as you see in Figure 11-2. Determine the operating profit Company Y would have earned if it had manufactured and sold 550,000 units in the year.

Solve It

10. Assume that Company Z's production output for the year is 2,000,000 units (instead of 2,500,000 units as in Figure 11-2). In other words, assume that the business manufactures the same number of units that it sells in the year. Assume all other manufacturing and operating factors are the same. Determine the company's operating profit for the year.

Solve It

Boosting profit by boosting production

In the Company X example shown in Figure 11-1, cost of goods sold expense for the year benefits from the fact that the business produced 10,000 more units than it sold during the year. These 10,000 units *absorbed* $3,500,000 of its total fixed manufacturing overhead costs for the year. The cost of goods sold expense escaped $3,500,000 in fixed manufacturing overhead costs because the company produced 10,000 more units than it sold during the year, thus pushing down the burden rate (see the preceding section for an explanation of burden rate). Until the units are sold, the $3,500,000 stays in the inventory asset account (along with variable manufacturing costs, of course).

The distribution of the company's fixed manufacturing overhead costs for the year is summarized as follows:

Total Fixed Manufacturing
Overhead Costs for Year $42,000,000
(Divided by 120,000 unit
production output gives
$350.00 burden rate)

$38,500,000   Cost of Goods Sold Expense
(110,000 units sold during the year
times $350.00 burden rate)

$3,500,000   Finished Goods Inventory
(10,000 units increase in inventory
times $350.00 burden rate)

Of its $42,000,000 total fixed manufacturing overhead costs for the year, only $38,500,000 ended up in cost of goods sold expense for the year ($350 burden rate × 110,000 units sold= $38,500,000). The other $3,500,000 ended up in the inventory asset account ($350 burden rate × 10,000 units inventory increase = $3,500,000). I'm not suggesting any funny business, but Company X did help its operating profit to the tune of $3,500,000 by producing 10,000 more units than it sold. Suppose that the business had produced only 110,000 units, equal to its sales volume for the year. All its fixed manufacturing overhead costs would have gone into cost of goods sold expense, and operating profit would have been that much lower.

It's entirely possible that Company X's 120,000 units production output level is justified as a way to have more units on hand for sales growth next year. But the production output decision can get out of hand. A manufacturer may deliberately pump up production output not to prepare for sales growth next year but to pump up profit this year, and that's *massaging the numbers,* pure and simple. It falls short of cooking the books, which involves fraudulent accounting practices that are untruthful or fictitious. Nevertheless, pushing up production output for the sole purpose of boosting profit definitely smacks of accounting manipulation.

You need to judge whether an inventory increase is justified. Be aware that an unjustified increase may be evidence of profit manipulation or just good old-fashioned management bungling. The day of reckoning will come when the products are sold and the cost of inventory becomes cost of goods sold expense.

In Figure 11-1, Company X's production capacity for the year is 150,000 units. It produced only 120,000 units during the year, which is 30,000 units fewer than it could have. In other words, it operated at 80 percent of *production capacity* (120,000 units output ÷ 150,000 units capacity = 80 percent utilization), which is 20 percent *idle capacity.* (The average U.S. manufacturing plant normally operates at 80 to 85 percent of its production capacity.) Production capacity, to remind you, is the maximum output that a business could achieve during a period of time given its machinery, equipment, buildings and land, labor force, and other necessary manufacturing factors. Idle capacity is the difference between actual output during the period and production capacity. The term "idle" may be too pejorative. Most manufacturers, as a matter of fact, do not run at full production capacity. So, some idle (unused) production capacity is normal.

Running at 80 percent of production capacity, this business's burden rate for the year is $350 per unit ($42,000,000 total fixed manufacturing overhead costs ÷ 120,000 units output = $350 burden rate). As I explain earlier in this section, the burden rate would be higher if the company produced only 110,000 units during the year. The burden rate, in other words, is sensitive to the number of units produced. This connection can lead to all kinds of mischief.

Suppose that Company X manufactures 150,000 units during the year and increases its inventory 40,000 units, which may be a legitimate move if the business is anticipating a big jump in sales next year. On the other hand, an inventory increase of 40,000 units in a year in which only 110,000 units were sold may be the result of a serious overproduction mistake, and the larger inventory may not be needed next year.

EXAMPLE

Q. In the Figure 11-1 scenario Company X manufactured 120,000 units during the year, which caused its inventory to increase 10,000 units. Suppose, instead, that the company had manufactured 150,000 units during the year, which is its production capacity. Assume sales and other factors were the same in this alternative scenario as shown in Figure 11-1 – only production output is different. What would be its operating profit for the year if it had produced 150,000 units?

A. The following operating profit report and summary of manufacturing activity for Company X shows what would have happened at the 150,000 units production output level. Remember that sales volume doesn't change in this scenario; only production output changes. Comparative data is presented for the 120,000 units production output level in the original scenario (see Figure 11-1).

	Company X	
Operating Profit Report For Year	**Per Unit**	**Totals**
Sales volume, in Units		110,000
Sales Revenue	$1,400.00	$154,000,000
Cost of Goods Sold Expense (see below)	(690.00)	(75,900,000)
Gross Margin	$710.00	$78,100,000
Variable Operating Expenses	(300.00)	(33,000,000)
Contribution Margin	$410.00	$45,100,000
Fixed Operating Expenses		(21,450,000)
Operating Profit		$23,650,000
Manufacturing Activity Summary For Year	**Per Unit**	**Totals**
Annual Production Capacity, in Units		150,000
Actual Output, in Units		150,000
Raw Materials	$215.00	$32,250,000
Direct Labor	125.00	18,750,000
Variable Manufacturing Overhead Costs	70.00	10,500,000
Total Variable Manufacturing Costs	$410.00	$61,500,000
Fixed Manufacturing Overhead Costs	280.00	42,000,000
Product Cost and Total Manufacturing Costs	$690.00	$103,500,000

Check out the $23,650,000 operating profit when production output is 150,000 units, compared with the $15,950,000 operating profit when production output is 120,000 units — a $7,700,000 difference even though sales volume, sales prices, and operating expenses all remain the same. Whoa! What's going on here? The simple answer is that the cost of goods sold expense is $7,700,000 less than before. How can cost of goods sold expense be less if the business sells 110,000 units in both scenarios, and variable manufacturing costs are $410.00 per unit in both cases?

The culprit is the *burden rate* component of product cost. In Figure 11-1, total fixed manufacturing costs are spread over 120,000 units of output, giving a $350 burden rate per unit. Note that total fixed manufacturing costs are spread over 150,000 units output, giving the much lower $280 burden rate, or $70 per unit less. The $70 lower burden rate multiplied by the 110,000 units sold reduces cost of goods sold expense $7,700,000 and increases operating profit the same amount.

WARNING!

If the business had produced 150,000 units (its production capacity), its inventory would have increased 40,000 units. This increase is quite large compared to the annual sales of 110,000 for the year just ended. Who was responsible for the decision to go full blast and produce up to production capacity? Do the managers really expect sales to jump up enough next year to justify the much larger inventory level? If their guess is right, they look brilliant. But if the output level was a mistake and sales don't go up next year . . . they have you-know-what to pay, even though profit looks good this year. An experienced business manager knows to be on guard when inventory takes such a big jump.

11. Towards the end of the year, the president of Company Y looks at the preliminary numbers for operating profit and doesn't like what he sees. He's "promised" the board of directors that operating profit for the year will come in at $4,850,000. In fact, his bonus depends on hitting that operating profit target. There is still time before the end of the year to crank up production output for the year. Therefore, he orders that production output be stepped up. The president asks you to determine what the production output level for the year would have to be in order to report $4,850,000 operating profit for the year. Of course, you have ethical qualms about doing this, but you need the job. So, you reluctantly decide to do the calculation. Determine the production output level that would yield $4,850,000 operating profit for the year.

12. Refer to your answer to Question 10, in which Company Z produces only 2,000,000 units during the year. In the scenario shown in Figure 11-2, the business manufactures 2,500,000 units, which is its maximum production output for the year. Do you think that Company Z cranked up production output to 2,500,000 units mainly to boost its operating profit for the year?

Solve It

Calculating Product Cost in Unusual Situations

The basic calculation model for product cost is:

Total manufacturing costs for period ÷ Total units produced during period = Product cost per unit

Total manufacturing costs for the period includes *direct* manufacturing costs that can be clearly identified with a particular product and *indirect* manufacturing costs that are allocated to the product.

This product cost calculation method is appropriate in most situations. However, it has to be modified in two extreme situations:

 ✔ When manufacturing costs are grossly excessive or wasteful due to inefficient production operations

 ✔ When production output is significantly less than normal capacity utilization

Suppose that Company X had to throw away $1,200,000 of raw materials during the year because they weren't stored properly and ended up being unusable in the production process. The manager in charge of the warehouse received a stiff reprimand.

Q. In Figure 11-1, which shows Company X's operating profit performance and summary of manufacturing activity for the year, it is assumed that there were no wasteful manufacturing costs. In this question, assume, instead, that the business had to throw away $1,200,000 of unusable raw materials. How should the $1,200,000 cost of raw materials that were thrown out be presented in the operating profit report and summary of manufacturing activity?

A. The $1,200,000 cost of raw materials that were wasted and not used in production should not be included in the calculation of product cost. The $1,200,000 cost of wasted raw materials should be treated as a *period cost,* which means that it's recorded as an expense in the period. The operating profit report and summary of manufacturing activity for the year in this scenario is as follows:

	Company X	
Operating Profit Report For Year	**Per Unit**	**Totals**
Sales volume, in Units		110,000
Sales Revenue	$1,400.00	$154,000,000
Cost of Goods Sold Expense (see below)	(750.00)	(82,500,000)
Gross Margin	$650.00	$71,500,000
Variable Operating Expenses	(300.00)	(33,000,000)
Contribution Margin	$350.00	$38,500,000
Fixed Operating Expenses		(21,450,000)
Cost of Wasted Raw Materials		(1,200,000)
Operating Profit		$15,850,000

Manufacturing Activity Summary For Year	**Per Unit**	**Totals**
Annual Production Capacity, in Units =		150,000
Actual Output, in Units =		120,000
Raw Materials	$205.00	$24,600,000
Direct Labor	125.00	15,000,000
Variable Manufacturing Overhead Costs	70.00	8,400,000
Total Variable Manufacturing Costs	$400.00	$48,000,000
Fixed Manufacturing Overhead Costs	350.00	42,000,000
Product Cost and Total Manufacturing Costs	$750.00	$90,000,000

The $1,200,000 wasted raw materials cost is recorded as an expense in the year, as you see in the operating profit report. As a result, the cost of raw materials is reduced the same amount in the manufacturing activity summary for the year with the result that product cost drops to $750 per unit.

13. The president of Company X is puzzled by the operating profit report and summary of manufacturing activity for the year, in which $1,200,000 raw materials cost was wasted and charged to expense in the year. He expected that operating profit would be $1,200,000 lower (as compared to the scenario in Figure 11-1, in which there's no wasted raw materials cost). Operating profit in the wasted raw materials scenario is only $100,000 lower than in Figure 11-1. Explain to the president why operating profit is only $100,000 lower.

14. After Company Y's operating profit report and summary of manufacturing activity for the year has been prepared (see Figure 11-2), you, the chief accountant, learn that $1,000,000 of raw materials were thrown away during the year because the items had spoiled and couldn't be used in the manufacturing process. The company's president knows about this loss and insists that no change be made in the operating profit report and summary of manufacturing activity. Do you go along with the president, or do you argue for changing the operating profit report and summary of manufacturing activity?

As I mention earlier, unused production capacity is called *idle capacity*. One argument is that the cost of idle capacity should be charged off as a period cost (that is, charged directly to expense in the year and not included in product cost). Generally, the cost of idle capacity is calculated as follows:

Percent of idle capacity × Fixed manufacturing overhead costs = Cost of idle capacity

Refer to Company Y's operating profit report and summary of manufacturing activity for the year (Figure 11-2). Its annual production capacity is 800,000 units, but it produced only 500,000 units during the year. The company's idle capacity is 37.5 percent. In this case, the idle capacity cost is calculated as follows:

37.5 percent idle capacity × $8,000,000 fixed manufacturing overhead costs = $3,000,000 cost of idle capacity

Q. How would Company Y's operating profit report and summary of manufacturing activity be revised if the cost of idle capacity is treated as a period cost in the year?

A. The $3,000,000 cost of idle capacity is taken out of fixed manufacturing overhead costs and moved up to the operating profit report as an expense in the period. The revised operating profit report and summary of manufacturing activity, which you may find somewhat surprising, is as follows:

	Company Y	
Operating Profit Report For Year	**Per Unit**	**Totals**
Sales volume, in Units		500,000
Sales Revenue	$85.00	$42,500,000
Cost of Goods Sold Expense (see below)	(50.00)	(25,000,000)
Gross Margin	$35.00	$17,500,000
Variable Operating Expenses	(12.50)	(6,250,000)
Contribution Margin	$22.50	$11,250,000
Fixed Operating Expenses		(5,000,000)
Cost of Idle Capacity		(3,000,000)
Operating Profit		$3,250,000

Manufacturing Activity Summary For Year	**Per Unit**	**Totals**
Annual Production Capacity, in Units		800,000
Actual Output, in Units		500,000
Raw Materials	$15.00	$7,500,000
Direct Labor	20.00	10,000,000
Variable Manufacturing Overhead Costs	5.00	2,500,000
Total Variable Manufacturing Costs	$40.00	$20,000,000
Fixed Manufacturing Overhead Costs	10.00	5,000,000
Product Cost and Total Manufacturing Costs	$50.00	$25,000,000

Allocating indirect costs is as simple as ABC . . . not!

Most manufacturers make many different products. Just think of General Motors or Ford and the number of different car and truck models they assemble. If a separate production plant (building, machinery, equipment, tools, workforce, and so on) were dedicated to making only one product, all manufacturing costs would be *direct* costs to that one particular product. But in reality, it's the other way around: One production plant is used to make many different products. The result is that many production costs are *indirect* to the different products manufactured by the business.

Indirect manufacturing costs are allocated among the products produced during the period. Therefore, product cost includes both direct and indirect manufacturing costs. Coming up with a completely satisfactory allocation method is difficult and ends up being somewhat arbitrary — but it must be done in order to determine product cost.

Accountants have developed many methods and schemes for allocating indirect overhead costs, many of which are based on some common denominator of production activity, such as direct labor hours. A different method that has gotten a lot of press is called *activity-based costing* (ABC).

With the ABC method, you identify each necessary, supporting activity in the production process and collect costs into a separate pool for each identified activity. Then you develop a *measure* for each activity — for example, the measure for the engineering department may be hours, and the measure for the maintenance department may be square feet. You use the activity measures as *cost drivers* to allocate cost to products. So if Product A needs 200 hours of the engineering department's time, and Product B is a simple product that needs only 20 hours of engineering, you allocate ten times as much of the engineering cost to Product A.

The idea is that the engineering department doesn't come cheap; including the cost of their slide rules and pocket protectors as well as their salaries and benefits, the total cost per hour for those engineers could be $150 to $200, or more. The logic of the ABC cost-allocation method is that the engineering cost per hour should be allocated on the basis of the number of hours (the driver) required by each product. In similar fashion, suppose the cost of the maintenance department is $20 per square foot per year. If Product C uses twice as much floor space as Product D, you charge it with twice as much maintenance cost.

The ABC method has received much praise for being better than traditional allocation methods, especially for management decision-making. However, you should keep in mind that it requires rather arbitrary definitions of cost drivers, and having too many different cost drivers, each with its own pool of costs, isn't practical.

Managers should be aware of which cost allocation methods are being used by their companies and should challenge a method if they think that it's misleading and should be replaced with a better (though still somewhat arbitrary) method. I don't mean to put too fine a point on this, but to a large extent, cost allocation boils down to a "my arbitrary method is better than your arbitrary method" argument.

Note that changing the handling of the cost of idle capacity produces no difference in the company's operating profit for the year. Is this surprising, or what? In this example, the company produces the same number of units it sells during the year. Thus, there's no "inventory effect." One-hundred percent of its manufacturing costs for the year end up in expense regardless of the way in which the idle capacity is handled. In Figure 11-2, the entire $8,000,000 fixed manufacturing overhead costs ends up in cost of goods sold expense. In this example scenario, $3,000,000 of the fixed costs end up in a period expense account (Cost of Idle Capacity), and the other $5,000,000 ends up in cost of goods sold expense.

15. Assume that Company Z manufactures 2,100,000 units during the year (instead of the 2,500,000 units production output shown in Figure 11-2). Determine its operating profit for the year. Assume that the cost of idle capacity is treated as a period cost and isn't embedded in product cost.

Solve It

---

16. Refer to Company X's operating profit report and summary of manufacturing activity presented in Figure 11-1. Note that its annual production capacity is 150,000 units, but the business manufactured only 120,000 units during the year. Therefore, it had 20 percent idle capacity (30,000 units not produced ÷ 150,000 units production capacity = 20 percent idle capacity). However, the cost of idle capacity isn't treated as a separate period cost; all the company's fixed manufacturing overhead costs are included in calculating its product cost.

Suppose that the business treats the cost of idle capacity as a period cost. Prepare a revised operating profit report and summary of manufacturing activity for the business.

Solve It

Answers to Problems on Manufacturing Cost Accounting

The following are the answers to the practice questions presented earlier in this chapter.

1 The company's total manufacturing costs for the year are $91,200,000 (see Figure 11-1), but only $83,600,000 is charged to cost of goods expense. What happened to the other $7,600,000 ($91,200,000 manufacturing costs for year – $83,600,000 cost of goods sold expense for year = $7,600,000)?

The business produced 120,000 units, which is 10,000 more units than the 110,000 units it sold during the year. Therefore, $\frac{1}{12}$ (10,000 ÷ 120,000) of its total manufacturing costs is allocated to the increase in inventory, and 11/12 is allocated to cost of goods sold during the year:

$\frac{11}{12}$ × $91,200,000 total manufacturing costs = $83,600,000 allocated to cost of goods sold expense

$\frac{1}{12}$ × $91,200,000 total manufacturing costs = $7,600,000 allocated to inventory

You can also answer this question by using product cost and number of units sold during the year:

$760 product cost × 110,000 units sold during year = $83,600,000 cost allocated to cost of goods sold expense

$760 product cost × 10,000 units increase in inventory = $7,600,000 cost allocated to inventory

2 As you can see in Figure 11-1, Company X recorded $42,000,000 fixed manufacturing overhead costs in the year. Suppose, instead, that its fixed manufacturing overhead costs were $45,600,000 for the year, which is an increase of $3,600,000. Would the company's operating profit have been $3,600,000 lower? (Assume that variable manufacturing costs per unit and operating expenses remain the same.)

No, operating profit would not be $3,600,000 lower. The following schedule shows that operating profit would be $3,300,000 lower. The higher fixed manufacturing overhead costs drive up the product cost per unit, from $760 to $790, or $30 per unit. However, the business sold only 110,000 units, so the $30 higher product cost per unit increases cost of goods sold expense only $3,300,000 ($30 increase in product cost × 110,000 units sales volume = $3,300,000). Therefore, operating profit decreases $3,300,000.

	Company X	
Operating Profit Report For Year	**Per Unit**	**Totals**
Sales volume, in Units		110,000
Sales Revenue	$1,400.00	$154,000,000
Cost of Goods Sold Expense (see below)	(790.00)	(86,900,000)
Gross Margin	$610.00	$67,100,000
Variable Operating Expenses	(300.00)	(33,000,000)
Contribution Margin	$310.00	$34,100,000
Fixed Operating Expenses		(21,450,000)
Operating Profit		$12,650,000

Manufacturing Activity Summary For Year	Per Unit	Totals
Annual Production Capacity, in Units		150,000
Actual Output, in Units		120,000
Raw Materials	$215.00	$25,800,000
Direct Labor	125.00	15,000,000
Variable Manufacturing Overhead Costs	70.00	8,400,000
Total Variable Manufacturing Costs	$410.00	$49,200,000
Fixed Manufacturing Overhead Costs	380.00	45,600,000
Product Cost and Total Manufacturing Costs	$790.00	$94,800,000

The operating profit decrease still leaves $300,000 of the total $3,600,000 fixed manufacturing overhead costs increase to explain. The 10,000 units increase in inventory absorbs this additional amount of fixed manufacturing overhead costs; including fixed manufacturing overhead costs in product cost is called *absorption costing*. Some accountants argue that product cost should include only variable manufacturing costs and not include any fixed manufacturing overhead costs. This practice is called *direct costing*, or *variable costing*, and it isn't generally accepted. Generally accepted accounting principles (GAAP) require that fixed manufacturing overhead cost must be included in product cost.

3 Suppose that Company X uses the FIFO method instead of the LIFO method shown in Figure 11-1. The company starts the year with 25,000 units in beginning inventory at a cost of $735 per unit according to the FIFO method. During the year, it manufactures 120,000 units and sells 110,000 units (see Figure 11-1). Determine Company X's cost of goods sold expense for the year and its cost of ending inventory using the FIFO method.

The business started the year with 25,000 units at $735 per unit for a total cost of $18,375,000, which constitutes one batch of inventory. The business manufactured 120,000 units during the year at $760 per unit for a total cost of $91,200,000, which constitutes the second batch of inventory.

Under FIFO, the cost of goods sold expense is determined as follows:

25,000 units × $735 = $18,375,000

<u>85,000 units</u> × $760 = <u>$64,600,000</u>

110,000 units sold   = $82,975,000

Under FIFO, the ending inventory consists of one layer:

35,000 units × $760 = $26,600,000

4 Company X produced 120,000 units and sold 110,000 units during the year (see Figure 11-1). Therefore, the company increased its inventory 10,000 units. Does this increase seem reasonable? Or is the company's production output compared with its sales volume out of kilter?

It's hard to say for sure whether the increased inventory is reasonable. The key factor is the forecasted sales volume for next year. If the business predicts moderate sales volume growth next year, then increasing inventory 10,000 units seems reasonable. On the other hand, if the sales forecast is flat for next year, why did the business produce more than it sold during the year just ended? The inventory increase could have been a mistake, or taking a more cynical view, perhaps the business deliberately manufactured more units than it sold in order to boost operating profit for the year.

5 Refer to Figure 11-2 for the operating profit report and manufacturing activity summary of Company Y for the year. Assume that the business had no work-in-process inventory at the start or end of the year. The business purchased $7,800,000 raw materials on credit during the year. Make the basic manufacturing entries for the business by following the series of entries explained in the section "Taking a Short Tour of Manufacturing Entries."

Note: The following manufacturing entries include short explanations.

Raw Materials Inventory	$7,800,000	
Accounts Payable		$7,800,000

Purchase on credit of raw materials needed in the production process.

Work-in-Process Inventory	$7,500,000	
Raw Materials Inventory		$7,500,000

Transfer of raw materials to the production process.

Work-in-Process Inventory	$10,000,000	
Cash		$x,xxx,xxx
Payroll Taxes Payable		$x,xxx,xxx
Accrued Payables		$x,xxx,xxx

To record direct labor costs for period.

Work-in-Process Inventory	$2,500,000	
Cash		$x,xxx,xxx
Accounts Payable		$xxx,xxx
Accrued Payables		$xxx,xxx

To record indirect variable manufacturing overhead costs for period.

Work-in-Process Inventory	$8,000,000	
Cash		$x,xxx,xxx
Accumulated Depreciation		$x,xxx,xxx
Accounts Payable		$x,xxx,xxx
Accrued Payables		$x,xxx,xxx

To record indirect fixed manufacturing overhead costs for period.

Finished Goods Inventory	$28,000,000	
Work-in-Process Inventory		$28,000,000

To record completion of manufacturing process and to transfer production costs to the finished goods inventory account.

Cost of Goods Sold Expense	$28,000,000	
Finished Goods Inventory		$28,000,000

To record cost of products sold during year.

6 Refer to Figure 11-2 for the operating profit report and manufacturing activity summary of Company Z for the year. Assume that the business had no work-in-process inventory at the start or end of the year. The business purchased $19,500,000 raw materials on credit during the year. Make the basic manufacturing entries for the business by following the series of entries explained in the section "Taking a Short Tour of Manufacturing Entries."

Note: The following manufacturing entries include short explanations.

Raw Materials Inventory	$19,500,000	
Accounts Payable		$19,500,000

Purchase on credit of raw materials needed in the production process.

Work-in-Process Inventory	$18,750,000	
Raw Materials Inventory		$18,750,000

Transfer of raw materials to the production process.

Work-in-Process Inventory	$6,875,000	
Cash		$x,xxx,xxx
Payroll Taxes Payable		$x,xxx,xxx
Accrued Payables		$x,xxx,xxx

To record direct labor costs for period.

Work-in-Process Inventory	$12,500,000	
Cash		$x,xxx,xxx
Accounts Payable		$xxx,xxx
Accrued Payables		$xxx,xxx

To record indirect variable manufacturing overhead costs for period.

Work-in-Process Inventory	$8,000,000	
Cash		$x,xxx,xxx
Accumulated Depreciation		$x,xxx,xxx
Accounts Payable		$x,xxx,xxx
Accrued Payables		$x,xxx,xxx

To record indirect fixed manufacturing overhead costs for period.

Finished Goods Inventory	$46,125,000	
Work-in-Process Inventory		$46,125,000

To record completion of manufacturing process and to transfer production costs to the finished goods inventory account.

Cost of Goods Sold Expense	$36,900,000	
Finished Goods Inventory		$36,900,000

To record cost of products sold during year.

7 Assume that Company Y uses the LIFO method to charge out raw materials to production. In this question, assume that supply shortages of raw materials meant that Company Y couldn't purchase all the raw materials it needed for production during the year, and it had to draw down its raw materials inventory. Fortunately, it had an adequate beginning inventory of raw materials to cover the gap in purchases during the year. In this situation, would the cost of raw materials issued to production be different than the $7,500,000 shown in Figure 11-2?

Yes, the cost of raw materials charged to production probably would be lower because the beginning inventory or raw materials probably is on the books at a lower cost per unit compared with current purchase prices. This "aging" of inventory cost is one disadvantage of the LIFO method, which I discuss in Chapter 9. When a business dips into its beginning inventory because it uses more materials than it was able to buy during the period, it has to charge out the raw materials at the costs recorded in its inventory account. These costs may go back several years, and in the meantime, the costs of raw materials have probably escalated to higher prices per unit. If the difference is significant, the chief accountant should warn managers that the raw materials component of product cost is lower than normal because of a *LIFO liquidation effect* — not because of more efficient production methods or lower raw material purchase prices during the year.

8 Determine what Company Z's operating profit would be if it had sold 2,100,000 units during the year, which is 100,000 more units than in the example shown in Figure 11-2. Assume that production output had remained the same at 2,500,000 units (the company's production output capacity).

The business manufactured 500,000 more units than it sold during the year (see Figure 11-2). Therefore, it certainly had 100,000 additional units available for sale; indeed, it had 500,000 additional units available for sale without having to reach into its beginning quantity of inventory. An additional 100,000 units of sales is only a 5 percent increase (100,000 additional units ÷ 2,000,000 units sales volume = 5 percent.) So, the company's fixed operating expenses probably would not increase at the higher sales volume level.

The company's product cost would be the same at the higher sales level and its fixed operating costs would hold the same. Therefore, its operating profit would increase $405,000:

$4.05 contribution margin per unit × 100,000 additional units sold = $405,000 operating profit increase

In other words, Company Z's operating profit would increase from $600,000 to $1,005,000, which is an increase of 67.5 percent. But don't get too excited — this large percent increase is due mainly to the low base of only $600,000 operating profit. Nevertheless, the business certainly could have reported a much better operating profit if it had sold just 5 percent more units.

9 Company Y was on track to sell 550,000 units in the year, but late in the year, a major customer canceled a large order for 50,000 units. The business reduced its production output to 500,000 units, as you see in Figure 11-2. Determine the operating profit Company Y would have earned if it had manufactured and sold 550,000 units in the year.

Company Y would have earned $4,875,000 operating profit, as the following schedule shows.

Operating Profit Report For Year	Company Y	
	Per Unit	Totals
Sales volume, in Units		550,000
Sales Revenue	$85.00	$46,750,000
Cost of Goods Sold Expense (see below)	(54.55)	(30,000,000)
Gross Margin	$30.45	$16,750,000
Variable Operating Expenses	(12.50)	(6,875,000)
Contribution Margin	$17.95	$9,875,000
Fixed Operating Expenses		(5,000,000)
Operating Profit		$4,875,000

Manufacturing Activity Summary For Year	Per Unit	Totals
Annual Production Capacity, in Units		800,000
Actual Output, in Units		550,000
Raw Materials	$15.00	$8,250,000
Direct Labor	20.00	11,000,000
Variable Manufacturing Overhead Costs	5.00	2,750,000
Total Variable Manufacturing Costs	$40.00	$22,000,000
Fixed Manufacturing Overhead Costs	14.55	8,000,000
Product Cost and Total Manufacturing Costs	$54.55	$30,000,000

The canceled order for 50,000 units hit operating profit hard: The company's operating profit fell $1,625,000 as the result, from $4,875,000 (see schedule above) to $3,250,000 (see Figure 11-2, in which only 500,000 units are sold).

The company has unused production capacity (see Figure 11-2), so producing an additional 50,000 units wouldn't have increased its fixed manufacturing overhead costs. And, its fixed operating costs would not have increased at the higher sales level. The company's *variable* operating expenses equal $12.50 per unit, and its *variable* manufacturing costs equal $40.00 per unit. Thus, its total variable costs equal $52.50 per unit. Manufacturing and selling 50,000 additional units causes costs to increase $2,625,000 ($52.50 variable costs per unit × 50,000 units = $2,625,000). Selling an additional 50,000 units increases sales revenue $4,250,000 ($85.00 sales price × 50,000 units = $4,250,000). Therefore,

Incremental sales revenue from additional 50,000 units = $4,250,000

Incremental costs from additional 50,000 units   = ($2,625,000)

Incremental operating profit from additional 50,000 units = $1,625,000

This calculation is an example of *marginal analysis,* on analyzing things on the edge. The focus is on the 50,000 units that the company didn't sell (but came close to selling).

10 Assume that Company Z's production output for the year is 2,000,000 units (instead of 2,500,000 units as in Figure 11-2). In other words, assume that the business manufactures the same number of units that it sells in the year. Assume all other manufacturing and operating factors are the same. Determine the company's operating profit for the year.

In this scenario, the company suffers a $1,000,000 operating *loss.* See the following schedule:

Operating Profit Report For Year	Company Z	
	Per Unit	Totals
Sales volume, in Units		2,000,000
Sales Revenue	$25.00	$50,000,000
Cost of Goods Sold Expense (see below)	(19.25)	(38,500,000)
Gross Margin	$5.75	$11,500,000
Variable Operating Expenses	(2.50)	(5,000,000)
Contribution Margin	$3.25	$6,500,000
Fixed Operating Expenses		(7,500,000)
Operating Profit Loss		($1,000,000)

Manufacturing Activity Summary For Year	Per Unit	Totals
Annual Production Capacity, in Units		2,500,000
Actual Output, in Units		2,000,000
Raw Materials	$7.50	$15,000,000
Direct Labor	2.75	5,500,000
Variable Manufacturing Overhead Costs	5.00	10,000,000
Total Variable Manufacturing Costs	$15.25	$30,500,000
Fixed Manufacturing Overhead Costs	4.00	8,000,000
Product Cost and Total Manufacturing Costs	$19.25	$38,500,000

By producing only 2,000,000 units, the company's burden rate increases to $4.00 per unit from the $3.20 burden rate when it produces 2,500,000 units (see Figure 11-2). This is an increase of $.80 per unit, which decreases Company Z's contribution margin per unit from $4.05 to $3.25 per unit. The company records $.80 less profit on each unit sold, so on its 2,000,000 units sales volume its operating profit drops $1,600,000 – from $600,000 profit (see Figure 11-2) to $1,000,000 loss. It appears that the business boosted production output to 2,500,000 units in order to show a profit for the year. As the result, Company Z's stuck with a surplus inventory that it will have to do something with in the year(s) ahead.

11 Towards the end of the year, the president of Company Y looks at the preliminary numbers for operating profit and doesn't like what he sees. He's "promised" the board of directors that operating profit for the year will come in at $4,850,000. In fact, his bonus depends on hitting that operating profit target. There is still time before the end of the year to crank up production output for the year. Therefore, he orders that production output be stepped up. The president asks you to determine what the production output level for the year would have to be in order to report $4,850,000 operating profit for the year. Of course, you have ethical qualms about doing this, but you need the job. So, you reluctantly decide to do the calculation. Determine the production output level that would yield $4,850,000 operating profit for the year.

The following schedule shows that if the business manufactures 625,000 units, its operating profit will be $4,850,000:

	Company Y	
Operating Profit Report For Year	**Per Unit**	**Totals**
Sales volume, in Units		500,000
Sales Revenue	$85.00	$42,500,000
Cost of Goods Sold Expense (see below)	($52.80)	(26,400,000)
Gross Margin	$32.20	$16,100,000
Variable Operating Expenses	($12.50)	(6,250,000)
Contribution Margin	$19.70	$9,850,000
Fixed Operating Expenses		(5,000,000)
Operating Profit		$4,850,000

Manufacturing Activity Summary For Year	**Per Unit**	**Totals**
Annual Production Capacity, in Units		800,000
Actual Output, in Units		625,000
Raw Materials	$15.00	$9,375,000
Direct Labor	$20.00	12,500,000
Variable Manufacturing Overhead Costs	$5.00	3,125,000
Total Variable Manufacturing Costs	$40.00	$25,000,000
Fixed Manufacturing Overhead Costs	$12.80	8,000,000
Product Cost and Total Manufacturing Costs	$52.80	$33,000,000

The president wants $1,600,000 more profit than shown in Figure 11-2 ($4,850,000 profit target – $3,250,000 profit at 500,000 units production level = $1,600,000 additional profit). The only profit driver that changes with a higher production level is the burden rate, which has to decline $3.20 per unit in order to achieve the additional profit ($1,600,000 additional profit wanted ÷ 500,000 units sales volume = $3.20 decrease needed in burden rate). The burden rate has to decrease $3.20, from $16.00 (see Figure 11-2) to $12.80. The production output level has to be 625,000 units to get the burden rate down to $12.80 ($8,000,000 fixed manufacturing overhead costs ÷ $12.80 burden rate = 625,000 units).

Whether it's ethical and above board to jack up production to 625,000 units when sales are only 500,000 units for the year is a serious question. The members of Company Y's board of directors should definitely challenge the president on why such a large inventory increase is needed. I would, that's for sure!

12   Refer to your answer to Question 10, in which Company Z produces only 2,000,000 units during the year. In the scenario shown in Figure 11-2, the business manufactures 2,500,000 units, which is its maximum production output for the year. Do you think that Company Z cranked up production output to 2,500,000 units mainly to boost its operating profit for the year?

No one wants to jump to conclusions, but it would appear that boosting operating profit very well may be the reason for Company Z's high production output level. Put another way, the chief executive of the business has to justify the large inventory increase based on legitimate reasons, such as a big jump in sales forecast for next year or a looming strike of employees that will shut down the company's production for several months. Otherwise, the ugly truth is that the business is engaging in some *earnings management,* also called massaging the numbers. Sophisticated readers of the company's financial statements will notice the large jump in inventory in the balance sheet, and they may press top management for an explanation. Therefore, the attempt at accounting manipulation may not work.

13   The president of Company X is puzzled by the operating profit report and summary of manufacturing activity for the year, in which $1,200,000 raw materials cost was wasted and charged to expense in the year. He expected that operating profit would be $1,200,000 lower (as compared to the scenario in Figure 11-1, in which there's no wasted raw materials cost). Operating profit in the wasted raw materials scenario is only $100,000 lower than in Figure 11-1. Explain to the president why operating profit is only $100,000 lower.

The president is asking about the impact on operating profit. If the $1,200,000 cost of wasted raw materials is included in the calculation of product cost $1,100,000 of it ends up in cost of goods sold expense because 110,000 of the 120,000 units produced were sold during the year. The other $100,000 is absorbed in the inventory increase. In contrast, if the $1,200,000 is charged to expense directly, none of it escapes into the inventory increase. So in one scenario, profit is hit with $1,100,000 expense and in the other scenario profit is hit with $1,200,000 expense. The operating profit difference is only $100,000.

14   After Company Y's operating profit report and summary of manufacturing activity for the year has been prepared (see Figure 11-2), you, the chief accountant, learn that $1,000,000 of raw materials were thrown away during the year because the items had spoiled and couldn't be used in the manufacturing process. The company's president knows about this loss and insists that no change be made in the operating profit report and summary of manufacturing activity. Do you go along with the president, or do you argue for changing the operating profit report and summary of manufacturing activity?

If you haven't read my answer to Problem 13, please read it. In that scenario the net error in operating profit is only $100,000 because most of the cost of wasted materials had flowed through to cost of goods sold expense. In this case *all* of the cost of wasted materials ends up in the cost of goods sold expense, so operating profit is correct. The reason is that all of the manufacturing costs for the year are charged to cost of goods sold because all of the company's output for the year was sold. Note that its entire $28,000,000 manufacturing costs is charged to cost of goods sold expense. (Remember that the company uses the LIFO method.)

Therefore, the argument in this situation is really about how to classify costs in the internal operating profit report to managers. Would it be better to report a separate cost of wasted raw materials? Yes, I think so. Hopefully, this is a cost the company can avoid from happening again. If the error is not corrected, the managers would be misled into thinking that the true product cost is $16.00, when in fact it is $2.00 lower ($1,000,000 cost of wasted raw materials ÷ 500,000 units production output = $2.00 per unit error).

15 Assume that Company Z manufactures 2,100,000 units during the year (instead of the 2,500,000 units production output shown in Figure 11-2). Determine its operating profit for the year. Assume that the cost of idle capacity is treated as a period cost and isn't embedded in product cost.

The company's operating loss is $680,000, as the following schedule shows.

		Company Z
Operating Profit Report For Year	**Per Unit**	**Totals**
Sales volume, in Units		2,000,000
Sales Revenue	$25.00	$50,000,000
Cost of Goods Sold Expense (see below)	(18.45)	(36,900,000)
Gross Margin	$6.55	$13,100,000
Variable Operating Expenses	(2.50)	(5,000,000)
Contribution Margin	$4.05	$8,100,000
Fixed Operating Expenses		(7,500,000)
Cost of Idle Capacity		(1,280,000)
Operating Profit		($680,000)

Manufacturing Activity Summary For Year	**Per Unit**	**Totals**
Annual Production Capacity, in Units		2,500,000
Actual Output, in Units		2,100,000
Raw Materials	$7.50	$15,750,000
Direct Labor	2.75	5,775,000
Variable Manufacturing Overhead Costs	5.00	10,500,000
Total Variable Manufacturing Costs	$15.25	$32,025,000
Fixed Manufacturing Overhead Costs (Net of idle capacity cost -- see above)	3.20	6,720,000
Product Cost and Total Manufacturing Costs	$18.45	$38,745,000

The company has 16 percent idle capacity in this scenario (400,000 units not produced ÷ 2,500,000 units capacity = 16 percent idle capacity). So, 16 percent of its $8,000,000 fixed manufacturing overhead costs, or $1,280,000, is removed from the calculation of product cost and treated as a period cost. This action reduces operating profit for the year by this amount, of course.

16 Refer to Company X's operating profit report and summary of manufacturing activity presented in Figure 11-1. Note that its annual production capacity is 150,000 units, but the business manufactured only 120,000 units during the year. Therefore, it had 20 percent idle capacity (30,000 units not produced ÷ 150,000 units production capacity = 20 percent idle capacity). However, in the Figure 11-1 scenario, the cost of idle capacity isn't treated as a separate period cost; all the company's fixed manufacturing overhead costs are included in calculating its product cost.

Suppose that the business treats the cost of idle capacity as a period cost. Prepare a revised operating profit report and summary of manufacturing activity for the business.

Company X's operating profit would be $15,250,000, as the following schedule shows.

Operating Profit Report For Year	Company X	
	Per Unit	Totals
Sales volume, in Units		110,000
Sales Revenue	$1,400.00	$154,000,000
Cost of Goods Sold Expense (see below)	(690.00)	(75,900,000)
Gross Margin	$710.00	$78,100,000
Variable Operating Expenses	(300.00)	(33,000,000)
Contribution Margin	$410.00	$45,100,000
Fixed Operating Expenses		(21,450,000)
Cost of Idle Capacity		(8,400,000)
Operating Profit		$15,250,000

Manufacturing Activity Summary For Year	Per Unit	Totals
Annual Production Capacity, in Units		150,000
Actual Output, in Units		120,000
Raw Materials	$215.00	$25,800,000
Direct Labor	125.00	15,000,000
Variable Manufacturing Overhead Costs	70.00	8,400,000
Total Variable Manufacturing Costs	$410.00	$49,200,000
Fixed Manufacturing Overhead Costs (Net of idle capacity cost -- see above)	280.00	33,600,000
Product Cost and Total Manufacturing Costs	$690.00	$82,800,000

Note that the company's operating profit decreases a relatively small amount, only $700,000, due to treating idle capacity as a period costs instead of a product cost. In Figure 11-1, operating profit is $15,950,000, and in this schedule, it's $15,250,000, or $700,000 less. This $700,000 is "buried" in the ending inventory cost under the method shown in Figure 11-1; in other words, in the scenario shown in Figure 11-1, the cost of idle capacity is included in the $760 product cost. The product cost is $70 higher than the $690 product cost in this schedule (in which idle capacity is pulled out of manufacturing and treated as a period cost). The company sold 110,000 units, and the other 10,000 units of its production output increase its inventory. These 10,000 units absorb $700,000 of the idle capacity cost (10,000 units inventory increase × $70 higher burden rate = $700,000 absorbed by inventory increase).

Chapter 12

Figuring Out Interest and Return on Investment

· ·

In This Chapter

▶ Getting the lowdown on interest

▶ Breaking the code on compound interest

▶ Examining installment loans and payments

▶ Figuring return on investment

· ·

*I*n my experience, most people are a little fuzzy on interest and return on investment. Sure, most people know that *interest* is the cost of borrowing money or the income from saving money. And they know that they should earn a return on their investments. However, when put in a specific borrowing, saving, or investing situation, people aren't sure how interest is calculated and exactly what different interest rates mean. And they're in a fog regarding how rates of return on investments are determined and the assumptions behind these measures of investment performance.

The better you understand interest and return on investment, the better economic citizen and intelligent investor you will be. In this chapter, I explain how interest works and how investment performance is measured using rates of return. I think you'll find more than a few surprises as you go through it.

The Apollo 13 astronauts became famous for their message, "Houston, we have a problem." The inherent problem in this chapter is that, by their very nature, interest and return on investment require calculations. However, most people have their enthusiasm for number crunching under control (except for accountants and actuaries). I don't throw a bunch of mathematical formulas at you in this chapter (that would turn you off for sure). Instead, I use transparent examples that demonstrate how interest works and how to determine return on investment. In sports, becoming a better player takes practicing and scrimmaging. In accounting, the best means for improving your understanding of interest and return on investment is practicing and scrimmaging with realistic examples.

Getting Down the Basics of Interest

Any explanation of interest has to start with what's called *simple interest* — although, it's not as simple as the term implies.

Keeping it simple with simple interest

The idea behind simple interest is that a certain amount of interest is paid or earned on a certain amount of money for a certain period of time, say one year. Suppose you put $1,000 in a savings account at the start of the year. At the end of the year your savings account was credited (increased) $40 for the interest you earned. The simple interest rate you earned is calculated as follows:

$40 interest earned ÷ $1,000 amount invested for one year = 4.0 percent simple interest rate

But, what if you earned $10 each quarter instead of $40 at the end of the year? Things get more complicated, as I explain in the chapter.

Q. Suppose you've filled out all the forms and convinced a bank to loan your business $100,000. The bank has examined your three "Cs": character, collateral, and cash flow. The terms of the loan are that the bank will put $100,000 in your checking account today; the maturity of the loan is one year later; and, the annual interest rate on the loan is 6 percent. (The loan is renewable, but that's another topic.) What amount do you have to pay the bank one year later, on the maturity date, to pay off this loan?

A. You can probably solve this problem in your head without doing any calculations on a hand held business/finance calculator or using Excel. I modify this simple example later in the chapter in order to explore several other important features of interest, so I want to be very clear about how interest is calculated for this basic example.

In this example, interest is added to the amount borrowed to determine the *maturity value* of the loan, which is the amount payable to the bank on the maturity date. The amount borrowed, which is called the *face value* or *principal* of the loan, is the basis for calculating interest. The amount of interest is calculated as follows:

$100,000 amount borrowed today × 6 percent annual interest rate = $6,000 interest on loan

$100,000 amount borrowed today + $6,000 interest on loan = $106,000 maturity value of loan one year later

How do you do those calculations?

You're probably asking, "How do I actually do the calculations in this chapter?" Well, you have two basic choices for doing interest and return on investment calculations: You can use either a business/financial calculator or the Excel spreadsheet program from Microsoft. I use both of these tools, with the complexity of the calculation making the actual determination. Hewlett-Packard and Texas Instruments make excellent hand held business/financial calculators. I recommend them highly. If you use a computer-based spreadsheet, Excel is basically your only option. Fortunately, Excel runs equally well on both Windows and Macintosh computer platforms.

With both a business/financial calculator and Excel, you have to spend a little time familiarizing yourself with the tool and how to use it — that's the rub. (When's the last time you actually read a users' manual?) As I proceed with the examples in this chapter — which get more and more complicated — I include useful hints about doing calculations either with a hand-held business/financial calculator or in Excel.

The legal instrument used for the contract between a borrower and a lender is fairly complicated and has many clauses and provisions. Generally, the borrower signs a *promissory note* to the lender. You need a lawyer to fully explain the terms, conditions, obligations, and rights of each party under the loan agreement.

Q. Suppose the lender does *not* refer to an annual interest rate and does not refer to the amount you borrow. You sign a legal instrument (probably a promissory note) that calls for the payment of $106,000 at the maturity date of the loan (one year later). The bank puts $100,000 in your checking account today. Is the annual interest rate on this loan still 6 percent?

A. Yes, the annual interest rate is still 6 percent. Why? Well, the interest rate is calculated on the basis of the amount received at the start of the loan. So, the interest rate is calculated as follows:

$106,000 maturity value of loan one year later – $100,000 received today when signing the note payable = $6,000 interest for one year

$6,000 interest for one year ÷ $100,000 received at start of loan = 6 percent annual interest rate

One year later you pay back to the bank 6 percent more than the bank loaned to you today, which means that the annual interest rate is 6 percent. Whether this interest rate is too high or not is up to you. You may want to shop around at different banks and other lenders to see if you can get a better interest rate.

1. Suppose your company borrows $500,000 from a bank, and that amount is deposited in your checking account today. The note that you sign calls for a 6.25 percent annual interest rate. Determine the *maturity value* (the amount you will pay the bank when the note comes due then) of the note one year from now.

Solve It

2. Suppose you sign a note that calls for $868,000 to be paid to the lender one year from today. (In other words, the maturity value of the loan one year from today is $868,000.) The lender gives you $800,000 today in exchange for this note. There's no mention of the rate of interest on this loan. What is the annual interest rate on this loan?

Solve It

3. Refer to Question 1. Suppose the date on the note is March 1, 2006 — this is the date the note was signed and the money was put in the company's checking account with the bank. It's now August 31, 2006, which is the close of the company's fiscal year. Should an adjusting entry for interest expense be recorded? If so, make the journal entry.

Solve It

4. Refer to Question 2. Because the note payable calls for a payment of $868,000 at the maturity date, the bookkeeper thinks that this amount should be recorded as a liability and that the difference between this liability amount and the $800,000 proceeds received by the business should be debited to the prepaid expenses asset account. Do you agree?

Solve It

Distinguishing nominal and effective interest rates

Assume a business borrows $100,000 for one year at an annual interest rate of 6 percent. One alternative is that the bank charges 6 percent simple interest that is payable at the end of the year. In this case the business pays the bank $106,000 (which includes $6,000 interest) at the maturity date one year later. Now here's a twist that happens all the time: Instead of 6 percent simple interest that is figured once a year, assume that the bank quotes a 6 percent annual interest rate that is *compounded quarterly*, which means it wants to be paid interest every three months. Does this make a difference? It sure does, and it makes the calculation of interest more complicated.

When used in reference to an annual rate of interest, *compounding* refers to the frequency of charging (or earning) interest during the year. The annual rate has to be converted into the interest rate per period. Assuming the lender charges interest quarterly, the 6 percent annual rate is divided by four to get the 1.5 percent interest rate per quarter. In the example just introduced, the business could pay $1,500 at the end of each quarter ($100,000 × 1.5 percent interest rate per quarter = $1,500 interest per quarter). This way, the bank collects interest income earlier and can put the money to work sooner. On the other hand, the main reason for quarterly compounding may be to raise the *effective* annual interest rate.

Suppose the business doesn't want to pay interest quarterly; it prefers to make just one payment at the maturity date of the loan one year later. The bank readily agrees as long as the compounding effect is included in the payoff amount (maturity value) of the loan. The bank demands quarterly compounding, which means there are four interest periods during the year.

Q. Assuming quarterly compounding of the quoted 6 percent annual interest rate, determine the amount the business has to pay the bank at the maturity date of the note one year from now.

A. The 6 percent annual interest rate quoted by the bank is often referred to as the *nominal* rate. Nominal means in name only. In the example, the lender insists on quarterly compounding, which means that it charges a 1.5 percent rate each quarter. If the business doesn't pay interest at the end of each quarter, the unpaid interest is added into the loan balance for the next quarter.

Accordingly, the amount owed to the bank one year later is calculated as follows:

Quarter	Loan Balance at Start of Period	Interest at 1.5%	Loan Balance at End of Period
First	$100,000.00	$1,500.00	$101,500.00
Second	$101,500.00	$1,522.50	$103,022.50
Third	$103,022.50	$1,545.34	$104,567.84
Fourth	$104,567.84	$1,568.52	$106,136.36

The business owes the bank $106,136.36 at the maturity date of the note. Therefore, interest on the note is $6,136.36, which is $136.36 higher than the $6,000.00 simple interest the bank would have charged if the entire year had been treated as just one interest period.

So, there are two interest rates at work in this loan: the *nominal* rate (6 percent per year in this example) and the *effective* annual interest rate that gives effect to the compounding of the nominal rate. The effective annual interest rate on the loan in the example is 6.13636 percent, and is calculated as follows:

$6,136.36 interest for one year ÷ $100,000.00 borrowed at the start of year = 6.13636 percent effective annual interest rate on loan

The true interest rate is the effective interest rate because this rate determines the actual payment of interest. The nominal interest rate is simply the point of departure for calculating the effective interest rate.

If the business in this example had agreed to a 6.13636 percent annual interest rate on the loan in the first place, the bank would have been willing to compound annually, which means once a year. At this higher rate, the bank would have ended up with the same amount of money. Essentially, the bank should be indifferent about whether it charges a 6.13636 percent annual interest rate that is compounded annually, or a nominal 6 percent annual rate that is compounded quarterly. It's six of one, or a half dozen of the other.

Is it misleading to quote a nominal annual interest rate of 6 percent that in fact is compounded quarterly? The effective or "real" annual interest rate isn't 6 percent, but 6.13636 percent. You could argue that compounding is a sleight of hand trick for jacking up the true annual interest rate. Financial institutions have to be careful to abide with federal and state laws for truth in lending in this regard. But these laws still leave lenders a fair amount of wiggle room in advertising interest rates. All I can do is to caution you that featuring nominal annual interest rates is common practice. If you're loan-shopping, be sure to find out whether the nominal annual interest rate is compounded more frequently than once a year.

5. Suppose a business borrows $100,000 for one year. The lender quotes a 6 percent annual interest rate that's compounded semi-annually (twice a year). Determine the annual effective interest rate on the loan. You may find the following form helpful.

Half-Year	Loan Balance at Start of Period	Interest at ?%	Loan Balance at End of Period
First	$100,000.00		
Second			

Solve It

6. A company borrows $250,000 from its bank for one year. At the maturity date, one year after the money's deposited in the company's checking account, it writes a check to the bank for $268,324 to pay off the loan. Determine the effective annual interest rate and the nominal annual interest rate assuming semiannual compounding. You may find the following form helpful.

Half-Year	Loan Balance at Start of Period	Interest at ?%	Loan Balance at End of Period
First	$250,000.00		
Second			$268,324.00

Solve It

Discounting loans

Banks (and other lenders) make loans to businesses on the *discount basis*. The business signs a note to the lender that calls for a certain amount, say $100,000, to be paid at the maturity date of the loan. But the note contains no mention of an interest rate and there is no mention of how much money the business receives. To determine the amount loaned to the business, the lender *discounts* the maturity value of the loan by deducting a certain amount from the maturity value. The difference between the maturity value and the amount loaned to the business is the interest.

EXAMPLE

Q. A business signs a note to its bank that calls for $100,000.00 to be paid on the maturity date one year later. The bank deposits $93,295.85 in the company's checking account on the day the note is signed. The note doesn't refer to an interest rate. Determine the effective annual interest rate on this loan and the nominal annual interest rate assuming that interest is compounded quarterly.

A. A problem like this isn't that technical. Nevertheless, the calculations required to solve the problem are demanding. I recommend using a hand-held business/financial calculator to get an accurate answer. Here are step-by-step instructions for using a hand-held calculator to answer this problem:

1. Select the TVM (time value of money) function.

2. To find the effective annual interest rate on the loan enter 1 for N, which is the number of periods (one year).

3. Enter $93,295.85 for the PV (present value).

4. Enter $100,000.00 as a negative number for the FV (future value); this amount is negative because it has to be paid out to the bank at maturity.

5. Press the INT (interest) key for the answer, which should be 7.19 percent (rounded). (On Hewlett-Packard calculators, this key is labeled I/YR, which stands for interest per year, but it really means interest per period.)

6. After finding the effective annual interest rate, keep the same values in the registers for PV and FV, but enter 4 for N, the number of interest periods (the number of compounding periods). Then hit the INT key, and you get the quarterly interest rate, which should be 1.75 percent. You multiply this percentage by 4 to get the nominal annual interest rate, which is 7 percent.

You can also use the RATE function in the financial set of functions in Excel to solve for the effective and nominal interest rates for this problem.

7. A business receives $235,648.98 today from its bank and signs a one-year note that has a maturity value of $250,000.00. Determine the effective annual interest rate on this loan, and determine the nominal annual rate assuming semiannual compounding. You may find the following form helpful.

Half-Year	Loan Balance at Start of Period	Interest at ?%	Loan Balance at End of Period
First	$235,648.98		
Second			$250,000.00

Solve It

8. Assume that your next paycheck will be $2,000.00 (net of all withholdings). Unfortunately, payday is two weeks off, so you go to a storefront business that offers to advance money on your next paycheck. (These loan sharks — well, that may be too harsh a term — loan you a certain amount today against the amount of your next payroll check.) The lender advances you $1,960.78 against your next paycheck. You're desperate, so you take the money and sign the note. Two weeks later, you sign over your $2,000.00 paycheck to the lender to pay off the loan. What is your nominal annual interest rate on this loan? (If you have time, you may also calculate the *effective* annual interest rate on this loan based on biweekly compounding, or 26 times per year.)

Solve It

Lifting the Veil on Compound Interest

In the "Distinguishing nominal and effective interest rates" section earlier in this chapter, I explain how quarterly compounding increases the *effective* annual interest rate compared with the quoted *nominal* annual interest rate. In this and following sections, the effective interest rate is taken for granted. Instead of focusing on what happens within one year, the following discussion look at the effects of compounding over multiple years for investing and borrowing examples.

Interest rates and you

In an old TV police show, the sergeant would remind his officers as they were about to go out on the streets for their shift: "Be careful out there." When borrowing and saving, I would offer you the same advice concerning quoted interest rates and effective interest rates. For an example, assume a lender quotes you a 6 percent annual interest rate on your home mortgage loan. You make monthly payments, so the actual interest rate is .5 percent per month. This equals a 6.168 percent effective interest rate on your mortgage. In contrast, if you save money in your credit union and it pays 6 percent interest that is compounded monthly, you do not earn 6 percent, but rather 6.168 percent effective interest. If you had $10,000 in your account at the start of the year your balance is not $10,600.00 at the end of the year, but rather

$10,616.80 — because of the monthly compounding effect.

In quoting mortgage interest rates, most lenders refer to the nominal annual rate (in this example, the 6 percent annual interest rate). They do not mention the effective annual interest rate, which takes into account the monthly compounding effect. The credit union in which you have a savings account probably advertises the 6.168 percent effective annual interest rate it pays on savings accounts. In general, lenders refer to their nominal annual interest rates, whereas institutions that want to attract your savings refer to their effective annual interest rates. But, you have to be careful out there and make sure you know which rate is being referred to.

Be careful: "compounding" in these longer-term contexts (which run 5,10, 20, or more years) takes on a different emphasis. Compounding in these long range settings refers to the exponential growth idea — that if something grows at a certain rate from year to year, over enough years its size will end up being two or more times larger than what you started with. For instance, if you start with a population of, say, 10,000 persons in a town and its population grows 6 percent per year, its population will double to 20,000 in 12 years.

You just invested your $10,000 year-end bonus in a 401(k) plan (a qualified tax-deferred retirement account). You don't pay income tax on the $10,000 or on the earnings in your retirement account until you withdraw money from the account sometime in the future. You plan to retire in 20 years. Being conservative, you put the money in a *savings account* that pays 5 percent annual effective interest. (The interest rate could change in the future, but assume that the interest rate remains the same over all 20 years.)

Q. Assuming that your retirement account earns 5 percent annual interest for 20 years, what will be the balance in your account when you retire in 20 years?

A. In order to answer the question for the 20-year lifespan of the investment, you need to understand how year-to-year compounding works. Compounding means that you don't withdraw your interest earnings each year. Instead, you reinvest the annual earnings. The result of compounding for, say, the first four years is shown as follows:

Year	Retirement Account at Start of Year	Interest Earnings at 5.0%	Retirement Account at End of Year
1	$10,000.00	$500.00	$10,500.00
2	$10,500.00	$525.00	$11,025.00
3	$11,025.00	$551.25	$11,576.25
4	$11,576.25	$578.81	$12,155.06

The total amount of your earnings over the first four years is $2,155.06. Someone may think that, at 5 percent, you earn $500.00 each year on your $10,000.00 investment, and over four years, you will have earned $2,000.00. But as you can see in the schedule, you earn $2,155.06. You reinvest your annual earnings, which means that,

year-to-year, you have more money invested in your retirement account.

Over 20 years, your retirement account balance grows to $26,532.98. This amount assumes an annual 5 percent annual earnings rate and assumes that the financial institution you have your retirement investment account with doesn't go belly up. (The FDIC may insure your account, but that still doesn't guarantee that you'll get all your earnings.)

Your total amount of earnings over 20 years is $16,532.98 (the future value less the $10,000.00 you started with). It may be useful to think of your total earnings as follows: At $500.00 per year interest, based on your initial investment, you earned $10,000.00 ($500.00 per year × 20 years = $10,000.00). The other $6,532.98 of earnings over the 20 years comes from compounding (reinvesting) your earnings every year.

How did I get the answer? To prepare the four-year schedule, I grabbed my trusty HP calculator: I entered 20 for N, 5 for I/YR, negative 10,000 for PV, and then I punched the FV key to get the answer. (By the way, be sure that the PMT [payment] key has zero entered.)

Before computer spreadsheet programs and hand-held business/financial calculators came along, you had to use a table look-up method to solve problems like this one. Some of the biggest disadvantages of this method are that tables of future values and present values don't cover every situation, they're clumsy to use, and they require you to do pencil and paper calculations by hand. Surprisingly, many college accounting and finance textbooks still include these tables. For the life of me, I don't know why — it's like teaching the Morse code when everyone has a telephone.

9. Refer to the preceding example question, the retirement savings account example in which you invest $10,000 today and earn 5 percent annual interest (compounded annually) for 20 years. That example assumes that the 5 percent annual interest remains the same over all years. Instead, assume that you earn 4.5 percent annual interest during the first ten years and 5.5 percent annual interest during the last ten years. Are you better off in this situation?

Solve It

10. Suppose you just received your $25,000 year-end bonus. Instead of buying a new car, you decide to put the entire $25,000 in a qualified tax-deferred retirement investment account. You're 55 years old and plan to retire when you're 65 years old. You've done some research and have come up with two options for where to put your money: One is a safe, conservative investment vehicle that should earn an annual 4.5 percent interest rate (compounded annually), and the other is a more risky investment that has a good chance of being worth $45,000 ten years later, but there's some chance that it could be worth less than this amount. Compare your two options.

Solve It

Borrowing and Investing in Installments

Borrowing and investing are most commonly done in *installments*. With this method, payments are made regularly to pay off a loan or to build an investment. In this section, I stick with *interest-based* investments and examples of *fixed income* investments and loans. (In the section "Measuring Return on Investment (ROI)" later in the chapter, I cover investments in which changes in the market value of the investment are an important part of the return [earnings or loss] on the investment.)

Paying off a loan

Your business borrows $100,000 from a bank. You and the bank negotiate an installment loan in which you will pay off the loan over four years. The effective annual interest rate is 6 percent. The bank wants your business to *amortize* one-fourth of the principal amount each year. Amortize means to pay down the principal value of the loan. At the end of the first year, for instance, your business has to pay $25,000 on the principal balance of the loan plus interest for that year, and so on for the following three years. You sign the note to the bank and receive $100,000, which is deposited in your business's checking account.

Q. How much is each annual payment to the bank?

A. Probably the best approach to answering this question is to prepare an Excel spreadsheet to do the year-by-year calculations. (Of course you could do the calculations with pencil and paper by hand, but the Excel program is much faster and less prone to calculation mistakes.) The loan payment schedule is as follows:

Year	Loan Balance at Start of Year	Interest at 6.0%	Principal Payment	Total Payment to Bank	Loan Balance at End of Year
1	$100,000.00	$6,000.00	$25,000.00	$31,000.00	$75,000.00
2	$75,000.00	$4,500.00	$25,000.00	$29,500.00	$50,000.00
3	$50,000.00	$3,000.00	$25,000.00	$28,000.00	$25,000.00
4	$25,000.00	$1,500.00	$25,000.00	$26,500.00	$0.00

Q. Using the basic premise of the preceding question, suppose the bank wants *equal* payments at the end of each year. (In the preceding answer, the total payment varies year to year.) What is the annual payment on the loan under these terms?

A. A question like this shows the value of a hand-held business/financial calculator, which is designed for the express purpose of solving problems like this one. You enter 4 for N (the number of periods); 6 in INT (the I/YR key on HP calculators); 100,000 in PV (the present value of the loan, or the amount borrowed); and 0 in FV (future value). The reason for entering 0 in FV is that you want the loan completely paid off and reduced to a zero balance at the end of the fourth year. Press the PMT (payment) key, and the answer pops up on the screen — $28,859.15. Each payment to the bank should be $28,859.15.

The following schedule shows the proof of this answer. Compared with the schedule in the answer to the preceding question note that the annual payments are equal in this schedule:

Year	Loan Balance at Start of Year	Interest at 6.0%	Principal Payment	Total Payment to Bank	Loan Balance at End of Year
1	$100,000.00	$6,000.00	$22,859.15	$28,859.15	$77,140.85
2	$77,140.85	$4,628.45	$24,230.70	$28,859.15	$52,910.15
3	$52,910.15	$3,174.61	$25,684.54	$28,859.15	$27,225.61
4	$27,225.61	$1,633.54	$27,225.61	$28,859.15	$0.00

You can see that the principal balance reduces to zero at the end of the fourth quarter. In this schedule, as the amount of interest goes down each quarter, the amount of principal amortization goes up.

11. Suppose a business borrows $1,000,000 from a bank. The annual interest rate is 7.5 percent and the loan is for four years. The bank wants the business to make payments at the end of each year such that the principal of the loan is amortized in four equal amounts. Determine the annual payments required under the terms of this loan. You may find the following form helpful:

Year	Loan Balance at Start of Year	Interest at 7.5%	Principal Payment	Total Payment to Bank	Loan Balance at End of Year
1	$1,000,000.00	$75,000.00	$250,000.00	$325,000.00	$750,000.00
2					
3					
4					$0.00

Solve It

12. Suppose a business borrows $1,000,000 from a bank. The annual interest rate is 7.5 percent and the loan is for four years. The bank wants the business to make equal payments at the end of each year such that the principal of the loan is completely amortized (paid off) by the end of the fourth year. Determine the amount of annual payment required under the terms of the loan. You may find the following form helpful:

Year	Loan Balance at Start of Year	Interest at 7.5%	Principal Payment	Total Payment to Bank	Loan Balance at End of Year
1	$1,000,000.00	$75,000.00			
2					
3					
4					$0.00

Solve It

Investing in a retirement account

Many people invest in tax-deferred retirement accounts on the installment, or serial basis. They put some money in their retirement accounts at the end of each pay period, and their employers may or may not make matching payments. The federal income tax law encourages setting aside money from wages and other sources of steady income to build up a retirement fund, such as a 401(k), IRA, and many other plans.

Assume that your employer encourages employees to invest money from their monthly salaries in retirement accounts, and you've decided to do so. Each month, you put $250 into your retirement account, and your employer adds $150, so $400 is invested each month.

Q. To be conservative, assume that your retirement account will earn 4.8 percent income per year, compounded monthly (because you make monthly contributions). Although you may increase your monthly contributions in the future if your salary increases, at the present time, you can't forecast an increase. So you assume that $400 will be contributed into your retirement account at the end of each month. Determine the balance in your retirement account at the end of 20 years.

A. One way you can do this computation is to go to one of many Web sites that have *retirement calculators*. You enter your monthly contribution, the assumed rate of income per period, the number of years, and presto — the answer comes up on the screen. You can also use a business/financial calculator or the Excel spreadsheet program. In Excel, the FV function asks you to enter the same variables as a Web site retirement calculator and a business/financial calculator.

The balance in your retirement account after 20 years is $160,670. How do you know this answer is correct? Does it pass the common sense test? You invest $4,800 per year for 20 years, which is a total investment of $96,000. If the answer is correct, you will earn more than $64,000 income over the 20 years. Does this amount seem reasonable? Your intuition isn't particularly helpful here. To be reasonably certain that $160,670 is correct, you could program an Excel spreadsheet to see how your retirement balance accumulates month by month for 20 years. Or you could do the calculation a second time, to see if you come up with the same answer. Frankly, there's no easy way to prove the calculation is correct. I'm 99.9 percent sure that my answer here is correct, but if you come up with a different answer please let me know as soon as possible!

13. Each month, you put $250 into your retirement account, and your employer matches $150, so $400 is invested each month. Looking ahead, you wonder how much your retirement account will be worth when you retire in 20 years. You assume that your annual rate of income will be 5.4 percent over the next 20 years. Determine the future value of your retirement account 20 years from now.

Solve It

14. Assume that your goal is to retire 20 years from today with $500,000 in your retirement account. At this time, you have $50,000 in your retirement account. You would like to know how much you need to put into your retirement account each year from now until retirement to meet your goal, assuming that your retirement investment account will earn 6 percent interest per year. Assume that you make one payment into your retirement account at the end of each year (although in actual practice, it's more likely that you make monthly contributions during the course of the year). Determine the annual contributions you need to make into your retirement account over the next 20 years to end up with a $500,000 retirement nest egg.

Solve It

Measuring Return on Investment (ROI)

There are many kinds of investments — precious metals, real estate, farms and ranches, art, small businesses, corporate bonds, United States Treasury debt securities, municipal bonds, life insurance policies, retirement annuities, stocks, mutual funds, hedge funds, and so on. One thing all these different investment alternatives have in common is that the investor wants to take more money out of the investment than the amount of money put into the investment.

Measuring investment performance can be as simple as reading a comic strip or as perplexing as reading a book on nuclear physics. The primary measure of investment performance is the *annual rate of return on investment,* or ROI. "Return" in ROI refers to the earnings, income, profit, or gain, depending on the type of investment.

A fundamental point in measuring investment performance is that you have to recover, or recoup, the amount of capital you put in the investment venture. Only the excess over and above recovery of capital is return on the investment. Another fundamental point is that calculating return on investment focuses on cash flows into and out of the investment — unless changes in the market value of the investment are an integral and important part of the investment, such as investments in marketable securities (stocks and bonds, for example).

In just a few pages, I couldn't possibly do justice to even one of the investment alternatives open to you. Each type of investment requires at least a full chapter to explain its nature, risks, and procedures. So in the remainder of this chapter, I focus on how to calculate ROI for *generic* investment examples. I begin with a simple investment as far as calculating its ROI goes. Then I move on to more complicated examples.

Example 1: Steady income flow; liquidation value equals entry cost

In this scenario, you invest $100,000 today, you receive $6,000 at the end of each year for four years, and at the end of the fourth year, the investment is liquidated (converted back into cash) for $100,000. This is about as simple an investment as you can find.

Q. What is the annual rate of return on investment in this scenario?

A. You can eyeball this example scenario and see that the annual ROI rate is 6 percent. You don't really need to do any calculations — the annual cash flow is $6,000, or 6 percent of the amount invested. And you get your $100,000 entry cost back in full — no more, no less — at the termination of the investment.

Because I'm using generic investment examples, Figure 12-1 uses a generic template to analyze this particular investment.

			Cash Flow at End of Year		
	Year	Investment Balance at Start of Year	Total Amount	Earnings at 6.0%	Capital Recovery	Investment Balance at End of Year
Figure 12-1: Investment analysis template.	1	$100,000.00	$6,000.00	$6,000.00	$0.00	$100,000.00
	2	$100,000.00	$6,000.00	$6,000.00	$0.00	$100,000.00
	3	$100,000.00	$6,000.00	$6,000.00	$0.00	$100,000.00
	4	$100,000.00	$106,000.00	$6,000.00	$100,000.00	$0.00

In Figure 12-1, turn your attention to the three columns under Cash Flow at End of Year. The first column is the total cash flow for the period (one year, in this example); the second column is for the earnings on the investment for the period (based on the ROI for the investment); and the third column is for capital recovery for the period. Capital recovery equals the excess of the total cash flow over the amount earnings for the period. In the first three years, capital recovery is zero because the cash flows equal earnings for the year. But in the fourth and final year, the investment generates $106,000 total cash flow; the first $6,000 of this is the amount of earnings for the year, and the remainder is capital recovery. The $100,000 capital recovery in the final year exhausts the investment project; the investment venture is completed at this point. The entry cost of the investment has been fully recovered, and there are no more future cash flows.

The template presented in Figure 12-1 can handle just about every investment problem you can think of — it's a very powerful tool of analysis. You can alter it for any number of periods. I use four periods in these examples because that's all I need to demonstrate the key points for return on investment analysis. (Of course, an investment could run for 20 or more years and therefore have many more periods.) In Examples 2, 3, 4, and 5, I present the solutions using the Figure 12-1 template. The template offers one key advantage: It shows the capital recovery and investment balance year-to-year.

15. You invested $1,000,000 today and receive $50,000 at the end of each year for four years. At the end of the fourth year, you liquidate the investment for $1,000,000. Determine the annual ROI for the investment, and prove your answer. You may find the following form helpful:

		Cash Flow at End of Year			
Year	Investment Balance at Start of Year	Total Amount	Earnings at ?%	Capital Recovery	Investment Balance at End of Year
1	$1,000,000	$50,000			
2		$50,000			
3		$50,000			
4		$1,050,000			$0

Solve It

16. You invested $250,000 four years ago. Unfortunately, you made a bad decision. At the end of each year for four years, you received no income. But the good news is that you liquidated the investment for $250,000 at the end of the fourth year. Determine the annual ROI for the investment. You may find the following form helpful:

		Cash Flow at End of Year			
Year	Investment Balance at Start of Year	Total Amount	Earnings at ?%	Capital Recovery	Investment Balance at End of Year
1	$250,000	$0			
2		$0			
3		$0			
4		$250,000			$0

Solve It

Example 2: Substantial cash flows each year

You invest $100,000 today. The year-end cash flows from the investment are as follows: year 1 = $31,000; year 2 = $29,500; year 3 = $28,000; and year 4 = $26,500.

Q. What is the annual rate of return on investment for this scenario?

A. The annual rate of return on investment is 6 percent. Check out the following schedule, which uses the Figure 12-1 template. There's $25,000 capital recovery every year, so the investment balance decreases year-to-year. This decrease may or may not be attractive to you as an investor because you recover your capital quicker, but you earn less on the investment year-to-year.

		Cash Flow at End of Year			
Year	Investment Balance at Start of Year	Total Amount	Earnings at 6.0%	Capital Recovery	Investment Balance at End of Year
1	$100,000.00	$31,000.00	$6,000.00	$25,000.00	$75,000.00
2	$75,000.00	$29,500.00	$4,500.00	$25,000.00	$50,000.00
3	$50,000.00	$28,000.00	$3,000.00	$25,000.00	$25,000.00
4	$25,000.00	$26,500.00	$1,500.00	$25,000.00	$0.00

Earnings are taken out of cash flow for the period first, before capital recovery is determined. In other words, the amount of capital recovery each year is subordinate to earnings. Earnings come first, and capital recovery is second.

17. You invest $100,000 today. You receive $29,656.22 at the end of each year for four years. Determine the annual ROI on the investment, and prove your answer. You may find the following form helpful:

		Cash Flow at End of Year			
Year	Investment Balance at Start of Year	Total Amount	Earnings at ?%	Capital Recovery	Investment Balance at End of Year
1	$100,000	$29,656			
2		$29,656			
3		$29,656			
4		$29,656			$0

Solve It

18. You invest $1,000,000 today. You would like to earn 6.5 percent ROI each year for four years and recover $250,000 capital each year. Determine the annual amounts of return for each year you need to meet your objectives. You may find the following form helpful:

		Cash Flow at End of Year			
Year	Investment Balance at Start of Year	Total Amount	Earnings at 6.5%	Capital Recovery	Investment Balance at End of Year
1	$1,000,000			$250,000	
2				$250,000	
3				$250,000	
4				$250,000	$0

Solve It

Example 3: Zero cash flow until final year

You invest $100,000 today. The year-end cash flows from the investment are as follows: year 1 = $0; year 2 = $0; year 3 = $0; and year 4 = $136,048.90.

Q. What is the annual rate of return on investment for this scenario?

A. The annual rate of return on investment is 8 percent. Check out the following schedule, which uses the Figure 12-1 template. Even though no cash flow is received in the first three years, earnings are assigned to each of the first three years at the rate of 8 percent per year. The negative numbers for the first three years in the capital recovery column mean that the imputed earnings are, in effect, compounded or added into the investment balance. For instance, at the start of year 2, the investment balance includes the amount of non-received earnings for the first year.

		Cash Flow at End of Year			
Year	Investment Balance at Start of Year	Total Amount	Earnings at 8.0%	Capital Recovery	Investment Balance at End of Year
1	$100,000.00	$0.00	$8,000.00	($8,000.00)	$108,000.00
2	$108,000.00	$0.00	$8,640.00	($8,640.00)	$116,640.00
3	$116,640.00	$0.00	$9,331.20	($9,331.20)	$125,971.20
4	$125,971.20	$136,048.90	$10,077.70	$125,971.20	($0.00)

This example brings out an exceedingly important point: There's no cash flow until the end of the investment, so from a strict cash flow point of view, you can argue that the annual earnings for the first three years are zero. Then in the fourth year, the investment earns 36.05 percent ROI ($36,048.90 cash flow in excess of the entry cost ÷ $100,000.00 entry cost = 36.05 percent). In summary, you can make the case that the annual ROI is as follows: year 1 = 0.0 percent; year 2 = 0.0 percent; year 3 = 0.0 percent; and, year 4 = 36.05 percent. Well . . . you could argue this point of view, but you'd be lonely because no one does it this way.

In the world of finance, the ROI for Example 3 is measured at 8 percent per year. The standard method for determining the ROI on the investment assumes that the annual earnings are theoretically received in cash but then immediately reinvested. Thus, you see the compounding effect from year to year; the investment balance increases year-to-year by the amount of reinvested earnings.

Don't think that because the investment earns 8 percent ROI each year, you actually have any cash flow from the investment. You don't. In short, the 8 percent ROI solution is a convenient way to express the annual rate of growth in the value of the investment. It's rather arbitrary, but it's the way things are done.

19. You invest $100,000 today. The year-end cash flows from the investment are as follows: year 1 = $0; year 2 = $0; year 3 = $0; and year 4 = $128,646.64. Determine the annual ROI for this investment. You may find the following form helpful:

		Cash Flow at End of Year			
Year	Investment Balance at Start of Year	Total Amount	Earnings at ?%	Capital Recovery	Investment Balance at End of Year
1	$100,000	$0			
2		$0			
3		$0			
4		$128,647			$0

Solve It

20. You invest $100,000 today. The year-end cash flows from the investment are as follows: year 1 = $0; year 2 = $0; year 3 = $0; and year 4 = $90,368.79. Determine the annual ROI for this investment. Does this answer make sense? You may find the following form helpful:

		Cash Flow at End of Year			
Year	Investment Balance at Start of Year	Total Amount	Earnings at ?%	Capital Recovery	Investment Balance at End of Year
1	$100,000	$0			
2		$0			
3		$0			
4		$90,369			$0

Solve It

Example 4: Irregular cash flows, both positive and negative

You invest $100,000 today. The year-end cash flows from the investment are as follows: year 1 = negative $15,000; year 2 = negative $25,000; year 3 = $50,000; and year 4 = $141.625.

Q. What is the annual rate of return on investment for this scenario?

A. The annual rate of return on investment is 10 percent. Check out the following schedule, which uses the Figure 12-1 template. This sort of investment may not be for you because you put $100,000 in the investment to get it started, and then at the end of the first and second years, you put additional money in the investment. These additional payments into the investment are called *negative cash flows*.

		Cash Flow at End of Year			
Year	Investment Balance at Start of Year	Total Amount	Earnings at 10.0%	Capital Recovery	Investment Balance at End of Year
1	$100,000.00	($15,000.00)	$10,000.00	($25,000.00)	$125,000.00
2	$125,000.00	($25,000.00)	$12,500.00	($37,500.00)	$162,500.00
3	$162,500.00	$50,000.00	$16,250.00	$33,750.00	$128,750.00
4	$128,750.00	$141,625.00	$12,875.00	$128,750.00	$0.00

Would you make this investment? You would have to pump $140,000 into the project before you see any positive cash flow at the end of year 3. You may or may not be in a position to do this. On the other hand, the investment yields 10 percent annual ROI, which is pretty good. Generally, most investments involving negative cash flows are riskier and, therefore, demand a higher than average ROI to justify taking on the risks.

21. You invest $100,000 today. The year-end cash flows from the investment are as follows: year 1 = $10,000; year 2 = negative $15,000; year 3 = $20,000; and year 4 = $109,992. Determine the annual ROI on this investment. You may find the following form helpful:

		Cash Flow at End of Year			
Year	Investment Balance at Start of Year	Total Amount	Earnings at 7%	Capital Recovery	Investment Balance at End of Year
1	$100,000.00	$10,000			
2		($15,000)			
3		$20,000			
4		$109,992			$0

Solve It

22. You invest $100,000 today. The year-end cash flows from the investment are as follows: year 1 = $25,000; year 2 = $48,000; year 3 = $75,000; and year 4 = negative $32,431. Determine the annual ROI on this investment. Is there anything unusual about this investment? You may find the following form helpful:

		Cash Flow at End of Year			
Year	Investment Balance at Start of Year	Total Amount	Earnings at 7%	Capital Recovery	Investment Balance at End of Year
1	$100,000.00	$25,000			
2		$48,000			
3		$75,000			
4		($32,431)			$0

Solve It

Example 5: Market value–driven investments

You invest $100,000 today in a mutual fund. All dividends are reinvested in additional shares. The performance of your investment over four years is as follows:

Year	Investment Value at Start of Year	Total Return for Year*	Investment Value at End of Year	ROI for Year
1	$100,000.00	$15,000.00	$115,000.00	15.0%
2	$115,000.00	($22,000.00)	$93,000.00	–19.1%
3	$93,000.00	$43,500.00	$136,500.00	46.8%
4	$136,500.00	($450.00)	$136,050.00	–0.3%

* Includes cash income and change in market value of investment portfolio.

The Total Return for Year column includes cash income and change in the market value of the investment portfolio.

Q. How would most mutual funds advertise ROI performance for the four years in this example?

A. Instead of presenting a year-by-year ROI summary, which would show wild swings, a mutual fund with the investment performance shown in the example would advertise that it earned an average annual 8 percent ROI over the last four years.

The mutual fund argues that the performance of the fund is equivalent to having invested $100,000 and earning a level 8 percent annual ROI. Indeed, earning 8 percent per year causes the investment to increase from $100,000.00 to $136,050.00 four years later, which is the ending value of the investment (see the preceding schedule of returns). In other words, the mutual fund says that if the investment had grown in value at a steady rate of 8 percent per year, then the end result would be the same. This claim is true, as the following schedule shows, but it certainly isn't the whole story. Investors need to be informed about the wide swings in ROI year to year.

Year	Investment Value at Start of Year	Return at 8.0%	Investment Value at End of Year	ROI for Year
1	$100,000.00	$8,000.00	$108,000.00	8.0%
2	$108,000.00	$8,640.00	$116,640.00	8.0%
3	$116,640.00	$9,331.20	$125,971.20	8.0%
4	$125,971.20	$10,077.70	$136,048.90	8.0%

23. Look at the schedule of returns for Example 5. In this example, the average annual ROI is 8 percent. Is this the average of the four annual rates of ROI (see the far right column in the schedule)?

Solve It

24. You invest $100,000 today. The annual ROI on the investment is: year 1 = 12 percent; year 2 = negative 24.6 percent; year 3 = 33.7 percent; and year 4 = 29.6 percent. Determine the average annual ROI on the investment. You may find the following two forms helpful:

Year	Investment Balance at Start of Year	Earnings for Year	ROI for Year	Investment Balance at End of Year
1	$100,000.00		12.00%	
2			−24.60%	
3			33.70%	
4			29.60%	See Note 1

Year	Investment Value at Start of Year	Return at ? %	Investment Value at End of Year	ROI for Year
1	$100,000.00			
2				
3				
4			See Note 1	

Note 1: These two amounts are equal.

Solve It

Answers to Problems on Interest and Return on Investment

The following are the answers to the practice questions presented earlier in this chapter.

1 Suppose your company borrows $500,000 from a bank, and that amount is deposited in your checking account today. The note that you sign calls for a 6.25 percent annual interest rate. Determine the *maturity value* (the amount you will pay the bank when the note comes due then) of the note one year from now.

$500,000 × 6.25 percent annual interest rate = $31,250 interest for year

$500,000 borrowed + $31,250 interest = $531,250 maturity value of note

2 Suppose you sign a note that calls for $868,000 to be paid to the lender one year from today. (In other words, the maturity value of the loan one year from today is $868,000.) The lender gives you $800,000 today in exchange for this note. There's no mention of the rate of interest on this loan. What is the annual interest rate on this loan?

$868,000 maturity value of note − $800,000 proceeds from loan = $68,000 interest on note

$68,000 interest ÷ $800,000 amount of loan = 8.5 percent annual interest rate

3 Refer to Question 1. Suppose the date on the note is March 1, 2006 — this is the date the note was signed and the money was put in the company's checking account with the bank. It's now August 31, 2006, which is the close of the company's fiscal year. Should an adjusting entry for interest expense be recorded? If so, make the journal entry.

Yes, an adjusting entry should be made to record the accrued interest — six months' worth — on the loan. The following adjusting entry should be made:

Interest Expense	$15,625
Accrued Interest Payable	$15,625

To record six months interest on note payable: $31,250 annual interest × ½ = $15,625 interest through August 31, 2006.

4 Refer to Question 2. Because the note payable calls for a payment of $868,000 at the maturity date, the bookkeeper thinks that this amount should be recorded as a liability and that the difference between this liability amount and the $800,000 proceeds received by the business should be debited to the prepaid expenses asset account. Do you agree?

Accountants don't agree with this recording practice. Of course, all notes payable have a maturity value greater than the amount borrowed, but only the amount borrowed, equal to the face value or principal of the loan, is recorded as a liability at the time of signing the loan. Then, as time passes, an additional liability (accrued interest payable) is recorded for the accrued (accumulated) interest on the loan. In a simple bookkeeping sense, recording the $68,000 interest on the note as a prepaid expense and then crediting (decreasing) this account as interest expense is recorded is fine, but interest isn't really prepaid. Financial statement readers expect that the balance in the prepaid expense asset account is, in fact, for expenses that have been prepaid.

5 Suppose a business borrows $100,000 for one year. The lender quotes a 6 percent annual interest rate that's compounded semi-annually (twice a year). Determine the annual effective interest rate on the loan. You may find the following form helpful.

The annual effective interest rate is 6.09 percent, which can be seen in the following schedule:

Half-Year	Loan Balance at Start of Period	Interest at 3.0%	Loan Balance at End of Period
First	$100,000.00	$3,000.00	$103,000.00
Second	$103,000.00	$3,090.00	$106,090.00

At the end of the year, the loan balance is $106,09.00, so interest for the year is $6,090. Therefore,

$6,090 interest for year ÷ $100,000 amount borrowed = 6.09 percent effective annual interest rate

6 A company borrows $250,000 from its bank for one year. At the maturity date, one year after the money's deposited in the company's checking account, it writes a check to the bank for $268,324 to pay off the loan. Determine the effective annual interest rate and the nominal annual interest rate assuming semiannual compounding.

$268,324 maturity value of note – $250,000 proceeds of note = $18,324 interest on note for one year

$18,324 interest ÷ $250,000 proceeds of note = 7.33 percent effective annual interest rate

Because the effective interest rate is 7.33 percent, the nominal annual interest rate is slightly less — 7.2 percent, which means 3.6 percent per half year. The following schedule proves that this rate is correct:

Half-Year	Loan Balance at Start of Period	Interest at 3.6%	Loan Balance at End of Period
First	$250,000.00	$9,000.00	$259,000.00
Second	$259,000.00	$9,324.00	$268,324.00

7 A business receives $235,648.98 today from its bank and signs a one-year note that has a maturity value of $250,000.00. Determine the effective annual interest rate on this loan, and determine the nominal annual rate assuming semiannual compounding.

$250,000.00 maturity value of note – $235,648.98 proceeds of note = $14,351.02 interest on note for one year

$14,351.02 interest ÷ $235,648.98 proceeds of note = 6.09 percent effective annual interest rate

Because the effective interest rate is 6.09 percent, the nominal annual interest rate is slightly less — 6 percent, which means 3 percent per half year. The following schedule proves that this rate is correct:

Half-Year	Loan Balance at Start of Period	Interest at 3.0%	Loan Balance at End of Period
First	$235,648.98	$7,069.47	$242,718.45
Second	$242,718.45	$7,281.55	$250,000.00

8 Assume that your next paycheck will be $2,000.00 (net of all withholdings). Unfortunately, payday is two weeks off, so you go to a storefront business that offers to advance money on your next paycheck. (These loan sharks — well, that may be too harsh a term — loan you a certain amount today against the amount of your next payroll check.) The lender advances you $1,960.78 against your next paycheck. You're desperate, so you take the money and sign the note. Two weeks later, you sign over your $2,000.00 paycheck to the lender to pay off the loan. What is your nominal annual interest rate on this loan? (If you have time, you may also calculate the *effective* annual interest rate on this loan based on biweekly compounding, or 26 times per year.)

$2,000.00 maturity value of advance − $1,960.78 = $39.22 interest for two weeks

$39.22 interest ÷ $1,960.78 advance = 2 percent interest for two weeks

2 percent interest for two weeks × 26 = 52 percent nominal interest rate for one year (52 weeks)

The effective annual interest rate is 67.3 percent, assuming biweekly compounding of the 52 percent nominal annual rate.

Keep in mind that getting an advance against your next payroll check involves other fees and charges, so you pay more than just the $39.22 interest.

9 Refer to example question in the section "Lifting the Veil on Compound Interest," the retirement savings account example in which you invest $10,000 today and earn 5 percent annual interest (compounded annually) for 20 years. That example assumes that the 5 percent annual interest remains the same over all years. Instead, assume that you earn 4.5 percent annual interest during the first ten years and 5.5 percent annual interest during the last ten years. Are you better off in this situation?

The "trick" to answering this problem is doing it in two steps and carrying over the answer from the first step to the second step.

For the first step, use your business/financial calculator to determine that $10,000.00 invested for ten years at 4.5 percent annual interest accumulates to $15,529.69 at the end of the tenth year (assuming *compounding,* or reinvesting of annual earnings).

For the second step, enter your answer from the first step as the starting amount (the PV, or present value) for the second leg of the investment, which is ten years at 5.5 percent annual interest. Your investment will accumulate to $26,526.96 at the end of this second ten years (assuming compounding, or reinvesting of annual earnings.

You may be interested that the average annual interest rate that would take a $10,000.00 investment to $26,526.96 at the end of 20 years is 5 percent. But your actual investment balance wouldn't grow at this constant rate; rather, it would grow at the 4.5 percent and 5.5 percent rates during the first and second ten-year segments of the investment.

10 Suppose you just received your $25,000 year-end bonus. Instead of buying a new car, you decide to put the entire $25,000 in a qualified tax-deferred retirement investment account. You're 55 years old and plan to retire when you're 65 years old. You've done some research and have come up with two options for where to put your money: One is a safe, conservative investment vehicle that should earn an annual 4.5 percent interest rate (compounded annually), and the other is a more risky investment that has a good chance of being worth $45,000 ten years later, but there's some chance that it could be worth less than this amount. Compare your two options.

The first thing to do is calculate the future value of your safe, conservative investment. Using a business/financial calculator, $25,000 invested today that earns 4.5 percent for ten years will grow to a balance of $38,824 at the end of the tenth year. The alternative investment may be worth $45,000 at that time, which is considerably more than the conservative investment. You have to assess the degree of risk that the alternative investment may be worth less than $38,824. Of course, this kind of speculation is difficult.

11 Suppose a business borrows $1,000,000 from a bank. The annual interest rate is 7.5 percent and the loan is for four years. The bank wants the business to make payments at the end of each year such that the principal of the loan is amortized in four equal amounts. Determine the annual payments required under the terms of this loan.

The following schedule shows the annual payments on the loan. I determined the annual amounts by adding the interest on the loan for the year and $250,000, which is one-fourth of the amount borrowed. A bank may or may not insist on equal principal reductions each year.

Year	Loan Balance at Start of Year	Interest at 7.5%	Principal Payment	Total Payment to Bank	Loan Balance at End of Year
1	$1,000,000.00	$75,000.00	$250,000.00	$325,000.00	$750,000.00
2	$750,000.00	$56,250.00	$250,000.00	$306,250.00	$500,000.00
3	$500,000.00	$37,500.00	$250,000.00	$287,500.00	$250,000.00
4	$250,000.00	$18,750.00	$250,000.00	$268,750.00	$0.00

12 Suppose a business borrows $1,000,000 from a bank. The annual interest rate is 7.5 percent and the loan is for four years. The bank wants the business to make equal payments at the end of each year such that the principal of the loan is completely amortized (paid off) by the end of the fourth year. Determine the amount of annual payment required under the terms of the loan.

The annual payments on the loan are $298,567.51. As you can see in the following schedule, the loan is fully amortized (paid off) after the business makes the fourth payment. You can determine the annual payment on the loan by using a business/financial calculator or using the PMT function in the financial functions in Excel. The important thing, however, is to make sure that you understand how each payment is divided between interest and principal reduction.

Year	Loan Balance at Start of Year	Interest at 7.5%	Principal Payment	Total Payment to Bank	Loan Balance at End of Year
1	$1,000,000.00	$75,000.00	$223,567.51	$298,567.51	$776,432.49
2	$776,432.49	$58,232.44	$240,335.07	$298,567.51	$536,097.42
3	$536,097.42	$40,207.31	$258,360.20	$298,567.51	$277,737.22
4	$277,737.22	$20,830.29	$277,737.22	$298,567.51	$0.00

13 Each month, you put $250 into your retirement account, and your employer matches $150, so $400 is invested each month. Looking ahead, you wonder how much your retirement account will be worth when you retire in 20 years. You assume that your annual rate of income will be 5.4 percent over the next 20 years. Determine the future value of your retirement account 20 years from now.

With a business/financial calculator or using the FV (future value) function in the financial functions in Excel, you can determine that the future value of your retirement account based on your assumptions will be $172,227.02.

One purpose of this question is to call your attention to how difficult it is to forecast the variables for such a relatively long period of time. The annual rate of earnings on your retirement investment is almost certain to fluctuate; it's unlikely that the earnings rate will remain constant at exactly 5.4 percent every year for 20 years. Also, the monthly amounts you contribute to your retirement account will probably increase over time. Nevertheless, making reasonable forecasts and "running the numbers" is instructive to see the approximate value of your retirement investment in 20 years. At least you have a ballpark figure to work with. Some retirement plan mangers even make this sort of forecast for you.

14 Assume that your goal is to retire 20 years from today with $500,000 in your retirement account. At this time, you have $50,000 in your retirement account. You would like to know how much you need to put into your retirement account each year from now until retirement to meet your goal, assuming that your retirement investment account will earn 6 percent interest per year. Assume that you make one payment into your retirement account at the end of each year (although in actual practice, it's more likely that you make monthly contributions during the course of the year). Determine the annual contributions you need to make into your retirement account over the next 20 years to end up with a $500,000 retirement nest egg.

To work this problem, you need a business/finance calculator or Excel. The following answer explains how to enter the data for this problem into a calculator.

You already have $50,000 in your retirement account (good for you!), which will be invested for 20 years. At a 6 percent annual ROI, the $50,000 will increase to $160,357, so you need to put more money into your retirement account to achieve your $500,000 retirement goal.

Specifically, you need to make annual contributions for 20 years that will accumulate to $339,643 ($500,000 retirement goal – $160,357 future value of the $50,000 already in your retirement account = $339,643 additional future value needed).

To solve for this annual contribution amount with a calculator, do the following:

- Enter 0 in PV (present value); this amount is zero because you start this part of your retirement account with nothing in it

- Enter 20 in N (the number of periods)

- Enter 6 in INT; this key assumes that you're entering a percent, so the 6 is converted into 6 percent

- Enter $339,643 in FV (future value); this is the amount of future value you want to accumulate

- Press the PMT (payment key), and $9,233 should appear on the screen

You need to make annual contributions of $9,233, or $769 per month.

15 You invest $1,000,000 today and receive $50,000 at the end of each year for four years. At the end of the fourth year, you liquidate the investment for $1,000,000. Determine the annual ROI for the investment, and prove your answer.

Perhaps you can figure the answer without doing calculations: $50,000 is 5 percent of $1,000,000, so your annual ROI equals 5 percent. This ROI hinges on getting your full $1,000,000 back at the maturity of the investment. To prove the answer, see the following schedule (which uses the template provided in Figure 12-1):

Year	Investment Balance at Start of Year	Cash Flow at End of Year			Investment Balance at End of Year
		Total Amount	Earnings at 5.0%	Capital Recovery	
1	$1,000,000	$50,000	$50,000	$0	$1,000,000
2	$1,000,000	$50,000	$50,000	$0	$1,000,000
3	$1,000,000	$50,000	$50,000	$0	$1,000,000
4	$1,000,000	$1,050,000	$50,000	$1,000,000	$0

16 You invested $250,000 four years ago. Unfortunately, you made a bad decision. At the end of each year for four years, you received no income. But the good news is that you liquidated the investment for $250,000 at the end of the fourth year. Determine the annual ROI for the investment.

As the following schedule shows, the annual ROI for this investment, I'm sorry to say, is zero (0.0 percent):

Year	Investment Balance at Start of Year	Cash Flow at End of Year			Investment Balance at End of Year
		Total Amount	Earnings at 0.0%	Capital Recovery	
1	$250,000	$0	$0	$0	$250,000
2	$250,000	$0	$0	$0	$250,000
3	$250,000	$0	$0	$0	$250,000
4	$250,000	$250,000	$0	$250,000	$0

17 You invest $100,000 today. You receive $29,656.22 at the end of each year for four years. Determine the annual ROI on the investment, and prove your answer.

A series of equal amounts received or paid at equal intervals is called an *annuity*. In this scenario, you have a four-year investment annuity. Business/financial calculators are designed to solve problems like this. Enter 4 in N (number of periods), negative $100,000 in PV (present value), 29,656.22 in PMT (payment per period), and 0 in FV (future value) because the future value of the investment at the end of the investment is zero (there's no liquidation value upon termination of the investment). Press INT (or I/PR on a HP calculator), and you should see 7.2 percent.

Your annual ROI on this investment is 7.2 percent, which the following schedule proves:

			Cash Flow at End of Year		
Year	Investment Balance at Start of Year	Total Amount	Earnings at 7.2%	Capital Recovery	Investment Balance at End of Year
1	$100,000	$29,656	$7,200	$22,456	$77,544
2	$77,544	$29,656	$5,583	$24,073	$53,471
3	$53,471	$29,656	$3,850	$25,806	$27,664
4	$27,664	$29,656	$1,992	$27,664	($0)

TIP Each cash return (total amount received) includes an *earnings* component and a *capital recovery* component. Therefore, your investment balance decreases year-to-year, causing the annual amounts of your earnings to decrease year-to-year.

18 You invest $1,000,000 today. You would like to earn 6.5 percent ROI each year for four years and recover $250,000 capital each year. Determine the annual amounts of return for each year you need to meet your objectives.

I used Excel to prepare the following schedule, which shows the annual amounts (returns) needed each year to earn 6.5 percent on the amount invested at the start of the year and recover $250,000 capital each year:

			Cash Flow at End of Year		
Year	Investment Balance at Start of Year	Total Amount	Earnings at 6.5%	Capital Recovery	Investment Balance at End of Year
1	$1,000,000.00	$315,000.00	$65,000.00	$250,000.00	$750,000.00
2	$750,000.00	$298,750.00	$48,750.00	$250,000.00	$500,000.00
3	$500,000.00	$282,500.00	$32,500.00	$250,000.00	$250,000.00
4	$250,000.00	$266,250.00	$16,250.00	$250,000.00	$0.00

19 You invest $100,000 today. The year-end cash flows from the investment are as follows: year 1 = $0; year 2 = $0; year 3 = $0; and year 4 = $128,646.64. Determine the annual ROI for this investment.

The answer is 6.5 percent annual ROI. I did this calculation on my business/financial calculator. If you solve the problem with a calculator, be sure to enter 0 for PMT because you don't receive any annual cash returns — only the final cash out amount of $128,646.64. The 6.5 percent annual ROI is the correct answer, as shown in the following schedule:

			Cash Flow at End of Year		
Year	Investment Balance at Start of Year	Total Amount	Earnings at 6.5%	Capital Recovery	Investment Balance at End of Year
1	$100,000	$0	$6,500	($6,500)	$106,500
2	$106,500	$0	$6,923	($6,923)	$113,423
3	$113,423	$0	$7,372	($7,372)	$120,795
4	$120,795	$128,647	$7,852	$120,795	($0)

20 You invest $100,000 today. The year-end cash flows from the investment are as follows: year 1 = $0; year 2 = $0; year 3 = $0; and year 4 = $90,368.79. Determine the annual ROI for this investment. Does this answer make sense?

Oops! Right away, you ought to see that the investment has a negative return — you lost money on this investment. Do you really need to know the exact negative annual ROI? Well, if you do, the annual *negative* ROI is 2.5 percent, as shown in the following schedule. Your investment balance decreases at the decline rate of 2.5 percent per year. (Normally, of course, you think of a growth rate when discussing investments.)

			Cash Flow at End of Year		
Year	Investment Balance at Start of Year	Total Amount	Earnings at −2.5%	Capital Recovery	Investment Balance at End of Year
1	$100,000	$0	($2,500)	$2,500	$97,500
2	$97,500	$0	($2,438)	$2,438	$95,063
3	$95,063	$0	($2,377)	$2,377	$92,686
4	$92,686	$90,369	$92,686	$92,686	($0)

21 You invest $100,000 today. The year-end cash flows from the investment are as follows: year 1 = $10,000; year 2 = negative $15,000; year 3 = $20,000; and year 4 = $109,992. Determine the annual ROI on this investment.

One way to solve this problem is to use the *internal rate of return* (IRR) function in Excel (it's in the financial set of functions). Many business/financial calculators include a similar function that allows you to enter a series of unequal future returns (both negative and positive) and solve for the internal rate of return. The IRR is simply the ROI rate that, when applied to the entry cost and future returns from the investment, makes the total capital recovery over the life of the investment equal to the entry cost.

In Excel, set up a schedule based on the Figure 12-1 template. Make an initial guess for IRR, and see what the ending investment balance is at the end of the investment. If it's positive, you haven't recovered all the capital, so lower the IRR. If the ending balance is negative, raise the IRR. It only takes a few iterations to zero in on the exact IRR answer.

The IRR, or annual ROI, on this investment is 6 percent, which is shown in the following schedule:

		Cash Flow at End of Year			
Year	Investment Balance at Start of Year	Total Amount	Earnings at 6.0%	Capital Recovery	Investment Balance at End of Year
1	$100,000	$10,000	$6,000	$4,000	$96,000
2	$96,000	($15,000)	$5,760	($20,760)	$116,760
3	$116,760	$20,000	$7,006	$12,994	$103,766
4	$103,766	$109,992	$6,226	$103,766	($0)

22 You invest $100,000 today. The year-end cash flows from the investment are as follows: year 1 = $25,000; year 2 = $48,000; year 3 = $75,000; and year 4 = negative $32,431. Determine the annual ROI on this investment. Is there anything unusual about this investment?

The annual ROI, or IRR for this investment is 8 percent, as shown in the following schedule:

		Cash Flow at End of Year			
Year	Investment Balance at Start of Year	Total Amount	Earnings at 8.0%	Capital Recovery	Investment Balance at End of Year
1	$100,000	$25,000	$8,000	$17,000	$83,000
2	$83,000	$48,000	$6,640	$41,360	$41,640
3	$41,640	$75,000	$3,331	$71,669	($30,029)
4	($30,029)	($32,431)	($2,402)	($30,029)	($0)

An unusual feature of this investment is the negative cash flow in the fourth and final year of the investment project. You recover more capital than the entry cost by the end of the third year. You need this over-recovery to provide for the negative cash flow in the final year. An implicit assumption is that the investor can put this over-recovery in an investment that can earn 8 percent. This assumption may or may not be true in an actual situation.

23 Look at the schedule of returns for Example 5. In this example, the average annual ROI is 8 percent. Is this the average of the four annual rates of ROI (see the far right column in the schedule)?

No, the average annualized ROI that you see referred to in advertisements and other material on the historical performance of mutual funds and other investments isn't equal to the average of the four annual ROI rates.

In Example 5, the average of the four annual ROI rates is:

(15 percent – 19.1 percent + 46.8 percent – 0.3 percent) ÷ 4 = 10.6 percent average of the four annual rates

The annualized ROI rate, which I explain in the section "Example 5: Market value-driven investments," is 8 percent.

24 You invest $100,000 today. The annual ROI on the investment is: year 1 = 12 percent; year 2 = negative 24.6 percent; year 3 = 33.7 percent; and year 4 = 29.6 percent. Determine the average annual ROI on the investment.

A good way to find the answer is to first "run out" the investment to its *terminal value,* which is the investment balance at the end of the fourth and final year, and then solve for the ROI rate that would produce the same terminal value.

Year	Investment Balance at Start of Year	Earnings for Year	Based on ROI for Year	Investment Balance at End of Year
1	$100,000	$12,000	12.0%	$112,000
2	$112,000	($27,552)	–24.6%	$84,448
3	$84,448	$28,459	33.7%	$112,907
4	$112,907	$33,420	29.6%	$146,327

The investment's value at the end of year 4 is $146,327. Solve for the ROI rate that would take $100,000 to $146,327 in four years. This rate is very close to 10 percent, as the following schedule shows:

Year	Investment Value at Start of Year	Return at 10.0%	Investment Value at End of Year	ROI for Year
1	$100,000	$10,000	$110,000	10.0%
2	$110,000	$11,000	$121,000	10.0%
3	$121,000	$12,100	$133,100	10.0%
4	$133,100	$13,310	$146,410	10.0%

There's a small difference between the $146,410 ending investment value in this schedule and the $146,327 ending balance, but as they say, it's close enough for government work.

Part IV
The Part of Tens

The 5th Wave

By Rich Tennant

"This is classic voodoo economics, Grace, right down to the chicken blood it's written in."

In this part . . .

The Part of Tens contains two shorter chapters: one directed to business investors and the other to accountants in carrying out their responsibilities to business managers. The former presents ten things everyone reading a business financial report should know and keep in mind. The latter chapter provides accountants a ten-point checklist for helping managers in their planning, control, and decision-making.

Chapter 13

Ten Things You Should Know About Business Financial Statements

inancial statements, which are one of the main products of the accounting system of a business, serve two broad purposes:

✔ They help managers manage the profit performance, cash flows, and financial condition of a business.

✔ They serve as a pipeline of information to business lenders and investors. Without this financial information, lenders would balk at loaning money to a business and investors would refuse to invest their hard-earned money in a business.

In short, financial statements are essential in managing a business and in raising the capital a business needs to operate.

Internal financial statements used by managers don't circulate outside the business if they contain confidential and proprietary information. Internal financial statements are distributed on a need-to-know basis within the business; they contain more-detailed information than the summary-level information presented in external financial statements distributed to lenders and shareowners of a business. But both the internal and external financial statements use the same accounting methods. Businesses keep only one set of books, but they "keep secrets" that aren't disclosed in their external financial reports.

Business managers, business lenders, and business investors should understand certain characteristics and limitations of financial statements. I explain ten of these important points in this chapter.

Rules and Standards Matter

I have seen very, very few maverick financial statements. Almost all financial statements are prepared using generally accepted accounting principles (GAAP) and/or international accounting standards. Financial statement readers can assume that American GAAP or the international equivalent have been applied in preparing the financial statements and that there aren't any significant deviations from these rules of the game. If financial statements are prepared on some other basis of accounting, the business should make this fact very clear in its financial report.

These accounting rules and standards don't put a business in an accounting straitjacket. A business still has wiggle room in the application of GAAP. For instance, both accelerated and straight-line depreciation expense methods are equally acceptable (see Chapter 9), and a business can adopt either conservative or liberal (aggressive) accounting methods for recording profit, which also affect the values reported for assets and liabilities in its balance sheet. A business has the choice among alternative methods in many areas of accounting.

Exactitude Would Be Nice, but Estimates Are Key

Looking at all the numbers in a financial statement, you may assume that they're accurate down to the last dollar. Not true. The balance in the cash account is exact, but virtually every other number you see in a financial report is based on an estimate. The amounts of expenses, revenue, assets, and liabilities are calculated down to the last dollar, but they're based on estimates, and estimates never turn out to be accurate down to the last dollar.

For example, consider depreciation expense. A business estimates the future useful life of a fixed asset (long-term operating asset) and allocates its cost over this useful life. Another example is accounts receivable — the business estimates how much of the total balance of its accounts receivable will turn out to be bad debts. Yet another example is the accrued liability for product warranty and guarantee costs that will be paid in the future. This amount is only an educated guess.

Estimates are unavoidable in accounting. Most businesses have enough experience to make pretty good estimates, and they consult experts when they need to. A business can nudge an estimate toward the conservative side or the liberal side. For instance, it can estimate that its future product warranty and guarantee costs will be fairly low or fairly high. Usually, arguments exist on both sides, and the business ends up having to make a somewhat arbitrary estimate.

Some estimates are particularly difficult to make, such as the liability for future post-retirement medical and health benefits that a business promises its employees. Another difficult estimate concerns product recalls. Estimating the cost of a major lawsuit in which the decision may go against the business is very difficult. My advice is to be alert in reading financial statements to see if the business is facing any issue that's particularly difficult to estimate.

Financial Statements Fit Together Hand in Glove

The three primary financial statements — the income statement, the balance sheet, and the statement of cash flows — appear on separate pages in a financial report and therefore may seem freestanding. In fact, the three financial statements are intertwined and interconnected (see Chapters 7 and 8). Accountants assume that the reader understands these connections, so they don't connect the dots between corresponding accounts in different financial statements. Understanding these tentacles of connection between the statements is extremely important, especially for interpreting the statement of cash flows (see Chapter 8). For example, an increase in accounts receivable during the year that's reported in the balance sheet causes a decrease in cash flow from operating activities.

For help in understanding financial statements and how all their elements work together, check out my book *How To Read A Financial Report* (Wiley), which has been in print for more than 25 years. The book clarifies the lines of connection between sales revenue and expenses in the income statement and the assets and liabilities in the balance sheet that are changed by sales revenue and expenses. Profit activities are reported in the income statement, but the results of profit are reported in the balance sheet. I explain why accrual basis profit differs from the cash flow from profit (operating activities) — which is a key point that business managers and investors should understand, but many don't. I use financial statement example templates that can be adapted to fit most businesses. I offer to send readers the Excel spreadsheets for the exhibits in my book. To date, I've received hundreds and hundreds of requests for the spreadsheets. Hands down, the most frequent comment in the e-mails I receive is that I make clear the lines of connection between accounts in the financial statements.

Accrual Basis Is Used to Record Profit, Assets, and Liabilities

The vast majority of businesses must use the *accrual basis of accounting* to determine profit or loss and to keep track of their assets and liabilities. Simply put, the accrual basis must be used to reflect economic reality. The following are three examples of the accrual basis at work:

- ✔ A business makes a sale on credit, accepting the customer's promise to pay at a later date and delivering the product. The accountant records the sale by an increase to an asset called accounts receivable.

- ✔ A business buys a building or machine that will be used many years in its operations and pays cash for the asset. The cost of the asset isn't charged to expense right away. Rather, the cost is allocated to expense over the estimated useful life span of the asset.

- ✔ A business records an expense now even though it will not pay for the expense until sometime later. To record the expense, a liability is increased; later, when the expense is paid, the liability is decreased.

Some small businesses don't sell on credit, don't carry inventory, don't invest in fixed assets (long-term operating resources), and pay their bills quickly. They may use the *cash basis of accounting* instead of the accrual basis. Basically, all they do is keep a checkbook.

Cash Flow Differs from Accrual Basis Profit

The accrual basis of accounting (see the preceding section), even though it reflects economic reality, causes one point of confusion: Many people look at the bottom-line profit or loss number in the income statement and jump to the conclusion that it's the amount that cash increased or decreased for the period. Indeed, the expression "a business makes money" suggests that making a profit increases the business's cash account the same amount. But cash flow from profit — the net increase or decrease in cash from the sales and expense activities of a business for a period — almost always differs from the amount of bottom-line profit or loss reported in its income statement.

In one sense, you can blame accounting for speaking with a forked tongue: The income statement reports one number for profit (net income), and the statement of cash flows reports another number for profit (cash flow from operating activities). There's the accrual basis number in the income statement and the cash basis number in the statement of cash flows. Essentially, a financial report has two versions of profit.

The amount of cash flow from profit (operating activities) in the statement of cash flows tells you what profit would have been on the cash basis of accounting. The statement of cash flows explains why the cash flow from profit is different from the net income for the period. The main (but not only) difference between cash basis and accrual basis profit accounting is *depreciation*. On the accrual basis, depreciation expense is deducted from sales revenue to determine profit, which is correct of course. From the cash flow point of view, in contrast, depreciation isn't bad but good. The cash inflow from sales revenue, in part, reimburses the business for using its fixed assets. In other words, depreciation for the year is recovery of the cash invested in fixed assets in prior years. Money is returning to the business.

Profit and Balance Sheet Values Can Be and Often Are Manipulated

I'm sure you've heard about business managers "massaging the numbers" to make profit for the year look better or to make the financial condition of the business look better. (My father-in-law calls this "fluffing the pillows.") Managers can and do lay a heavy hand on the accounting process — to pump up sales revenue or to deflate expenses for the year in order to meet pre-established profit goals or to dampen the volatility of reported earnings year to year. There's no end to the tactics for manipulating accounting numbers.

Rather than presenting a litany of the techniques for massaging the numbers, I offer two observations:

- ✔ Massaging the numbers is expected, and one may even argue that business lenders and investors encourage it — mainly on the grounds that a business is entitled to put its best face forward. Independent CPA auditors go along with a reasonable amount of accounting manipulation.

- ✔ There's a big difference between massaging the numbers and *cooking the books.* Cooking the books is the playful name for a serious crime, accounting fraud, in which fictitious sales are recorded, expenses aren't recorded, liabilities are hidden, or assets are overstated. Accounting fraud is a felony (if one gets caught and convicted, that is).

Financial Statements May Be Revised Later to Correct Errors and Fraud

One ominous financial reporting development over the last decade bothers me a great deal: An increasing number of businesses revise their financial statements after releasing them to the public. I'm speaking about businesses whose securities are traded in public markets (such as the New York Stock Exchange and NASDAQ). Private businesses don't release their financial reports to the public at large, so their financial reports probably aren't revised and restated as frequently as those of public businesses.

By their very nature, financial statements are tentative and conditional. One of the first things you learn in studying accounting is the *going concern assumption*. The accountant assumes the business will continue to operate for an indefinite period of time and isn't planning to shut down and liquidate its assets. Financial statements are conditional — the condition being that business will continue to operate in a normal fashion. (If a business is in the middle of bankruptcy proceedings, on the other hand, the accountant has to reckon the chances of the business continuing in operations.)

It's amazing to me that most financial report revisions are made to correct major accounting errors and accounting fraud. How did these errors slip through the system in the first place? Undoubtedly, the Enron scandal has made people more aware of the possibility of accounting fraud. But even before Enron happened, the pace of financial report revisions had accelerated. All you can do is to take any financial report with a grain of salt and keep in mind that the financial statements may contain serious errors.

Some Asset Values Are Current, but Others May Be Old

The balance (amount) of an asset in a balance sheet is the result of the entries (increases less decreases) recorded in the account. A balance sheet doesn't disclose whether the ending balance in an asset is from recent entries or from entries made years ago. How recent an ending balance is depends on which asset you're talking about and which accounting method is used for the asset. For example, if a business uses the FIFO method for its cost of goods sold expense, its inventories balance is from entries recorded recently. In contrast, if the company uses the LIFO method, its inventories balance is from older entries. How much older? Well, one major equipment manufacturer has been using LIFO for many years and part of its inventories balance goes back more than 50 years.

The balance of property, plant, and equipment typically consists of fixed assets that have been on the books for 5, 10, 20, or more years. You should never confuse the original costs in this asset account with the current replacement value of the assets. On the other hand, the accounts receivable balance is current, as is cash, of course.

The footnotes to the financial statements may include information on the current replacement values of certain assets. For example, if a business uses LIFO and has a large gap between the FIFO and the LIFO balances. In this situation, the business discloses an estimate of the FIFO amount for its inventories.

Financial Statements Leave Interpretation to Readers

One guiding rule of financial reporting is to let the financial statements speak for themselves. The financial statements and footnotes report the facts but don't interpret what the facts mean or what the facts portend. The assessment and forecast of a company's financial performance and condition are left for the readers to tackle.

Having said that, I should quickly point out that the chief executive and other top-level offi-cers of *public* companies include a good deal of commentary and their interpretations of the company's financial performance in annual financial reports. Indeed, it's useful to carefully read the Management Discussion and Analysis (MD&A) section in a public company's annual financial report. But keep in mind that getting the top officers' take is like asking the captain of a ship how the voyage went when the passengers may have quite a different opinion.

Financial Statements Tell the Story of a Business, Not Its Individual Shareowners

Financial statements tell the story of the business. How well or poorly individual investors in the business have done isn't information you can find in the financial statements. Some shareowners in a business may have had their money invested in the business from day one, whereas other original investors may have sold their shares. The business doesn't record the prices they received for the shares; in other words, dealings and transactions among share-owners aren't recorded or reported by the business. This activity is none of the business's business.

The owners' equity accounts in a balance sheet report only the original amounts invested by shareowners. What has happened since then in the trading of these ownership shares isn't captured in the financial statements — unless the business itself bought some of the shares from its shareowners. You might find it very interesting to compare the current market price of stock shares you own with the stockholders' equity balances reported in the company's balance sheet. In a rough sort of way, this is like comparing the current market value of your home with the cost you paid many years ago.

Chapter 14

A Ten-Point Checklist for Management Accountants

In a business, accounting has several functions. The responsibilities of the chief accountant and the accounting department include the following:

- ✔ Complying with the manifold requirements of federal and state income taxes, state and local sales taxes, property taxes, and payroll taxes.

- ✔ Designing and operating a system to capture, record, process, and store all relevant documents and information about the financial activities of the business.

- ✔ Ensuring the integrity and reliability of the information system, and preventing fraud from inside and outside the business (the latter being directed at the business).

- ✔ Preparing financial statements that are reported outside the business to its lenders and shareowners. (If the business is a public company, the accountants are also responsible for preparing filings with the Security and Exchange Commission, or SEC.)

- ✔ Preparing financial statements and accounting reports for distribution to the business's managers for their planning, control, and decision-making needs.

The last function listed here is referred to as *management* or *managerial accounting*. It concerns accounting's role in helping business managers carry out their functions. This chapter offers a ten-point checklist for accountants in fulfilling their functions for managers, somewhat like the checklist for pilots before take off. Accountants are saddled with the several functions listed above, and under the pressures of time they may end up giving short shrift to their duties to managers — which is understandable. However, the very continuance of the business depends on accountants providing managers information they need to know for making decisions and maintaining control. If managers don't get what they need from their accountants, the business could fail or spin out of control. In this sense, management accounting functions are the most central — if the business fails, the other accounting functions are beside the point.

Designing Internal Accounting Reports

In designing internal accounting reports for managers, the accountant should ask, "Who's entitled to know what?" Generally speaking, the board of directors, the chief executive officer, the president, and the chief operating officer are entitled to know anything and everything. (This sweeping comment is subject to exceptions in business organizations that tightly control the flow of financial information.) By virtue of their positions, the financial vice president and chief accountant (often called the controller) have access to all financial information about the business.

Other managers in a business have a limited scope of responsibility and authority. The accountant should report to them the information they need to know, but no more. For example, the vice-president of production receives a wide range of manufacturing information but doesn't receive sales and marketing information. The accountant should identify a particular manager's specific area of authority and responsibility in deciding the information content of accounting reports to that manager. The reporting of information to individual mangers should follow the organizational structure of the business; this practice is called *responsibility accounting*.

From the accounting point of view, the organizational structure of a business consists of *profit centers* and *cost centers:*

✓ **A profit center could be a product line, or even a specific product model.** For example, a profit center for Apple Computer is its iPod line of products; another profit center is its iTunes Music Center (where customers download audio and video files). Within each broad product line, Apple has sub-profit centers. For example, each type of iPod is a sub-profit center.

✓ **A cost center is an organization unit that doesn't directly generate sales revenue.** For example, the accounting department of a company is a cost center.

The accounting reports that go to the manager of a profit center should be oriented to the profit performance of that organization unit. The accounting reports that go to a manager of a cost center should be oriented to the cost performance of that organization unit.

Helping Managers Understand Their Accounting Reports

Most managers have limited accounting backgrounds; their backgrounds are usually in marketing, engineering, law, human resources, and other fields. Not to sound critical, but most business managers have their desires to learn accounting under control. Furthermore, they're very busy people with little time to spare. Yet accountants often act as if managers fully understand the accounting reports they receive and have all the time in the world to read and digest the detailed information they contain. Accountants are dead-wrong on this point.

One of the main functions of the management accountant is to serve as the translator of accounting jargon and reports to business managers — to take the technical terminology and methods of accounting and put it all into terms that non-accounting managers can clearly understand. Of course, being an author of accounting books for non-accountants, I may be biased, but I believe that management accountants can perform a very valuable service by improving their communication skills with non-accounting managers.

Involving Managers in Choosing Accounting Methods

Some business managers take charge of every aspect of the business, including choosing accounting methods for their businesses. But many business managers are passive and defer to their chief accountants regarding the accounting methods their businesses should use. In my opinion, the hands-off approach is a mistake. Chapter 9 explains three critical accounting issues for which a business has to choose between alternative accounting methods. Ultimately, the chief executive officer of the business is responsible for these decisions, as he or she is responsible for all fundamental decisions of the business. But such accounting decisions may not be on the radar screen of the chief executive.

In choosing accounting methods, the chief accountant shouldn't allow managers to sit on the sidelines and be spectators. The chief accountant shouldn't select an accounting method without the explicit approval and understanding of top-level managers. In particular, the head accountant should explain the differences in profit and asset and liability values between alternative accounting methods. The business's accounting methods should reflect its philosophy and strategies, so if the business is conservative in its policies and strategies, it should use conservative accounting methods.

The chief accountant can find himself or herself between a rock and a hard place when top-level managers intervene in the normal accounting process. This interference may be referred to as *massaging the numbers*, *managing earnings*, *smoothing earnings*, or good old-fashioned *accounting manipulation*. If the accountant accedes to management pressure, he or she should make clear to the manager what the consequences will be the following year. Generally speaking, there's a *compensatory effect,* or trade-off, between years; pumping up profit this year, for instance, causes profit deflation next year. Massaging the numbers produces a robbing Peter to pay Paul effect, and the accountant should make this very clear to the manager.

Designing Profit Performance Reports for Managers

The accountant needs to read the mind of the manager in designing the layout and content of reports to the manager. Ideally, the profit report should reflect the manager's profit strategy and tactics. For example, a manager of a profit center focuses on two main things — *margin* and *sales volume*. Therefore, the profit report should emphasize those two key factors. It sounds simple enough, but one impediment exists in designing internal profit reports for managers based on management thinking.

In designing internal profit reports for managers, accountants too often follow the path of least resistance. They use the format and content of the income statement reported outside the business, but this won't do. An external income statement conceals as much information as it reveals. External income statements don't disclose information about margins and sales volumes for each profit center of the business.

The accountant has to break out of his or her external income statement mentality and think in terms of what managers need to know for analyzing profit performance and making profit decisions. My main advice on this point is straightforward: Listen to how the manager explains his or her profit strategy, which is called the "business model." Get inside the manager's head. Do your best to understand the mindset of the manager regarding how he or she sees the formula for making profit. Listen carefully to which particular factors the manager thinks are the most important drivers (determinants) of profit. Don't try to remodel the manager's thinking into the accountant's way of thinking. Don't forget that the manager is the boss — even though you might think the manager should go back and learn accounting. In short, don't try to educate the manager on accounting; let the manager educate you on what he or she needs to know in order to make profit.

Designing Cash Flow Reports for Managers

The conventional statement of cash flows is far too technical and intimidating for most managers to make sense of. What managers don't understand, they don't use. In my view, accountants are too bound by their "debits and credits" thinking when it comes to the statement of cash flows. The statement of cash flows is designed to reconcile changes in the balance sheet during the period with the amounts reported in the statement. But should this function also be the purpose of reporting this financial statement to managers? I don't think so.

In mid-size and large businesses, the financial officers of the business manage cash flow. Other managers don't have any direct responsibility over cash flow — although their decisions impact cash flow. Managers of profit and cost centers should have a basic understanding of the cash flow impacts of their decisions. They don't necessarily need cash flow statements, but they need to know how their decisions impact cash flow.

The cash flow reports to managers of profit and cost centers should focus mainly on the key factors that affect *cash flow from operating activities* (see Chapter 8). These internal management reports should concentrate on changes in accounts receivable, inventory, and operating liabilities (accounts payable and accrued expenses payable). These are the main factors for the difference between cash flow and profit that the managers of profit and cost centers have control over and responsibility for.

Designing Management Control Reports

Management control is usually thought of as keeping a close watch on a thousand and one details, anyone of which can spin out of control and cause problems. First and foremost, however, management control means achieving objectives and keeping on course toward the goals of the business. Management control covers a lot of ground — motivating employees, working with suppliers, keeping customers satisfied, and so on. But there's no doubt that managers need control reports that include a lot of detail.

The trick in management control reports is to separate the wheat from the chaff. Being very busy people, managers can't afford to waste time on relatively insignificant problems. They have to prioritize problems and deal with the issues that have the greatest effect on the business. Therefore, the accountant should design management control reports that differentiate significant problems from less serious problems. In control reports, the accountant should use visual pointers to highlight serious problems. In other words, control reports shouldn't be flat, with all lines of information appearing to be equally important.

Developing Models for Management Decision-Making Analysis

For decision-making purposes, business managers need a model of operating profit that, theoretically, fits on the back of an envelope. Here's an example of such a compact profit model, which I adapted from "Analysis method #1: Contribution margin minus fixed costs" in Chapter 10:

(Unit Margin × Sales Volume) – Fixed Expenses = Operating Profit

Suppose the sales price is $100 and variable costs equal $65 per unit. Therefore, unit margin is $35. Assume the business sells 100,000 units, so its total contribution margin for the period is $3,500,000 ($35 unit margin × 100,000 units = $3,500,000 total contribution margin). Last, assume its fixed expenses for the period equal $2,500,000. So its operating profit is $1,000,000 for the period.

The accountant should develop a condensed profit model, which is limited to the critical factors that tip profit one way or the other. This profit model helps the manager focus on the key variables that drive profit behavior. For example, continuing with the example just mentioned, suppose the manager is contemplating cutting sales price 10 percent to boost sales volume 20 percent. Using the profit model the manager can quickly do a before and after comparison of the proposed sales price cut:

Before: ($35 unit margin × 100,000 units) – $2,500,000 fixed expenses = $1,000,000 operating profit

After: ($25 unit margin × 120,000 units) – $2,500,000 = $500,000 operating profit

Giving up 10 percent of sales price for a 20 percent gain in sales volume may have intuitive appeal, but this decision would cripple profit. Operating profit would drop from $1,000,000 to only $500,000; the manager would give up $10, or 29 percent of the $35 margin per unit. The sacrifice is too great in exchange for only 20 percent gain in sales volume.

Working Closely With Managers in Planning

One of the most important managerial functions has two parts: forecasting changes that will affect the business and planning the future of the business. This task includes plotting the sales trajectory of the business, the need for additional capital, and shifts in size and makeup of its workforce and other factors. The accountant should be involved in the planning process from the get-go. Otherwise, the accountant is at a disadvantage in preparing budgets and financial projections. The better the accountant understands the planning process, and the closer the accountant works with managers in developing plans, the more useful the financial forecasts and budgets will be.

Establishing and Enforcing Internal Controls

Internal controls are the forms and procedures established in a business to deter and detect errors and dishonesty (see Chapter 4). (Internal control certainly isn't the most glamorous accounting function in a business organization.) Even if everyone in the business and everyone the business deals with are as honest as the day is long every day of the year, errors are bound to happen.

Here's a personal example: I recently started receiving retirement income from the organization that manages my retirement investment account. I completed a rather lengthy form giving the organization all the information it asked for, and being an accountant, I appreciated that it needed all this information. No problem. But the organization made a data input error, entering my wife's year of birth as 1963 instead of 1936. This is called a *transposition error*, and it's a common error in accounting systems.

Every business should have internal control procedures in place to prevent, or at least to quickly catch, this type of error. I caught the error because I'm an old auditor at heart. Well, to be honest, I noticed that the amount of money I received was too low and knew something was wrong. I called the error to the company's attention, and it took 15 telephone calls and over two months to get the error corrected! What bothered me is that the company didn't have internal control procedures in place to prevent or to quickly catch the error.

A business is the natural target of all sorts of dishonest schemes and scams by its employees and managers, its customers, its vendors, and others. To minimize its exposure to losses from embezzlement, pilfering, shoplifting, fraud, and burglary, the accountant should establish and enforce effective internal controls in the business. As my father-in-law once said, "There's a little bit of larceny in everyone's heart." Internal controls are an example of the principle that an ounce of prevention is worth a pound of cure.

Keeping Up-to-Date on Accounting, Financial Reporting, and Tax Changes

Accountants are very busy people because they carry out many functions in a business. Like business mangers, they don't have a lot of time to spare. One thing that gets short shrift in a crowded schedule is keeping up with changes in accounting and financial reporting standards. However, it's absolutely essential that accountants stay informed of the latest changes. Accountants simply have to set aside time to read professional journals, peruse Web sites, and keep alert regarding developments in accounting and financial reporting. Things don't stand still.

Index